LADIES OF LABOR, GIRLS OF ADVENTURE

Popular Cultures, Everyday Lives
Robin D. G. Kelley and Janice Radway, Editors

LADIES OF LABOR, GIRLS OF ADVENTURE

*Working Women, Popular Culture, and Labor Politics
at the Turn of the Twentieth Century*

NAN ENSTAD

COLUMBIA UNIVERSITY PRESS
NEW YORK

Columbia University Press
Publishers Since 1893
New York   Chichester, West Sussex
Copyright © 1999 Columbia University Press
All rights reserved

Library of Congress Cataloging-in-Publication Data
Enstad, Nan.
    Ladies of labor, girls of adventure : working women, popular culture, and labor
politics at the turn of the twentieth century / Nan Enstad.
        p. cm. — (Popular cultures, everyday lives)
    Includes index.
    ISBN 978-0-231-11103-4 (pbk.)
    1. Working class women—United States—History—20th century. 2. Popular
culture—United States—History—20th century. 3. Women consumers—United
States—History—20th century. 4. Fashion—United States—History—20th century.
I. Title. II. Series.
    HD6058.E57 1999
    305.42'0973—dc21   98-8572
                                    ∞
        Casebound editions of Columbia University Press books
        are printed on permanent and durable acid-free paper.

                    Printed in the United States of America

Columbia University Press gratefully acknowledges permission to use the following photographs:
Fig. 2.1: Courtesy of The Library of Congress; Fig. 2.2: Courtesy of the Lewis W. Hine Collection,
United States History, Local History and Genealogy Division (The New York Public Library, Astor,
Lenox, and Tilden Foundations); Fig. 2.3: Courtesy of the Lewis W. Hine Collection, United States
History, Local History and Genealogy Division (The New York Public Library, Astor, Lenox, and
Tilden Foundations); Fig. 2.4: Courtesy of the International Ladies Garment Workers Union
Archives (Kheel Center, Cornell University); Fig. 3.1: Courtesy of the Tamiment Institute Library,
New York University; Fig. 3.2: Courtesy of the Tamiment Institute Library, New York University;
Fig. 3.3: Courtesy of the Tamiment Institute Library, New York University; Fig. 4.4: Courtesy of the
International Ladies Garment Workers Union Archives (Kheel Center, Cornell University); Fig. 4.5:
Courtesy of the International Ladies Garment Workers Union Archives (Kheel Center, Cornell
University); Fig. 5.1: Courtesy of the Billy Rose Collection, The New York Public Library for the
Performing Arts (Astor, Lenox, and Tilden Foundations); Fig. 5.3: Courtesy of the Billy Rose
Collection, The New York Public Library for the Performing Arts (Astor, Lenox, and Tilden
Foundations); Fig. 5.4: Courtesy of The Museum of Modern Art (Film Stills Archive); Fig. 5.5:
Courtesy of the Billy Rose Collection, The New York Public Library for the Performing Arts
(Astor, Lenox, and Tilden Foundations).

For Anne

CONTENTS

ACKNOWLEDGMENTS

Long before this book became a three-dimensional product, available for sale and consumption, it existed as a set of rather unformed ideas, an inchoate rage, and vague but persistent hopes. I relied on a variety of kinds of help in getting from there to here.

Economically, this book was generously supported by an American Association of University Women Fellowship, an American Council of Learned Societies Fellowship, and two Summer Excellence Grants and a New Faculty Research Grant from the University of North Carolina at Greensboro. I conducted some of the research for this book while a graduate student at the University of Minnesota, supported by a Harold Leonard Memorial Film Fellowship and Travel Grant, and a William W. Stout Endowed Fellowship.

Archivists and librarians at the following institutions provided assistance in locating sources: the Tamiment Library, New York University; the Billie Rose Theater Collection at the New York Public Library; the Museum of Modern Art; the Kerlan Collection of Children's Literature,

University of Minnesota; the Immigration History Research Center, University of Minnesota; the Library of Congress, Motion Picture Division; the International Ladies Garment Workers Union Archive, Cornell University; and the Edison Archives. When I was on the road, Deirdre Fishel and Cinder Hypki housed me in New York and Baltimore, respectively, and made the research trips feel like vacations. My colleagues in the History Department at the University of North Carolina, Greensboro, have been ever-supportive. Thanks especially to Steven Lawson for going many extra miles. Derek Krueger helped me gain a home at UNC Greensboro. I also benefited from the support of research assistants. Thanks to Kelly Hardin and Brett Rumble who read microfilm for this project. Much appreciation and respect to Brenda MacDougall, who chased down elusive facts, scouted research territories, and always returned with crucial information. Her creative abilities and fine research skills have improved this project. I also am indebted to two scholars who graciously took time from their own work to translate material from the ethnic presses in New York City: Jennifer Guglielmo researched and translated Italian newspapers and Linda Lipsky researched and translated the Yiddish *Forverts*.

I was fortunate as a graduate student to find excellent mentors from whom I gained crucial gifts as I created and pursued my interests. From David W. Noble, one of my dissertation coadvisers, I gained a healthy irreverence toward just about everything. It is largely owing to David that I sought a Ph.D. in history: when I was still an undergraduate biology major, he captivated me with his critique of U.S. history and his view of historical writing as narrative. Both still undergird my basic approach to history and cultural studies.

From Sara M. Evans, my other dissertation coadviser, I gained a model of political engagement through the rigorous pursuit of social and women's history. I hope that I have learned the excellent lessons in historical methods that she endeavored to teach me. Sara also gave me the great gift of respecting my ideas and my politics, even when they differed from her own, and so expanded my sense of the possibilities for meaningful exchange in and out of academics.

I owe a special word of thanks to George Lipsitz. On the first day of George's popular culture course at the University of Minnesota over a decade ago, I scribbled madly to capture his lecture and thought with some euphoria, this is what I've been looking for: a way to talk about how people make meaning under oppressive, unacceptable conditions. George left Minnesota before I began my dissertation, yet he read many drafts of dissertation and book chapters and his feedback and support have been invaluable at every stage of my work. I cannot imagine what this book would look like without his stunning example and his exceptionally generous involvement.

People who took the time to read my work literally gave me the energy to continue. For their interest, critical engagement, and influence I would like to thank the following: my feminist studies writing group in Minnesota—Tomoko Kuribayashi, Sally Lieberman, and Nancy Potter; my writing group at UNC Greensboro—Bill Blair, Colleen Kriger, John Tolan, and Lisa Tolbert; Rachel Buff, Miriam Cohen, Cindy Davis, Margaret Finnegan, Jennifer Guglielmo, Jane Healey, Robin D. G. Kelley, Carolyn Mathews, M. J. Maynes, Riv Ellen Prell, Paula Rabinowitz, Brian Riedel, John Sayer, Birgitte Soland, Kathy Wallerstein, and Patrick Wilkinson. A big and special thanks to Steve Peterson, who read countless early drafts and talked over these issues with me from a zillion angles. John D'Emilio read my dissertation and gave great suggestions for overhaul. Of equal importance, he and Jim Oleson also fed me innumerable bowls of homemade soup which warmed my heart and my belly. Janice Radway gave incisive comments on a draft of the book at a critical moment in my thinking, and Barbara Melosh and Vicki Ruiz read a draft for Columbia University Press and gave suggestions which greatly influenced the book's final form. Susan Cahn bravely plowed through some remarkably rough drafts, provided indispensable advice and humor, and was still willing to read final copies as well. Anne Enke read every word of multiple drafts; I relied daily on her exuberant support of my creative efforts and her shrewd critical abilities.

My students at UNC Greensboro in the past five years have provided inspiration, excitement, brilliance, and radicalism. I regret that I cannot list them all here. For all that they have taught me and for their companionship along the way I would like especially to thank Bryan Duncan, Donyelle Eller, Cat Hagarty, Pamela Gaddy, Bert Vanderveen, Carolyn Mathews, Neil Soiseth, and Brian Riedel.

Over the years of writing this book, my family developed amazing abilities to support my efforts by asking questions and by commiserating or celebrating, depending on the drama of the moment. With ever-growing love and appreciation I thank my father Jim Enstad, my brother Chris Enstad, and my sister Patty Enstad. I wish my mother, Cathy Enstad, could see this book; before her death in 1995 she had such vicarious hope for it.

Sometimes what helped me most were people who kept my imagination company, who inspired me to take necessary risks and color outside the lines. For being distinctively themselves and sharing their journeys with me, I gratefully acknowledge Jane Healey, Ben Ramsey, Pippa Holloway, Rachel Buff, Steve Peterson, Susan Cahn, and John D'Emilio. Also Cinder Hypki, who has been there from the beginning, sharing creative vision, poetry, politics and tomato-cheese sandwiches— her light is all through this book. Finally, Anne Enke, who has shared all the daily downs and ups—she believed in this book even when I was too tired to. The warmth of her deeply generous spirit has changed me into the kind of person who can write a book. Our endless magical conversations about the universe and everything and our physical and nonphysical travels make life a joy and an adventure.

LADIES OF LABOR, GIRLS OF ADVENTURE

INTRODUCTION
Mud in Our French Heels

At a recent American Studies Association conference, I attended a session entitled, "Does Cultural Studies Neglect Class?" The panelists presented a variety of views, but one argued "yes," and urged historians and cultural critics to make sure we have "materialist mud on our boots." This fashion metaphor captured my attention, immersed as I was in researching the fashions of working women at the turn of the twentieth century. That brief phrase conjured in my mind a very specific image of boots: *work* boots, with tough, thick soles and heavy leather uppers, a man's boots, well worn from labor and the "mud" of daily life. The presenter argued that, as scholars, we wear boots, and they ought not be clean and pretty. This suggested to me an ideal of a strong identification between scholar and working-class subject. The presenter warned that cultural studies threaten to remove us from the materialist mud, as scholars lose touch with the suffering of workers in favor of the fun of popular culture studies.

Because of my research, I experienced a dissonance with the opposition between "materialist mud" and "cultural studies" this metaphor created. The most stylish working women at the turn of the twentieth century wore cheap French heels, not boots, which they bought for one or two dollars on pushcarts in urban, working-class neighborhoods. French heels signaled Americanization and "ladyhood" for these mostly immigrant women. Young women often chose the pretty shoes as one of their first purchases in the United States, and proudly wore them for work and leisure. The middle class disdained these delicate high heels; the style was worn predominantly by the wealthy and the working classes. The French heels seemed woefully flimsy and too pretty to carry the "materialist mud" of the presenter's metaphor. When I tried to substitute them in my imagination for the boots in the metaphor, I realized that my mind had supplied an entire archetypical image of a worker wearing such muddy boots: a large male with muscular arms, engaged in physically demanding labor. While there was nothing in the presenter's words that overtly coded a gender or race connotation to these boots, my mind drew on well-established labor iconography and supplied an image of a white male worker.[1] French heels lacked the connotations of labor and heroic hard struggle that the boots conveyed to me.

I would like to suggest, however, that French heels provide an apt metaphor for how historians should approach class and cultural studies. Women's French heels represented both the promises and limitations of American capitalism. Working women wore them and declared themselves "American ladies." They invested French heels with great meanings of entitlement and belonging: they actively rejected the class ideologies that excluded women from the privileged label of "lady," and embraced America's promise that immigrants could escape the oppression and caste systems of the "old country." At the same time, the cheap shoes had paper-thin soles that could not withstand the walking and standing that women's work required. The grit from the streets quickly wore through, so that women literally had mud *in* their shoes. The capitalist marketplace both offered working women utopian promises and contained painful limitations. Indeed, the two cannot be separated. To see French heels simply as part of working women's "culture," which threatens to divorce us from their material life, is to pull apart aspects of daily life that the women necessarily experienced together. Indeed, by understanding the contradictions and connections between the promises and the limitations of consumer culture we can recover a rich matrix of meanings in working women's daily lives. As historians, perhaps we should metaphorically keep French heels on our feet, attuned to the tangible connections between the pleasures and the pains of consumer capitalism.

The American Studies Association panelist's fear that popular culture will take us away from serious class politics is an old one, and is reflected in the labor history sources I examine here. Labor leaders in the International Ladies Garment Workers Union (ILGWU) and the Women's Trade Union League (WTUL) routinely chastised working women for their ceaseless pursuit of fashion, their avid dime novel reading about working heroines who married millionaires, and their "affected" style, which included aristocratic airs and accents. While these practices had an array of diverse meanings, most leaders saw them as wholly negative. Leaders feared that such practices kept women from serious and practical concerns like labor organizing, and exacerbated middle-class perceptions of working women as too frivolous to be taken seriously as workers or political actors. Leaders urged working women to adopt a more serious demeanor and more sensible shoes. In doing so, they were asking women to more closely fit ideals of "worker" and "political actor" already deeply entrenched in U.S. culture.

Closely related ideals structured the raced and gendered image my mind supplied to the panelist's metaphor. While the word "worker" appears not to exclude but simply to describe, the *ideal* of "worker" in the nineteenth century was male. In addition, it was often *as workers* that working-class people claimed access to the political process, either through union representation or through the vote. As Judith Butler has argued, the dominant understanding of political action is that it requires a coherent and fixed identity already in place. That is, many assume that people must first fully identify with the category "worker" before they will engage in political action around working conditions. But Butler and others have noted that this idea of a coherent subjectivity, traceable to Enlightenment thought, carries an inherent tyranny. Identity categories such as "workers" or "women" are necessarily based in exclusions: as they define the inside they also define the outside. In doing so, they establish a new norm that becomes oppressive when they exclude others, or when they require people to fit themselves to the fiction of the category in order to be included. Far more than simple descriptions, labels shape identities and experiences.[2]

For example, Elizabeth Spelman has argued that the phrase "as women" has both enabled and undermined feminism's goal of emancipation. Feminism has seemed to require simply that a woman identify as a woman. But Spelman argues that when feminism, lacking a race or class critique, asked a diversity of women to think or act "as women," it unwittingly replaced the cultural norm of "man" (white and middle class) with a norm of white middle-class woman. Women of color, working-class, or otherwise "different" women became the deviation from that norm. Thus, feminism replicated the oppression that women experienced in the dominant culture. Spelman's point is not simply that we need to be more inclusive, but rather that the insistence on a coherent subject position at the root of political action itself tends toward oppressive exclusions.[3]

Perhaps the phrase "the worker" has had the same insidious role in the labor movement: this seemingly descriptive category is also based in exclusions, ways in which some workers can seem less serious than others and less deserving of the name. As David Roediger argues, male labor unions in the antebellum era developed a heroic category of "worker" for white males, in direct contrast to "slave labor." Their language of class, according to Roediger, formed around concepts of "manly" and "free" labor that explicitly excluded African American laborers and all women.[4] The long-term impact of this was to grant dignity to the name "worker" but reserve it for "serious" (white, male, and usually skilled) laborers.[5] By the late nineteenth century, most unions sought the advancement of the working classes by advocating a living wage for men, who served as heads of families. In this ideal, male wages were sufficient to support women and children, removing the necessity for their employment. Though the ideal of the living wage was never realized, the notion of the worker became more intricately tied to masculinity. For example, when Samuel Gompers of the American Federation of Labor talked about the rights of "workers" in the early twentieth century, he usually meant white, male, skilled industrial workers. Gompers overtly identified this most privileged group as the true backbone of the working class, and the AFL limited its organizing largely to this group. Correspondingly, many leaders believed women lacked dedication to their jobs and desired only marriage. In other words, many people did not consider women *real* workers, and they therefore did not expect political action from them.[6] Clearly, the category of the worker carried gender and race assumptions that replicated dominant hierarchies and undermined the oppositional potential of the labor movement.

Working women's participation in consumer culture exacerbated the perception of them as frivolous and their exclusion from the category of worker. Consumer culture can seem inherently opposed to serious political subjectivity. As Tania Modleski argues, our ways of thinking about consumer culture are intricately connected to conceptions of the feminine.[7] The nineteenth-century white middle class saw consumption as the feminine counterpart to productivity, a valued ideal associated with masculinity. Labor and production formed the basis of male identity and workers' dignity; consumer culture was seen as feminized, unproductive, irrational, and even emasculating. Of course, the dichotomy was false: this ideal formulation obscured men's consumption as well as women's productive activities in and out of the home. A man's work boot is as much a commodity as is a French heel, but high heels are typically associated with commodity culture while men's boots are associated with work. When working women engaged in consumer activities, they threatened their already provisional status as workers by participating in a part of culture associated with femininity.

Many contemporary scholars accept and extend the opposition between production and consumption. However, as Modleski points out, they differ on whether a "feminine" consumer culture is positive or negative. Historian Ann Douglas argues that the advent of a mass culture at the turn of the century "feminized" all of American society. She decries this transition for undermining the best Calvinist values of work and for obfuscating the process of industrial production. Critic Michel de Certeau, in contrast, celebrates the potentials of consumer culture but fundamentally agrees with Douglas's acceptance of that culture as feminine. The logic of the realm of popular culture, claims de Certeau, is not linear and rational; rather it is more "natural," "primitive," and "feminine," which allows it to resist the regimented "logic" of industrial capitalism. As Modleski notes, these very different critics maintain and perpetuate the nineteenth-century construction of consumerism as feminine.[8] It is little wonder then that women have been most often the symbol of the mindless consumer, from the turn of the century to today. Little wonder too that radicals at the turn of the century might mistake women with pretty hats for women with empty heads.

However, women workers in the early twentieth century went on strike in very large numbers. How can we account for this? Clearly, their participation in consumer culture did not preclude their political activism. Although contemporaries consistently bemoaned working women's consumer culture activities as detrimental to their identification and acceptance by others as serious workers, women did take political action in their workplaces and on public streets. Indeed, this book will argue that it was not so much clear and coherent identities as workers that supported women's political consciousness and actions, but the very contradictions they experienced as they found themselves excluded or only provisionally included in powerful cultural categories such as "worker," "lady," or "American." The dissonance between their experiences and the categories available to describe them proved to be a source of creativity as they fashioned a particular form of radicalism and their own gender and class language. The very interests in fashion, film, and fiction that labor leaders condemned became resources as women wrested identities from the contradictions they faced. The dissonance and contradictions they experienced, while painful, were not their only liability. An additional liability was that the radicalism they shaped was unintelligible to many contemporaries and has continued to be unintelligible to historians. Thus, it failed to transform dominant understandings of political activism at the time. Working women's politics remains misconstrued if we look only to how and when women acted according to our preconceived idea of political subjectivity and within our established category of worker.

To argue, as I do in this book, that consumer culture is serious and material business is not to claim it as an arena of freedom, nor to claim that it made women radical. Neither is it to say popular culture always functioned in opposition to the dominant culture for working women. Certainly, producers did not wish to champion the working woman but to sell goods. And sometimes women created popular practices with these products that reinforced social hierarchies. However, consumerism was not inevitably a sign of women's mass deception.[9] Consumer culture offered working-class women struggling with extremely difficult material and ideological constraints a new range of representations, symbols, activities, and spaces with which to create class, gender, and ethnic identities. Working women embraced these new resources and created practices that were in themselves a form of politics, in that they shifted the cultural terrain to the women's interests.[10]

Women's labor historians have not tended to view women's popular culture activities as potential political resources. Rather, like the labor leaders of the time, they have been suspicious of consumerism's trivializing effects. In an effort to defend the legitimacy of women as *workers*, most women's labor historians writing about this time period marginalize evidence about the centrality of popular culture to working-class women.[11] At the same time, Kathy Peiss's important book about working women's popular culture activities in New York does not address the fact that this same cohort of pleasure-seeking women produced some of the most dramatic strikes of the century.[12] Indeed, the labor histories that stress the seriousness of the strikers and Peiss's documentation of a world of pleasure-seeking seem so at odds that it is hard to believe these books are about the same women.

When historians have interrogated the use of consumer culture in the lives of historical actors, however, they have found people using it to gain identity, dignity, resources, and justice. For example, Jacqueline Dowd Hall finds that young Appalachian women strikers in the 1920s created a dramatic rebellious style on picket lines and in courtrooms, partly through their innovative and proud use of modern fashion. Stephen Norwood similarly documents the flamboyant use of fashion by striking female Irish-American telephone operators in 1910s and 1920s Boston. George Sanchez reveals that consumer culture became a site for young Mexican Americans to create their own version of Americanization, and Vicki Ruiz shows that young Mexican American women used consumer culture to push against restrictions for women even as they reinterpreted Mexican American identity. Robin D. G. Kelley argues that Malcolm X's early adulthood in Detroit's hipster subculture, which included oppositional cultural practices such as wearing the zoot suit and the conk hairstyle and speaking in a distinctive "hep cat" language, profoundly shaped his radicalism. And Tricia Rose demonstrates that rap artists create a "black idiom" that articulates the struggles of urban black life precisely within the highly commercialized music industry.[13] These historians argue that participation in consumer culture usually has multiple and even contradictory meanings. Nevertheless, all suggest that diverse groups of people have wrested meaning from difficult and oppressive conditions. As George Lipsitz writes, "People fight with the resources at their disposal, and frequently their pain leads them to quite innovative means of struggle."[14] Popular culture is one resource (among many) that people use to create community, pleasure, and sometimes politics.

The challenge of analyzing the kind of mass-produced popular culture that working women consumed has perhaps been the most acute. Fashion and mass-produced narratives for women have the reputation of being particularly silly or trite. Consider, for example, the reputation of soap operas and romances as opposed to televised sports. Indeed, mass-produced narratives for women and women's fashion are cited variously as evidence of both the triviality of these forms and the silliness of women consumers.[15] However, as critic Angela McRobbie argues, mass-produced narratives and fashion can allow women to actively create leisure and personal spaces that are female-centered, and are locations for developing positive identities.[16] And as Lisa Lewis and Janice Radway demonstrate in their studies of MTV and romances respectively, such spaces are often *productive* of ideologies that exceed those found in the texts themselves. Women are not, therefore, passive consumers.[17] An examination of working women's relationship to these most denigrated forms of consumer culture can shed light on how women shaped cultural practices in their own interests, and perhaps even on why they seemed willing to walk off their jobs at the drop of a hat.

As I began to study turn-of-the-century working-class women's consumer culture activities, first among my observations was that these women did not attach the same meanings to consumer products that their critics did. For these northern workers in industrial centers, a concern with fashion was not antithetical to "true" radicalism. Like the telephone workers documented by Stephen Norwood, female garment workers incorporated their love of fashion with their political styles. In fact, when more than 20,000 female garment workers of New York City staged the great shirtwaist strike of 1909, the dynamic young striker Clara Lemlich included a defense of fashion in a list of grievances. Young women needed a place to put their hats, Lemlich told a reporter from the *New York Evening Journal*, so that they would not get trampled by the traffic of the shop during work hours. "Sometimes a girl has a new hat," said Lemlich. "It is never much to look at because it never costs more than fifty cents, but it's pretty sure spoiled after its been at the shop. . . . We like new hats as well as other young women. Why shouldn't we?"[18]

What might seem like a small or trivial request was actually closely tied to the central issues of the strike. Workers' grievances focused not only on wages and hours, but also on the treatment they received from mostly male bosses and supervisors. Female garment workers were paid an average of six dollars per week for ten to fourteen hours of labor per day; many earned less than they needed to support themselves.[19] However, women also routinely endured arbitrary extensions of working hours, the demeaning fine system for "mistakes" in their work, and sexual harassment, which ranged from constant insinuations to intrusive touch. Working conditions were often uncomfortable or dangerous, and doors were sometimes locked to keep workers from taking breaks. (One such locked door led to the death of 146 workers in the Triangle Shirtwaist Factory fire in 1911.) Most workers had no cloakrooms to protect their clothes from the grime and bustle of the factories, and had to pile their coats and broad-brimmed hats on single, exposed hooks.[20]

All of these offenses and indignities epitomized the oppressive nature of the women's jobs. As *The Survey* reporter Mary Brown Sumner put it, "What outraged [Lemlich] most from the beginning were the petty persecutions, the meannesses, and the failure to recognize the girls as human beings."[21] Lemlich's demand for a place for women to put their hats was consistent with the strikers' insistence that they be treated "like ladies," that is, that they be accorded respect by supervisors and bosses. Lemlich invoked women's hats, consumer products, in articulating notions of collectivity and worker dignity. Her representation of hats as icons of respect due to women workers rhetorically linked consumer products to her broader concept of liberation for working-class women.

In order to fully understand the meanings Lemlich's demand carried, we need to understand the ways that fashionable hats signified freedom for young working women as well as in the wider culture. Women's hats carried varied meanings within working women's families, on the street, and in mass-produced narratives such as magazine stories and films.

Young immigrant women's hats held two particular meanings at home, among their families. First, hats signaled women's status as workers who earned their own money. Hats, dresses, and shoes were symbols of a generational struggle in which young women believed that, as workers, they deserved a portion of their pay for their own use, just as was customary for men. Expendable income was one of the primary privileges that accrued to a male breadwinner. Mothers and fathers, however, tried to hold the line that said that a daughter's labor belonged to her father's household—unless she was married, in which case her labor belonged to her husband. When women insisted on their own money from their pay envelopes, they insisted that the heretofore masculine label of "worker" be extended to them.[22]

Second, hats could signal Americanization within the immigrant family, as women adopted modern styles sometimes at odds with their parents' traditions. Lemlich, a Jewish immigrant from the Ukraine, was undoubtedly personally familiar with these struggles among her mostly Jewish and Italian immigrant co-workers. For these women, clothing was the first sign of a new American identity; seasoned relatives often bought newcomers American clothes, including shoes, on the day of their arrival. Indeed, many employers would not hire women who did not wear American clothing. Sometimes immigrant parents criticized stylish daughters' seeming disregard for the ways of the old country. Other times parents themselves embraced the new American styles of dress and appearance. But whether in consort with parents or in rebellion against family-based power structures, young women signaled their modernity and Americanism through dress. Fashion could be a way of making connections across ethnic boundaries, as immigrants from various backgrounds adopted similar styles, as well as a way to reinterpret a specifically Jewish or Italian identity in a new context. When an immigrant woman bought a fashionable hat and put it on at home, then, she created herself as a "worker" and as an "American," with various potential connotations.[23]

When young working women wore these same hats out on the streets, however, they took on additional meanings. Middle- and upper-class women critiqued working women's display of fashion as "putting on airs" and "playing the lady." Working women countered that they *were* ladies, and should be treated as such. For middle-class women, fashion served as a display of class distinction and taste, a cultural marker of privilege that differentiated them from working-class women and women of color. When working-class women dressed in elaborate styles, they staged a carnivalesque class inversion that undermined middle-class efforts to control the definition of "lady." The right to untrammeled hats, as chapter 2 will argue, was part of a larger and ongoing gender and class language among working women that appropriated the status of middle- and upper-class women. Thus, their hats could mean something different as they dressed to go out to work, to amusements, to parade in front of parents, or to promenade on Fourteenth Street or Essex Street. Both Jewish and Italian women took part in these activities, though Jewish women typically had more freedom of movement than Italian women, and could wear their fashions to a range of public amusements. Despite Italian women's more limited mobility, they regularly attended motion pictures and purchased dime novels and fashion items.[24] Working women's hats could thus signal them as "workers," "Americans," or "ladies," or all three at once.

These varied associations were enough to prompt Lemlich to bring up hats as a powerful symbol for working-class women's freedom and entitlement. But the broader popular culture also associated hats with women's freedom, albeit in quite different terms. Lemlich may have been familiar with the prevalent narratives in print and film media; certainly readers of the *New York Evening Journal* were. As John D'Emilio and Estelle Freedman have noted, producers had to promote increased consumption as rigorously as the products themselves: "Americans did not automatically respond to factory output by multiplying their desires for material goods; an ethic of consumption had to be sold."[25] Promising women liberation from family-based patriarchy was one common means of making this sale and gaining loyal consumers.[26]

This consumer ethic is conveyed in a 1912 short film, *The New York Hat*, directed by D. W. Griffith.[27] In the film, a young woman (Mary Pickford) lives with her old-fashioned, cheap, tyrannical father. Mary's dying mother left a secret bequest with the young, attractive minister of her church, placing a small savings in his hands to provide for occasional finery for Mary. The note reads:

My Beloved Pastor: My husband worked me to death, but I have managed to save a little sum. Take it, and from time to time buy my daughter the bits of finery she has always been denied. Let no one know.

The minister honors the bequest, and secretly purchases an elaborate hat, made in New York, for Mary. Town "busybodies" see him buy the hat and later observe Mary proudly wearing it. They spread rumors of scandal that get back to Mary's father. Furious at her apparent affair, Mary's father destroys the hat, and Mary is crushed. When her father confronts the minister, however, the minister produces the bequest. Mary's father is ashamed at his excessive frugality and his tyranny over his wife and daughter, and the minister and the daughter become engaged.

The consumer product, the New York hat, occupies the center of this narrative. It is both the cause of family discord and the means of the daughter's liberation from her tyrannical patriarch. The father is steeped in nineteenth-century values of frugality and hard work. However, in twentieth-century consumer culture, such values were outmoded, and the father is not portrayed as a responsible head of the family but as a cruel miser. The fact that the male suitor is a minister could assure an audience that the new system of consumerism was not only more liberating for women than thrift, but also morally superior. Consumer culture industries, here at once the fashion *and* film industries, were invested in affirming women's consumerism in terms that neutralized traditional critiques of spending. They therefore promoted consumption as a means of liberation from family-based patriarchy, even as they re-established family harmony by the end of the film. In a limited way, *The New York Hat* presented a critique of patriarchal authority within the family. At the same time, it affirmed the *right* of women, even poor women, to consumer products. The producers of *The New York Hat*, however, presented this liberation as highly individualistic. They portrayed no striking or clearly immigrant workers, and reinforced dominant notions of romance. Thus the movie sidestepped the more controversial issue of a woman's right as a worker and erased ethnicity altogether.

When Clara Lemlich invoked women's hats in her plea for liberation from oppressive workplace conditions, she put these already existing cultural associations to her own purpose. She widened the sphere of struggle beyond the family or immigrant group to the workforce, making the hat a symbol of gender and class struggle. Lemlich seemed to invoke poor women's "right" to consumer products when she said, "We like new hats as well as any other young women. Why shouldn't we?" But she did not simply imbibe the individualist ethic represented in *The New York Hat*. Rather, Lemlich imbued the right to have hats with a collective meaning for women workers, operating within a class conflict. Lemlich's demand is evidence that even as popular culture and fashion industries develop mass-produced products and the ideologies to justify and sell them, such products take on specific meanings within a social world.

I present this discussion of hats to suggest that it is possible to reconstruct the symbols and tropes important to working women in the past, to retrace the ways they understood their world. While cultural forms can have multiple meanings, these meanings are historically and socially constructed, and are not infinite. Historians can recover much of what Judith Walkowitz calls the "cultural repertoire" of historical actors.[28] But as Angela McRobbie has noted, too often critics see culture "as texts, images and representations rather than as social relationships."[29] My goal in this book is to link social history and cultural studies by examining consumer culture in the context of its social circulation.

To see consumer culture within social circulation refers to much more than "audience response" or even "reception." Rather, it involves understanding how products are shaped and imbued with meanings at various points of production and consumption. I look first at the economic and social factors at work in the production process and how they shaped the kinds of products available for working women, and those products' possibilities and limitations. Focusing on mass-produced fiction, fashion, and film means I am studying goods with a wide, often national or international, distribution.

To see culture in circulation also requires a focus on a specific group of consumers and the ways they wove the products into the fabric of their lives. It includes understanding the extent and nature of consumers' purchases, the particular ways they created social practices around their daily use of products, the content and qualities of products and, when possible, consumers' response to these products. Textual analysis thus is an important part of this method, but not its primary focus. Tracing the social circulation of consumer culture necessitates a specific regional and ethnic focus, as there certainly was great variation in the ways people responded to mass-produced popular culture. I focus on women in urban centers in the Northeast and Midwest between 1890 and 1920, paying particular attention to Jewish and Italian immigrant women in New York City.[30] I chose this group particularly because they have been the heroines of many labor histories and offer ample opportunity to explore women's practices in both popular culture and labor politics. Once we understand the meanings women made with consumer commodities, we can explore how those meanings operated within political events and discourses.

This study is not only about how working women used consumer culture products; it is also about how their interaction with products shaped who they were. Working women formed subjectivities in relationship to commodities. Their use of products was a central aspect of their self-construction and self-expression as women, as workers, and as Americans. This was not a passive process: the commodities did not *make* women behave in a particular way or become particular sorts of selves. However, neither was the process autonomous. Working women formed subjectivities from the limited resources available to them in their daily lives, including the myriad of ways they were addressed by popular culture industries, labor unions, reformers, and family members. The term "subjectivity" is important. By it I mean the particular way that an individual becomes a social person, part and product of the corner of the world she or he inhabits. Subjectivity is thus related to the concepts "self" and "identity," with a crucial distinction: subjectivity emphasizes a *process* of becoming that is never completed. It is based on the premise that *who one is* is neither essential nor fixed, but is continually shaped and reshaped in human social exchange. The notions of self and identity can be used in this way, but they typically connote some internal essence (self) or something that develops and is achieved, or even socially constructed, at which point it is static (identity). I will use all three terms in this study to explore working women's process of becoming in relationship to their social context.

Working women formed subjectivities as ladies by using the fiction and fashion commodities available to them. Mass-produced clothing allowed them to create elaborate modifications of current styles, and dime novels offered them fantasies of working heroines who became great ladies through inheritances and marriages to millionaires. Their style was not an imitation of middle-class identity but an appropriation of a valued set of class codes. When working women declared themselves "American ladies" they formed class, gender, and ethnic identities that engaged the exclusions the women faced in U.S. society. This subjectivity cannot be extricated from commodity purchase and use, but it affected women far beyond the realm of leisure activities. While subjectivities formed through commodity consumption are typically dismissed as superficial, this book argues that working women used popular culture as a resource to lay claim to dignified identities as workers, sometimes from the very terms used by others to degrade them. In addition, when working women went on strike, they utilized the subjectivities and languages they developed through popular culture practices to claim formal political status. Their new identities supported their participation in strikes; however, they did not make their way into the broader language of radical politics. Thus, I also reveal the painful limits of women's social practices and subjectivities. Working-class women were unable to transform radical rhetoric or to ensure the preservation of their particular experiences and understandings in historical narratives.

The following chapters argue that we have not understood the politics that working-class women made because we have not understood the ways women used consumer culture to do political work. My argument is not that popular culture activities led in any direct way to political activism, but that a reassessment of both is needed to understand how working-class women shaped their experiences in both realms. A number of cultural critics have called upon historians to view historical sources as *representations* of the past rather than as transparent reflections of events.[31] As representations, sources always emerge from interested positions and work to produce meanings and realities rather than simply to record them. Part of the task of seeing sources as representations is tracing the ways that some identities become widely culturally intelligible and seen as natural and self-evident, while others recede into epistemological obscurity. Indeed, we have perhaps been hasty in our recognition of working-class women as labor heroines, because in celebrating and categorizing them as exemplary workers, a status they did not generally hold in their own time, we obscure crucial contradictions and multiple identities at the center of their cultural and political maneuvers.

This book begins by tracing the development of the first mass-produced commodities made for working-class women: dime novel romances and inexpensive clothing. Industries began specifically to target working women as consumers as early as the 1860s. By the 1880s, producers fully established the economic niche for working women's fashion and formula fiction. Though these products opened up new possibilities and pleasures in working women's lives, they had limitations as well. Chapter 1 explores the social and economic forces that categorized cultural forms as "tasteful" or "cheap" and shaped the qualities of the products available for working women's use.

In chapter 2, I turn to working women's consumption of fashion and dime novel fiction. Working women created complex social practices around fashion and fiction consumption that connected the commodities to a collective workplace culture. Within social circulation, these products became part of working women's subjectivities as ladies. Working women's version of ladyhood differed greatly from middle-class ideals: it challenged middle-class perceptions of labor as degrading to femininity and created a utopian language of entitlement rooted in workplace experiences.

Chapters 3 and 4 examine the great New York shirtwaist strike of 1909–1910. Chapter 3 shows how women's dramatic fashion and distinctive cultural style became central to the public debate around the strike. To many, flamboyant fashion seemed incongruous with the effort to claim a formal political identity. The popular press represented striking women in sensational terms that accentuated their fashion. For many middle-class readers, such an emphasis on fashion signaled that the strikers were irrational and incapable of serious political action. In response, strike leaders created publicity that obscured working women's investment in consumer culture. In doing so, they failed to incorporate much of working women's own rhetoric into union rhetoric. Additionally, they left union records that painted the strikers as highly serious to match middle-class ideals of political actors. These sources subsequently led historians to represent the strikers similarly as serious, "rational" participants and to miss the importance of their cultural practices to the strike. Chapter 4 revises labor leaders' and historians' earlier accounts, focusing on working women's own efforts to construct political subjectivities in the shirtwaist strike. The massive walkout of over 20,000 workers, the development of grievances, and the style of picketing all become more clear with an understanding of working women's popular culture experiences. While working women's popular culture activities did not prompt their radicalism, working women drew upon the resources and identities that they had formed in relationship to commodities when they created themselves as strikers.

The fifth chapter returns to daily life outside of a strike context and explores working women's relationship to the dramatic new medium of motion pictures. Working women developed distinctive fan practices and fantasies when they incorporated the movies into their daily lives. Motion picture theaters became important new public spaces for working women across ethnic differences. Women imbued motion pictures, posters, and stars with an imaginative element, creating a public consumer identity closely connected to the dime novel fantasies and fashion displays of ladyhood. Thus, motion pictures became an additional site of social change for working women, and a resource as they continued to form public identities.

The political languages we employ in the late twentieth century are limited. Unwittingly, we tend to create a privileged definition of political actor, most often male and white, but always serious, who can stand best as "hero." This can either blind us to political potentials and actions in the past or present altogether, or require that people and their histories conform to dominant fictions in order to be recognized. For

Clara Lemlich and thousands of other young women who faced painful material struggles, concern with hats or French heels was not necessarily evidence of trivial desires. Rather, their passion for products could operate as powerful representations of female workers' dignity. If women's fifty-cent hats could remain untrammeled, so, perhaps, could their bodies and spirits. We need new political narratives to help us perceive languages of class, gender, and race that we may not otherwise recognize as such.[32] This book is an effort in that direction.

CHAPTER ONE

CHEAP DRESSES AND DIME NOVELS
The First Commodities for Working Women

"You see, I have always had my suits from a pushcart or sometimes from a little store in Hester Street. It is wonderful to have one from Wanamakers [a New York department store]. I wish I could wear the label on the front."   —Jewish working woman, 1915[1]

"Stephen, there's only one thing I love—outside of you! [said Peg] . . . Just coming home tonight I stopped in front of the Nonpareil Theater . . . and stood looking at the posters. One was a picture of Nellie Malone, the juvenile actress—" She half closed her eyes; then she went on in an intense low voice: "It should have been my picture . . ."
—James Oppenheim, "Peg O' the Movies," *The Ladies' World* (1913)[2]

In the 1870s, industries for the first time mass produced two types of commodities expressly targeted to a young working female audience: inexpensive fashion and formulaic fiction. Working-class women certainly had been consumers before this time. They, like their middle-class counterparts, often purchased food, cloth, and other durables for their families. In addition, working-class women consumed both fashion and fiction before the 1870s: some purchased inexpensive and quickly made dresses from "slop" dressmakers by the early nineteenth century and, along with other family members, read fiction in family story papers by the 1840s. Working women's consumption differed after 1870, however, because they increasingly purchased mass-produced products created specifically for them. The ready-made clothing industry, which initially focused on men's clothing, successfully extended to the more complicated clothing for women, replacing dressmakers' goods with mass-produced fashions. Story papers and dime novels simultaneously developed a set of formulas about and primarily for working women, a subset of cheap fiction that continued to grow in popularity and profitability into the twentieth century. As mass-produced clothing replaced slop dressmakers' products and formulas for working women supplemented earlier types of fiction, working women moved into a new relationship with mass-produced goods that hailed them as individuals rather than as family members.[3] Along with their labor, consumption of fashion and fiction constituted a new and specific relationship between working women and the market.

Working-class women, as much as their more wealthy counterparts, wound these commodities into their own culture based in display, self-statement, and glamour. The young woman quoted above, who probably made about six dollars per week, clearly wished not only to have a fine suit but also to display it. Years before manufacturers thought of it, she wanted to wear the label emblazoned on her chest, presumably to associate the brand of the suit with her self. By the 1890s, the garment industry produced a variety of "grades" of fashions, allowing women of various incomes to wear the latest styles. However, there was great diversity in cultural associations of class, gender, and ethnicity with these different grades. These associations had their roots in the early nineteenth-century expansion of middle-class fashion, and developed over time through the social uses of fashion by different classes and ethnicities. The relative status associated with different grades of clothing was not lost on the young worker who wished to display the Wanamaker label, which represented a full step up from the grade of suit she usually could afford. Her desire for this commodity was not automatic. Rather, it emerged from the economic and cultural history of the development of ready-made fashion products.

Formulaic magazine serial stories like "Peg O' the Movies," the source of the second epigraph, both fueled and exploited such desires. The reader of "Peg O' the Movies" was invited to identify with the heroine, Peg, a clerical worker who becomes a movie star and encounters exciting adventures on the job. When the fictional Peg sees the poster of the young, successful actress, she desires to become that object of fame and awe: "It should have been my picture [on the poster]." The mode of production and the narrative strategies of "Peg O' the Movies" can be traced to the development of "cheap" fiction formulas in the nineteenth century. Story paper and dime novel publishers actively created formulas beginning in the 1840s, when the advent of new printing technologies made it possible to mass-produce publications at low cost. The formula for working women that emerged in the 1870s combined narrative elements from the penny press, from romances and working men's dime novels, and from middle-class advice manuals. This formula spawned some of the most successful dime novels of the 1880s and 1890s, which continued to be reprinted in the twentieth century. By the 1910s, publishers translated dime novel formulas into popular magazine fiction, like "Peg O' the Movies," which was printed in *The Ladies' World*, as well as into early motion picture serials. The stories invoked the difficulty of working-class women's lives—toiling at jobs that offered low pay, dirty and dangerous working conditions, and little hope for advancement—and offered them fabulous fantasies of wealth, fashion, success, and love. When a 1913 woman read "Peg O' the Movies," she consumed a fiction product with a complex history.

Working women's relationship to consumerism, then, was shaped in part by the effects of production already inhering in the goods they bought. This is not to say that working women simply imbibed ideological messages conveyed by these commodities; on the contrary, they wound the products into their own social context and imbued them with their own meanings. However, the workings of the market dramatically shaped the range and nature of the commodities available to working women. As Martyn Lee has pointed out, commodities have a "dual nature." They bear the commercial and cultural influences that shaped their production and they become instruments for use in a separate arena of consumption, within particular consuming communities and contexts. Consumption is a moment when an individual interacts with the possibilities and limitations of the capitalist marketplace, yet the purchased product becomes a "material and symbolic resource" when it is integrated into an individual's daily life.[4] This chapter explores one part of the dual nature of goods: the ways that the nineteenth-century economy generated particular fashion and fiction commodities.

Fashion and fiction products for working women were not simply less expensive versions of those for middle-class women. There were significant differences in the quality and styles of fashions as well as in the narrative structure and content of novels. This chapter traces the development of those differences and argues that early efforts by the middle class to obscure their own consumption shaped the way the capitalist marketplace produced and categorized cultural commodities for both middle- and working-class people. This argument challenges a prevalent interpretation of the transition to a twentieth-century consumer culture. Many scholars have followed the lead of historian Warren Susman in describing a nineteenth-century "culture of character," as opposed to a twentieth-century "culture of personality" rooted in commodities. Susman argues that both the character model and the personality model of the self were constructions, but sees the character model as formed in relationship to morals, work, and citizenship, while the personality model could be "best developed in leisure time," in relationship to commodities like motion pictures. Many historians and cultural critics decry the centrality of commodities to the self in the twentieth century, dismiss the so-called "culture of personality" as superficial, and harken back to the "culture of character" as a mode of being in which values, rather than products, mattered.[5] However, the "culture of character" was also a culture of commodities. The notion of character served in part to distinguish middle-class "tasteful" consumption from other consumption, and to camouflage the fact that the middle class defined itself in large part through product purchase and use. By taking this ideology as an accurate description of social relations, historians have missed how the middle class designated the use of certain commodities as superficial, as a fantasy escape, or as immoral, while denying its own commodity consumption. This middle class tactic not only categorized products, it also spurred differential production methods for those emerging categories, and by the late nineteenth century had significant effects on the fashion and fiction available for working women's purchase.

A brief example will serve to dramatize the limitations of goods produced for working-class women. James Oppenheim, the author of "Peg O' the Movies," also published in middle-class journals, where his writing was markedly different. He published his poem "Bread and Roses" in *American Magazine*, a muckraking journal read largely by the middle class, in December 1911, in response to the new wave of strikes among women factory workers, particularly in New York, Philadelphia, and Chicago. Such subjects were popular and profitable in magazines of this sort that catered to an audience of concerned and usually politically aware middle-class citizens. Indeed, while mass-produced print material for the working classes rarely contained overt political content by 1900, mass-produced print material for the middle class allowed, and sometimes even required, such content as emblematic of a democratic society. "Bread and Roses" has gained an esteemed place in radical literature. Labor myth, in fact, holds that Oppenheim wrote the poem for the Lawrence, Massachusetts, textile strike of 1912, and that strike itself is often termed "The Bread and Roses Strike."[6] Oppenheim's poem celebrated the political activism of young working-class women:

As we come marching, marching, we bring the greater days.
The rising of the women means the rising of the race.
No more the drudge and idler—ten that toil where one reposes,
But a sharing of life's glories: Bread and Roses! Bread and Roses ...

A year and a half later, Oppenheim published "Peg O' the Movies" in *The Ladies' World*, a cheap magazine largely read by the working class. A different set of market conventions shaped this story, and the narrative elements of "Peg O' the Movies" bear only slight resemblance to those in "Bread and Roses." While both pieces focused on heroic young working women, in "Peg O' the Movies" Oppenheim portrayed no women strikers, no poignant political pleas. Oppenheim, a supporter and chronicler of the women's strikes, only celebrated them in texts destined for middle-class audiences, while he wrote stories of adventure, fame, and romance for working-class women themselves. Both "Peg O' the Movies" and "Bread and Roses" were literary products, shaped by market interests. Why then, despite their common authorship by a radical writer, do the two pieces look so different? The production process of fashion and fiction commodities for working women reveals the limitations and possibilities in these first products for working women.

It is important to explore the emergence of fashion and fiction for women in tandem, despite the very different nature of these types of commodities. Both developed at the same time due to similar economic and social changes. While industrialization in the early nineteenth century was largely fueled by the processing of raw materials, such as textile production, the boom after 1870 was driven increasingly by growth in industries providing goods for individual consumption. Increased mechanization of clothing manufacturing, combined with advances in sizing and fitting, prompted the expansion of mass production of clothing for women by the 1870s. Similarly, story paper and dime novel publishing grew dramatically due to printing and paper-making technologies by the 1860s, and producers sought new narratives and more specialized audiences by the 1870s. Thus, the fiction and fashion industries participated in the same large economic trends.

The development of fiction and fashion should also be studied together because working women became an increasingly important market for both. The numbers of women workers rose steadily in the 1870s, and many of the new jobs for them were in precisely the rapidly growing industries making consumer goods. As more women earned money of their own, impetus grew for some industries to draw them into consumption as individuals rather than only as family members. Indeed, the garment industry depended on working- and lower middle-class buyers during the first decades of its development, when problems of sizing and fit persuaded the more affluent to continue patronizing tailors. It is not surprising that the fiction and fashion industries would target some of their own workers (as well as other women) as consumers, thus recapturing a margin of the often meager wages paid to young women. In addition, the social relations of the production of ready-made clothing and dime novels categorized them both as "cheap" products, and thus shaped their potential meanings in similar ways.

The mechanization of textile production in the early nineteenth-century United States initiated dramatic changes in the types of clothing available for middle- and working-class people and the meanings associated with that clothing. In the eighteenth century, fine fabrics were woven by hand and were very expensive. The wealthy usually imported them from Europe and employed highly skilled tailors to construct complex and ornate styles for men and women. Most women of middling income employed tailors only for their best dresses, if at all, and made most of their families' clothing themselves from cheaper grades of fabric. Eighteenth-century ready-made clothing was made quickly by "slop" tailors and was reserved for men who had no female family members available to sew for them: sailors, male slaves, soldiers, and male laborers. This clothing was coarse, usually fit badly, and signaled to some the stigma of manual labor. With the implementation of the mechanized loom, the prices of all cloth, including fine cloth, dropped dramatically. This expanded the market of people who could afford tailor-made clothing.[7]

Tailors, in response to these changes, began to rationalize their production process by sending simple sewing and finishing to outworkers, usually working-class women, who sewed by hand in their homes. The tailors retained the more skilled tasks of measuring, sizing, and cutting. This rationalization (but not yet mechanization) of the labor process further lowered the price of tailor-made clothes. By the 1830s, the middle class could consistently afford a variety of such clothing in the latest styles. In addition, most tailors began to carry ready-made clothes as well, especially for men. Such clothing could be cut out quickly by the tailor, sewn for low wages by outworkers, and sold in the tailor's shop. This clothing still lacked a close fit, but served well the growing market of men who worked in urban centers, away from their families and the women who sewed for them. The finer, inexpensive cloth available meant that ready-made clothing could be made for occasions other than manual work, and both middle- and working-class men purchased ready-made business and evening wear. Thus, the mechanization of textiles expanded the choices and quality of clothing for the middle class and, to a more limited extent, the working class.[8]

Ready-made clothing allowed working men to dress very stylishly, or "high," for low prices. The young working men of New York City's Bowery neighborhood became notable as "Bowery b'hoys," largely for their distinctive use of ready-mades. The Bowery b'hoy wore, as one contemporary described it, a black broad-brimmed hat, a black frock coat that extended below the knee, a "flashy" vest of satin or velvet worn over a loose-fitting shirt with collar turned down to expose the neck, tight pantaloons, and "a profusion of jewelry as varied and costly as the b'hoy could procure."[9] Although urban working-class people could still rarely afford tailor-fitted garments, they experienced as dramatic a growth in clothing choices relative to earlier periods as did the middle class.

Ready-made clothing for women was not as extensive as that for men, probably because the market for it was not as great, since most women did their own sewing. Fashion histories argue that the extremely complex process of fitting women's garments precluded ready-mades for women until after the Civil War. However, this conclusion only holds for the middle class. Christine Stansell has shown that urban working women in the 1840s purchased ready-made dresses from slop tailors for two or three dollars per dress. Stansell argues that by the 1840s, there were enough domestics and other working women who had limited time in which to do their own sewing to support a large group of slop dressmakers. Like other ready-made clothing, the dresses probably did not fit as well as tailored dresses, and middle-class women did not buy them. However, these dresses did approximate the current styles. Like the clothing worn by the Bowery b'hoy, they allowed purchasers to dress "high."[10]

The meanings associated with this new availability of clothing emerged from the developing class structure, as both the middle class and the working class incorporated the commodities into their daily lives. The mechanization of textile production was just one facet of the industrialization that spawned new working and middle classes. Factories slowly displaced the artisan system, consigning the children of many self-employed artisans to poorly paid, dead-end factory jobs. Meanwhile, a new middle class took shape as the numbers of merchants and clerks grew in response to economic diversification.[11] Middle- and working-class meanings associated with fashion did not develop in isolation. The potential meanings of working women's fashion choices relate in part to middle-class notions of "character" and "taste," which became part of a very powerful ideology underpinning middle-class identity by mid-century. This ideology distinguished consumption with values (i.e. "tasteful" consumption) from consumption seen as lacking values and deriving solely from crass market interests.

By the 1840s, the middle class adopted consumer practices, such as the purchase of fine fashions, that in the eighteenth century had connoted gentility and had been largely confined to the wealthy.[12]

Because the middle class could now participate in the purchase of fine clothing and other consumer products, it declared this transition to be "democratic," emblematic of the new nation, and celebrated it as "egalitarian," as opposed to elite consumption, which it saw as hierarchical.[13] Unfortunately, most recent fashion histories have accepted middle-class rhetoric as historically accurate and celebrate the "democratization of clothing" in the nineteenth century, despite the overwhelming historical evidence that clothing has remained a key point of class and race conflict through the twentieth century.[14]

Indeed, members of the middle class did not see the different and inferior clothing of workers, servants, and slaves as contradicting this "democracy," but still sought to maintain distinction through dress from those "lower" in status than themselves. While gaining power, they were by no means economically secure in this early period. Lacking sufficient capital to ensure their children's economic futures, middle-class people needed to culturally distinguish themselves from the working class. Cultural capital, including education, manners and morals, and a middle-class standard of taste in consumption, could increase the likelihood of good business connections and marriages for their children.[15] Distinction in clothing had not disappeared; rather, it stood in tension with the democratic rhetoric. Thus, the middle class encountered a key contradiction that greatly shaped women's fashion practices: How could they maintain their egalitarian ideals even as they promoted class distinction?

In part, this contradiction was contained, if not resolved, through the ideal of the white middle-class "lady," who consumed but was by definition virtuous and pure. As historians have argued, women served as moral bulwarks for the middle-class family, providing guidance and stability to men and boys who ventured into the competitive and potentially corrupt public arena for business. Middle-class women in the 1840s created an ideal of "sincere" fashion based in domesticity: it served not to display beauty or wealth, but to reveal inner virtue. "Your dress is a sort of index to your character," preached *Godey's Lady's Book* in 1852,[16] and women were advised to make purchases that would display this character. This nineteenth-century understanding of identity and character as essential and emanating from within led to the idea that the inner truth about oneself manifested outwardly in one's appearance. Why not, then, pursue character through fashion? This ideal transformed fashion from the pursuit of status into, in historian Karen Halttunen's words, "a form of moral self-improvement."[17]

The historically specific nature of this middle-class view of fashion reveals that commodities are always consumed symbolically as well as to satisfy needs and wants. Indeed, those needs and wants, and how they are understood, are shaped within culture, in part through consumer practices. Thus, the act of consumption engages consumers in the prevailing social order, potentially but not inevitably valorizing that order. For the nineteenth-century middle class to maintain a symbolic association of their consumption as "democratic," the undemocratic labor relations that produced the commodities had to be obscured. Indeed, this was a characteristic of the entire emerging economic system. Capitalist production mystified the labor process and presented commodities seemingly devoid of meanings stemming from production. This allowed employers to emphasize the exchange value of the commodity over the labor that went into it, and thus validate keeping wages as low as possible, even when achieving high profits.[18]

The mystification of fashion commodities in the 1840s also specifically pushed against earlier meanings for such commodities.[19] Eighteenth-century aristocratic clothing had signaled high status both because it was extremely labor intensive to produce, and because it *appeared* to be: men's and women's clothing alike was intricately cut and elaborately trimmed. The 1840s middle-class "sentimental" styles were still expensive, using fine fabrics and employing skilled tailors, but they omitted the elaborate trim of earlier, aristocratic fashions. Thus, they obscured the labor required to produce them. As Halttunen states:

> In the sentimental period, rouge became unfashionable; heeled shoes went out of style; elbow-length gloves grew shorter; parasols, muffs and folding fans all shrank in size; and unmarried women began to wear very little jewelry. The overall effect generated by sentimental dress was demure self-effacement.[20]

One contributor to *Godey's Lady's Book* contrasted the moral nineteenth-century styles with decadent eighteenth-century fashion: "The nineteenth century with its darker colors and more thoughtful energy, seems even now, when nearly half of its years are sped, to wear mourning for the criminal folly of its predecessors."[21]

The new middle-class women's magazines of the 1840s disseminated information about fashion and played a key role in the formation of new meanings of commodities. This was particularly true because advertising, which would increasingly take on this role through the nineteenth century, was still in its infancy and was not highly sophisticated. Women's magazines like *Godey's Lady's Book* not only promoted the "sincere" style, they also developed a distinctly middle-class aesthetic that they called "good taste," or, alternately, "American" fashion. By claiming universal terms, the magazines again obscured the classed nature of their ideology. Indeed, editor Sarah Josepha Hale refused to include any fashion plates at all in her first magazine, the *American Ladies Book*, because she believed fashion was dictated by "foreign courts" and produced vanity in women. By 1830, the *American Ladies Book* did contain fashions, but only in "American versions," which often meant simply that there was a time lag between the presentation of new fashions in French and English magazines and in the *American Ladies Book*. Some "extreme" styles never were adopted.[22] When Hale later became editor of *Godey's*, she wrote:

> Here we have the opportunity of consulting individual taste, without reference to any arbitrary standard of high rank to sanction the adoption of extravagant, inconvenient or immodest modes, and we should be careful that our fashions are not inconsistent with good sense and pure morals.[23]

Thus, fashion that was American or in good taste had "moral value" and was by definition above the corrupting influence of the market.

Middle-class standards in taste kept an element of the "sincere" style long after it had been replaced by styles with more elaborate trimmings and accessories: to be tasteful one did not become an object of display by using "too much" ornamentation or color. Middle-class taste required women to *follow* the fashions, but not *lead* them. As one article in *Godey's* said, "The best dressers are generally those who follow the fashions at a great distance."[24] Indeed, as long as one dressed with taste, the simplicity of the 1840s was not required. By the early 1850s, styles again became very elaborate, requiring cumbersome hoopskirts with more petticoats and a plethora of ruffles, flounces, lace, and fringe trimmings.[25]

It is not surprising that middle-class women's styles so quickly became elaborate again, because the ideal of democracy stood in uneasy contradiction with the other function of fashion, which was distinction from those "below." The "democratization of fashion" was not, in fact, to extend to the working class. Hale unapologetically lamented the difficulty of maintaining distinction in a consumer economy:

> O the times! O the manners! Alas! How very sadly the world has changed! The time was when the *lady* could be distinguished from the *no-lady* by her dress, as far as the eye could reach; but now, you might stand in the same room, and, judging by the their outward appearance, you could not tell "which was which." Even gold watches are now no sure indication—for they have been worn by the lowest, even by "many of the factory girls." No lady

need carry one now, for any other than the simple purpose of easily ascertaining the time of day, or night, if she so please.[26]

A "lady's" dress marked not only her sincerity and good taste, but also her class and race privilege. In particular, the lady did not work outside the home, a status that her body and fashion reflected. The ideal lady had a narrow waist, arched back, and delicate hands and feet. Fashion enforced this fiction with corsets, petticoats, padding, and encumbering styles that restricted movement. In addition, the ideal sexual purity of the lady, North and South, served as an icon of race and class privilege and patriarchal control. In contrast, middle-class representations of white working-class and African American women usually depicted them as either large, coarse, and matronly or as sexually "impure." They could not be ladies. The constricting fashion that so marked the middle-class woman's lack of manual labor has often been critiqued on gender terms: the corsets, high heels, tight sleeves, and weighty skirts and petticoats not only hampered movement but often endangered health. But these very symbols of femininity that could be highly oppressive also served as the central signals of privilege and status.[27]

The middle class, then, obscured the hierarchy it created through clothing both by erasing the laborer behind the commodity and by insisting (except in rare revealing moments) that "tasteful" dress was available to all. Whether middle-class people tried to exclude the working classes from their modes of dress or to reform working-class fashion, the fact remained that the middle class set the standard it promoted as dominant, creating class ideology under the guise of democracy. This analysis is very much in keeping with Stuart Blumin's understanding of the emergence of middle-class culture in the nineteenth century. Blumin, drawing on Anthony Giddens, argues that the nineteenth-century middle class can be considered a class unto itself, even though it often denied its own existence. That is, the middle class largely defined itself through ideals of individualism and classlessness, even as it promoted class-based ideals as universal truths.[28]

In this way, middle-class people used notions of character and taste to make a distinction between commodities with values and those without values. They believed the former were shaped by morals rather than by market interests, whereas the latter were formed simply by the profit motive, and therefore were potentially dangerous. Fashion without middle-class taste was not only tacky, from a middle-class perspective it was morally suspect. Thus, while the middle class depended on commodities for its own identity, that identity included an ongoing attack on commodities that it believed sprang from economic interests rather than from (middle-class) values.

When working women bought the first ready-made dresses from slop dressmakers in the 1840s and 1850s, they may have worn the latest fashions, but they felt little need to conform to middle-class standards of taste. Historian Christine Stansell notes that the "Bowery g'hals" offended the writers for *Godey's Lady's Book* in their combinations of color and their "studied departure from ladyhood." Working-class women's fashion did not carry "moral value." Middle-class critics therefore saw it as immoral, and decried the purchase of such "outlandish, hot-looking dresses."[29] Working women, however, saw the same purchase as, according to Stansell, "a celebration of the possibilities of working-class life."[30] Very little research has been done on this early period of women's ready-made clothing, but it is clear that urban working women not only wore the latest styles, but regularly *exceeded* them, at once dressing like "ladies" and in "bad taste." Unrestrained by middle-class dictates, working women could emphasize the aspect of display present in the products.

The range and quality of ready-made clothing for women expanded greatly after the Civil War, as the sewing machine allowed for the mechanization of the clothing production process and as advances in sizing improved the fit of the garments. In addition, the numbers of working women continued to rise, particularly in the urban Northeast and Midwest. Increasingly, these women lived apart from family and/or did not have time to sew for themselves—which, as noted above, had long been the case for single working men. They constituted a significant new market of consumers for women's ready-made clothing; available products rapidly increased in variety, and quality of fit. As sizing improved, middle-class women began purchasing some forms of ready-made clothing but still visited tailors for their best clothes. By the 1870s, women could purchase most types of undergarments and cloaks ready-made; in the 1880s, they could purchase suits (dresses made of two or more pieces) and some gowns. By the 1890s, women could purchase most of the clothing they needed, including walking costumes, fancy ball dresses greatly favored by working women, and new fashionable shirtwaists, the fancy blouses worn with plain dark skirts that became the staples of working women's wardrobes.[31]

The garment industry provided the latest fashions in a number of grades, with hopes of capturing the full range of the market. This set up a tension between middle-class women, who needed to maintain a tasteful distinction between themselves and workers, and middle-class businessmen, who made a tidy profit by selling inexpensive versions of distinctive styles to working women. Some middle-class women responded by disparaging the cheaply made goods. Bertha Richardson noted the grades of fashion with some disdain:

> Purposeless imitation! . . . The Fourth Avenue shop says to the Fourth Avenue buyer: "Behold my clever imitation. For less than you could pay in a Fifth Avenue shop, I can give you a perfect imitation. You would not be behind the styles, I know. I can make you look like the real peacock." The Third Avenue shop scans the windows of the Fourth Avenue shop and returns the same to its customers. The First Avenue shop has a still cheaper imitation, and in Hester Street, on the pushcarts, ghosts of the real are "Going, going, going" for thirty-nine cents.[32]

The ready-made evening gowns that working women regularly bought particularly confounded some middle-class women's ideas of distinction, because such styles were worn more by the rich than the middle class. Middle-class writer Katherine Busbey wrote: "Evening frocks are not in common use except among the rich here, and so, naturally, there is no type of evening frocks at once in good taste and finish and of moderate price to be found in American shops."[33] Nevertheless, working women displayed their evening gowns with pride at dances such as a Lower East Side ball attended by Rose Pastor in 1903. She recounted one conversation she had about the dresses worn by the Jewish immigrant women in attendance:

> "Who is the girl in that elegant gown of violet crepe de chine, trimmed in velvet and fine laces?" "She works in the same factory as my cousin Jennie; she's a necktie maker." . . . "If I didn't know that all the girls here are working girls, I would think her papa was a railroad magnate of someone who owned a few millions at the least."[34]

By the late nineteenth century, middle-class women created a widespread literature promoting the idea that consumption without "taste" could lead to working women's moral "fall." White slavery narratives described the road to prostitution as paved with fine dresses and petticoats, alluring hats and charming shoes. In part the middle class believed the desire for clothing would lead women to "immoral" means of getting the money to buy them, but it also clearly saw the consumption itself as immoral. Lillian Wald, founder of the Henry Street Settlement on New York's Lower East Side, watched young women for the telltale sign of trouble: conspicuous apparel. For example, she wrote, "Annie began to show a pronounced taste in dress, and gave unmistakable signs of restlessness. She confided her aspirations toward the stage."[35] For the middle class, consumer desire unbounded by middle-class values of taste led to moral deterioration; thus, cheap fashion consumption made women themselves cheap, lowering their value and threatening their virtue even in the absence of sexual activity. The middle class could attempt to maintain distinction by reading the richest-appearing clothing on working women as signs of moral disorder.

Even as the marketplace offered working women the appearance of wealth, it did not provide the higher quality of goods enjoyed by middle- and upper-class consumers. Indeed, much of the ready-made clothing within working women's budgets fell apart soon after purchase. Thus, the possibilities for creative expression through dress offered by the garment industry were matched by the limitation that no standards existed to ensure clothing that was functional. Consumer League representatives reported that because working women rarely had a bulk of money, they often paid more for substandard clothing that quickly wore out than middle-class women did for similar items. One working woman reportedly bought twenty-four shirtwaists in one year at a cost of ninety-eight cents each.[36] No consumer item received more attention in immigrant accounts than flimsy and worn-out shoes. Typically bought for one to two dollars per pair in the early twentieth century, the shoes usually could not withstand the walking and standing required for work and travel to and from the workplace. Though the best-appearing French heels were available, one worker wrapped her feet in cardboard at work because her shoes had become so unserviceable. It was not uncommon for workers to require six or more new pair of shoes in one year.[37]

When the garment industry provided the latest styles to working women, it extended the oppressive elements of women's restrictive fashions to them as well. Despite the fact that the original purpose of such fashion was to signal that the "lady" did not labor, some women wore these styles to work. For those who wished to dress fashionably, codes of style and femininity, combined with what was available ready-made, ensured discomfort. In addition, many were underdressed in winter months. They purchased suits of fine, thin fabrics, but often could not afford the more expensive overcoats.[38] They adapted their clothes to working conditions by pinning up long trains (when long trains were in style) and by shedding undergarments or tight-fitting jackets that restricted movement. Working women could purchase certain ready-made clothes to use as they wished, but they did not have access to a range of quality goods for reasonable prices.

Nor did women have the options of alternative dress. Efforts to reform women's dress were largely confined to the middle class and did not penetrate the ready-made industry. "American dress reform" advocated a costume that featured a shorter, less corseted dress with pants and sensible shoes. These were not available ready-made; reformers urged women to convert their dresses themselves. It is questionable whether working-class women, particularly immigrants, ever heard about this movement. Since American dress reform also built upon middle-class notions of character, it is not likely that these clothes would have appealed to working women in any case. The "artistic dress" movement featured willowy, looser, elegant gowns for evening wear. Even if working women liked them, such dresses remained quite expensive and unavailable ready-made.[39]

The market thus shaped and limited the kinds of clothing available to working women, and sold them some of the necessary components of ladyhood. Both working- and middle-class women participated as consumers in the same clothing industry, but the middle class categorized working-class consumption as cheap when working women arranged the components of ladyhood into their own style. Despite the fact that clothing worn by both groups of women came from the same set of middle class-owned businesses, this designation became attached only to the clothes that working-class women wore. As Bertha Richardson said, "to those who have little and try to look as if they had more, we teach morals and standards."[40] Thus, the notion of taste served to maintain distinction even after industrialization reduced the extreme differences in the types of fabrics and styles between classes.

Industrialization and the rationalization of the labor process similarly shaped and categorized popular fiction. As with fashion, books and periodicals became more widely available for a broad segment of the population by the 1840s, as the printing press and paper-making technologies reduced production costs. Penny newspapers, domestic fiction for middle-class women, story papers, and dime novels all developed in the wake of these technological advances. As with fashion, even though these fiction commodities emerged from the same publishing industry, those consumed primarily by a middle-class audience became associated with character and moral value, while those consumed primarily by a working-class audience came to be seen by the middle class as cheap. Fiction for both middle- and working-class people had formulas and developed in relationship to market interests. However, the two types of products differed considerably. Middle-class fiction needed to be profitable, but it had to appear not to seek profit but rather to offer moral guidance and uplift.

Authors had to appear free to speak their own, original truth. Penny newspapers, story papers, and dime novels, however, did not need to answer to such imperatives of value, and their publishers could more fully and overtly rationalize the labor process to maximize profits.

Formulas emerged in popular fiction as a logical extension of the mechanization and rationalization of the publishing process, beginning with the penny newspapers in the first half of the nineteenth century. As with the expansion of fashion, technological innovation lowered the price of a valued commmodity and expanded the range of consumers. The new steam-driven cylinder presses mechanized the printing process, and cheaper paper made from wood pulp lowered costs for materials. By the 1840s, the telegraph enabled instantaneous communication between cities, which made news from afar immediately available but also reduced newspapers' reliance on their own cadres of reporters. The penny press put the telegraph to use earlier and more extensively than the more reputable newspapers. The Associated Press, founded in the late 1840s, standardized news products and made news stories widely available and relatively inexpensive. Reporters and writers in newspapers usually remained anonymous, a policy that reduced the personal investment in the articles they produced; they also received specific instructions on what kind of news to seek. And, in an attempt to further rationalize the production process, by the late nineteenth century the employee writing the article often was not the reporter who had gained the information firsthand. Such labor practices laid the groundwork for rationalizing fiction writing and decreasing individual innovation through set plot formulas in story papers and dime novels.

The result of mechanization and rationalization was a broader audience for the news. Whereas in the colonial era the news in print form was expensive and therefore largely restricted to elites, by the 1830s one-cent papers became available to both middle- and working-class people. In addition, rising literacy rates through the nineteenth century meant that publishers could count on a diverse audience.[41] By the 1840s, owners imported cheap paper made from wood pulp, a product available within the United States by the 1860s. By the 1850s, most northern cities had more than one newspaper, each boasting increased circulation. New York had fourteen dailies in 1850, with a combined daily circulation of over 150,000.[42]

The expansion of the newspaper audience led to a transformation in the content of the news. Owners and editors of penny newspapers such as the *New York Sun*, the *New York Herald,* and the *Philadelphia Public Ledger* packed their papers with local and sensational news about city life, particularly news focusing on crime and sex. As historian Daniel Czitrom has argued, newspapers no longer had to satisfy standards of respectability and shifted their emphasis to enlist a wide audience, in particular the literate working class.[43] These new formats seized upon the diversity of the industrial city, creating news narratives that invoked anxieties and desires about class, gender, and urban adventure. Indeed, these types of narratives formed the basis of many dime novels that promised to tell readers about real-life problems. Many middle-class people read penny newspapers, although the papers transgressed middle-class standards of taste. One critic argued in 1866 that the newspapers'

> flippancy and triviality are weakening to the mind that feeds upon it, impairing its power of sustained thought and application. They lower his taste. Again, they present a largely distorted view of society. The horrible accidents of a world are spread before him, day by day; he is entertained with the swindles, the vices, and the crimes of the earth; his paper immerses him in all sorts of abnormal things.[44]

Despite such criticisms, the huge circulations of the penny newspapers suggest that they did not appeal only to the working class. Indeed, because editors did not have to answer to codes of middle-class taste, they could engage middle-class anxieties about an urban order in flux. Penny newspapers can be seen as the psychological underworld of Victorian ideologies. As Peter Stallybrass and Allon White have argued, middle-class culture rejected the "low"—that is, dirt, disorder, accident, and sex—to maintain definitions of bourgeois culture as "high." These rejected forms become the most powerful "symbolic repertoires" in the culture. Thus, the tabloids seized upon what middle-class culture denied but also desired.[45] The penny press engaged a populace excited by the possibilities and dangers of the increasingly diverse industrial city, and narrativized the very elements that lay outside bourgeois social order: unpredictable loss or inheritance, crime, illicit sex, and cross-class romance, all of which threatened to blur class boundaries and weaken middle-class control. The penny papers were so successful, then, because they engaged both an overt working-class and an illicit middle-class readership, capitalizing on the lurid fascination among working- and middle-class people alike for sensational news. Likewise, because penny papers did not fall within the hallowed sphere of middle-class culture, middle-class critics could associate their sensationalism with working-class culture.

Because the penny press sought to please such a diverse audience, like other popular forms, it contained many contradictions and seemed to espouse various ideological positions. However, some historians have argued that the penny press, particularly before the 1850s, often expressed working-class interests. Alexander Saxton bases his argument on the fact that many early penny newspaper publishers had artisan printer backgrounds and were involved in labor politics of the 1830s. Benjamin Day, who started the first massively successful penny paper, the *New York Sun*, had been active in the New York Workingmen's Party. He and others earlier published a short-lived political paper overtly championing a worker's perspective, the *New York Sentinel*. However, when Day started the *Sun* he included very little political material, focusing instead on sensational stories. The *Sun* achieved great success and other papers followed Day's lead. Saxton aptly finds some working-class perspectives remaining in these sensational papers; the penny press did respond to its working-class readers.[46] But its goal to please a heterogeneous audience served in this case to blunt overt political content, foreshadowing the future for popular literature.

The same technological changes that made cheap dailies possible also spawned weekly story papers in the 1840s. By the 1850s, publishers such as Street and Smith and Robert Bonner established a format that endured through much of the nineteenth century. With titles like *Fireside Companion* and *Family Story Paper*, producers aimed their eight-page product to a family audience. Costing five or six cents, each edition contained installments of five to eight serial stories, including Westerns, domestic romances, historical romances, and adventure stories.[47] Dime novels followed quickly on the heels of story papers, as producers often reprinted serialized stories in dime novel form to sell the narrative again. Dime novels were usually published in series, with a new book issued each month. Each contained about 100 pages and measured four inches by six inches. Beadle and Adams, the first company to produce dime novels in great numbers, printed four million by 1865, with average sales ranging from 35,000 to 80,000 copies.[48] Later in the century, publishers issued novels in the "cheap library" format, pamphlets of sixteen or thirty-two pages that replaced the story papers, and in inexpensive book form, with the entire story on 200 to 300 pages. The inexpensive book usually cost ten to twenty-five cents. Buying in bulk helped: George Munro's Sons, Publishers, offered nine Laura Jean Libbey novels for the price of fifty cents in 1896. The novels could be bought at newsstands, through the mail, or by subscription.[49]

Publishers' desire to reduce the costs of paying writers shaped the kinds and the content of the narratives. Of course, it is particularly difficult to rationalize creative labor like fiction writing.[50] The easiest and most cost-effective way to reduce labor costs for books was simply to reprint the narratives from already-published material. Because of the lack of copyright protection, early publishers could pirate stories, usually from European novels, changing the titles and the authors' names. Publishers even reprinted novels they had already published once, changing the titles, authors, and series in which the novels were released to make them appear to be new books. In addition, they regularly reprinted narratives found in other venues and formats. For example, as Cathy Davidson has argued, the book *Charlotte Temple*, originally published in England, was first published in the United States by the reputable publisher Mathew Carey in 1794, and sold at the typical high price for books of fifty cents to one dollar. In the nineteenth century, publishers reprinted *Charlotte Temple* many times: in *Family Story Paper* number 211 in 1877, as a cheap library dime novel in the early 1890s, as well as in book form again for middle-class domestic fiction readers.[51] The effort to cut labor costs meant that dime novels available to working women consisted of a variety of types of narratives.

Most dime novel authors, however, were hired by the publishers to produce series for story papers that would later be reprinted in book form. Fiction formulas emerged from the labor relationship of the literary worker and the editor, as a variety of methods of rationalizing labor developed into what some people called the "fiction factory." As with all labor control, the goal was to guarantee a successful product while relying as little as possible on individual innovation or talent. Rationalization certainly did not *eliminate* creativity from the process of storytelling; rather, rationalization served to segment the creative process into steps to make it maximally predictable. Publishers assumed the role of director in the creative assembly. They often instructed authors to copy successful plots in already-published dime novels. Publishers also supplied authors with plots, in the form of either sensational newspaper story clippings or paragraph-long plot descriptions. Sometimes publishers asked authors to continue serials begun by other authors, using pen names. In such cases, the authors had to be especially attuned to the style and content of writing already established.[52] All of these techniques controlleded the individual innovation of the authors and tended to create a standardized product. While market research was primitive in the nineteenth century, publishers did keep track of sales and simply canceled serials or series that had not shown sufficient success. Once a particular kind of story became a hit with the public, publishers likely developed it into a formula.

Editors exerted increasingly tight control over manuscripts as the industry developed, and they shaped the content and style of dime novel fiction through their written responses to stories and their requests for revisions. In order to produce enough to make a living, writers had to work quickly and revise little or not at all. Thus, it was in their interest to anticipate and meet editors' demands so as to minimize costly revisions. The speed required prompted authors to standardize their own output. William Wallace Cook reported that he wrote drafts and final copies of his manuscripts in 1893, the first year he wrote popular fiction, but by 1894 he made the "first copies clean enough for the compositor" because otherwise he could "never have accomplished such a large amount of work." The economic risk inherent in this publishing method was largely absorbed by the literary workers. Writers had no job security: an unsuccessful serial, for example, could be "pulled" at a moment's notice, the author instructed to wrap everything up, with several planned or perhaps already written installments left unpublished and unpaid for.[53]

Standardization not only ensured that formulas would develop, it also tended to make dime novel fiction packed with sensational thrills, rather than politics or other controversial issues. The lack of an "original" in dime novels, however, did not mean that all narratives were the same, nor did it mean that they duped their readers. Rather, as Fredric Jameson argues, they had to contain a "utopian moment," some element that spoke to unfulfilled longing, in order to be popular.[54] Engaging popular desires and creating fantastic stories ensured both a pleased audience and many sales.

The first highly successful dime novel formula, the "mysteries of the city," illustrates these dynamics. The formula began with Eugene Sue's novel *Les Mysteres de Paris*. Popular fiction writers in Germany, Great Britain, and the United States quickly copied it, replacing Paris place names with local references. The formula did not entirely originate with Sue, however. As Michael Denning shows, the early mysteries of the city narratives altered Samuel Richardson's bourgeois novels *Clarissa* and *Pamela* by posing a conflict not between the bourgeois and the aristocracy, but between labor and capital. In addition, mysteries of the city authors filled their stories with crimes and curiosities of industrial urban life lifted from the penny newspapers.[55]

George Lippard wrote the first mysteries of the city in the United States in the 1840s, and infused his narrative with an overt working-class perspective, exposing middle-class corruption in the industrial city. Lippard's early stories centered on complex and sordid interactions, mostly among the wealthy, in a fictitious great mansion, distilling capitalist relations and the bourgeois home into a single form. Lippard also introduced two stock working-class characters of later dime novels: the vulnerable working woman who encountered a bourgeois or rich seducer, and the honest male mechanic who defended working-class integrity against bourgeois foes. Denning credits Lippard with creating many of the narrative conventions that would give dime novels throughout the nineteenth century "mechanic accents," the capacity to be read in a working-class perspective. Working-class readers embraced Lippard as their own, while middle-class critics decried the voyeuristic representations of sex and crime so similar to those they objected to in the penny press.[56]

Like the penny newspapers, mysteries of the city dime novels were highly contradictory narratives and certainly held appeal for a clandestine middle-class audience. Narrative contradictions allowed the stories to be read in different ways by different people. The narrators seemed to speak from a middle-class perspective but often promoted working-class views; villains and virtuous heroes often shared remarkably similar motivations of vengeance and resentment; and heroes did not consistently represent working-class perspectives. This element of contradiction is especially clear in the stock working-class female character, who was pursued by an evil bourgeois or aristocratic man. Denning argues that the plight of the helpless woman in the hands of the seducer could operate as an allegory for working-class exploitation by capitalists. Likewise, Alexander Saxton argues that similar news stories in the penny press used a working-class female character to stand for the entire working class. However, the sexually vulnerable working-class woman was a stock character in middle-class fiction as well, and reinforced middle-class views of working women as morally compromised. Thus, the same fictional device could shore up some middle-class mechanisms of class distinction, even as it challenged others. Dime novel romances for working women would innovate on this stock plot line to defend the working heroine from middle-class disparagement.[57]

The dime novel formula working women avidly consumed by the 1880s featured a working heroine who was *not* primarily a victim: she was never successfully seduced, and her vulnerability was paired with exceptional heroism. The formula developed from early narrative conventions in the penny press and mysteries of the city and bore the imprint of the dime novel production process. Laura Jean Libbey, the author credited with popularizing the working-girl formula in the United States, successfully copied and combined aspects of established popular narratives of the 1860s and 1870s, including working-girl stage melodramas, honest mechanic stories, and dime novel romances that did not feature working women.

Imagine the 1880s story: A working-class woman who toils at a factory suddenly finds herself, through a remarkable chain of calamities, without work, home, or family, usually by page 10. Thus vulnerable, she is pursued by two men: a dastardly villain of the upper class who wishes to compromise her virtue, and a noble hero, usually the factory owner's son, who falls madly in love with her. Our working-girl heroine, who is named Rosebud, or Ione, or Leonie, returns the affection of her rich hero, but fate parts them tragically over some misunderstanding, usually by page 60. Our hero then disappears, often to Europe, for most of the remainder of the book. The working girl must now face a series of unpredictable adventures and mishaps in the city, usually pursued by the villain and a jealous villainess, also of the upper class. Our heroine proves herself equal to every adventure through physical strength and bravery, with a little luck and help from occasional gentlemen. In the midst of abductions, poisonings, accidents, and attacks, she discovers that she is really an heiress and gloriously claims her riches by one third to one half of the way through the novel. She continues to evade the many traps of her enemies, and in her spare time attends sumptuous balls and other social events. Through another twist of fate, she is reunited with the rich hero, usually in the last twenty pages of the book, and misunderstanding melts away as they join in marriage.[58]

Producers added working female heroines to the ranks of dime novels' central characters in part because of increased newspaper coverage of women's wage work. In 1855, the *New York Tribune* exposed a scandal in needleworkers' conditions. Declaring itself the protector of working girls, the *Tribune* dedicated a number of news articles to the problem, drawing on established character types to describe the nasty bosses and the women victims. However sensationalized, the articles did attract attention to the growing phenomenon of women workers.[59] This attention increased in the 1860s, and both the penny press and story papers championed the "poor seamstress." In 1871, Francis S. Smith of Street and Smith Publishing wrote a story entitled "Bertha, the Sewing Machine Girl; or, Death at the Wheel," and its popularity spawned a plethora of copies in other story papers in the 1870s.[60] "Bertha, the Sewing Machine Girl" was adapted to the popular stage, becoming a quick hit at the Bowery Theater in New York in August of 1871. A number of similar working-girl stage plays followed, and the genre lasted until about the turn of the century.[61]

"Bertha" included many qualities that would carry over into the working-girl dime novel formula, including a flawlessly virtuous working heroine, dastardly villains who seek to ruin her reputation and keep her from marrying the man she loves, and a hero from whom she is parted for most of the story. In the tradition of melodrama, Bertha is naturally good and faced structures of oppression, twists of fate, and intentional attacks beyond her control. Like the vulnerable working-class woman in the mysteries of the city, she could represent the entire working class. This working girl heroine, however, is not simply a victim: she evades her enemies, finds she is really an heiress, is reunited with her working-class lover (who has since become wealthy) and is liberated from labor. Bertha does not change or grow in the course of the novel; rather, she perseveres against her enemies and meets each adventure with virtue. As a reward, she experiences a "magical transformation" in the form of wealth and triumph.

The working-girl stage drama established several lasting narrative features: the virtuous heroine who is both vulnerable and heroic, the secret inheritance, and the marriage to a (now) wealthy hero. While middle-class fiction increasingly stressed character development in the nineteenth century, many popular stage dramas and dime novels remained melodramatic. Like Bertha, dime novel heroines would not change or grow. They did not need to, for they were already perfect, and their adventures served to demonstrate their virtue. However, the stage-drama formula also differed in several respects from the later working-girl dime novel formula. Bertha and other stage heroines were much more given to speeches that revealed their virtue than the later dime novel heroines, including speeches aimed to reform their male counterparts, perhaps reflecting Francis Smith's investment in middle-class ideals of womanhood. The working girl was a suffering protagonist, challenged by relentless villains and calamities, though she ultimately triumphed. Her story was sad, meant to provoke tears (which may be why this genre of working-girl stage dramas was called the "weepies"). Finally, the working-girl stage dramas also featured a host of working-class charac-ters. In the later dime novels, the heroine was usually cast adrift from family and co-workers. In particular, the stage drama heroine had a working-class boyfriend, whom she married. Virtually no working-class male characters appeared in the later dime novel formula.[62]

The later working-girl formula was also influenced by the honest mechanic narrative of the 1880s, exemplified by the novels of Fred Whittaker. Michael Denning calls these stories "narratives of working-class manhood," spurred in part by challenges to masculinity caused by industrialization. The honest mechanic story, according to Denning, featured a heroic mechanic who meets various tests and challenges, develops and struggles upward, and by the end has achieved economic advancement, often becoming owner or foreman of the factory. Denning argues that these stories combined the "aristomilitary" or adventure romance—in which the hero must prove himself in a series of tests and contests including, in this case, a strike or election—and the bourgeois *Bildungsroman*, the novel of education and character development. In Whittaker's *Larry Locke, the Man of Iron*, Larry proves his masculinity by being able to achieve individual advancement without abandoning the mutuality of working-class unions. Indeed, Larry is a member of the Knights of Labor, a role he defends with ardor. If Larry's masculinity is not stated clearly enough, it is ever-present in another Whittaker hero, Job Manly. Workers always win strikes in these novels, and often belong to the Knights of Labor.[63]

Finally, the working-girl formula was also influenced by the romance genre of dime novels, typified by such highly popular authors as Mrs. Georgie Sheldon, May Agnes Fleming, Mrs. Harriet Lewis, Emma Garrison Jones, Bertha M. Clay, and E.D.E.N. Southworth. Like the working-girl dime novels, these romances continued to be reprinted into the 1920s, and working women read them voraciously. (As with many dime novels, most of these "authors" are really pseudonyms. At least seven men and women contributed to the 500-plus novels written under the name Bertha M. Clay.)[64] These dime novel romances usually featured wealthy women, rather than women workers, as protagonists. However, the heroines often confronted similar issues: sudden changes in wealth and status, conflicts about marriage for love or money, and discoveries of "true" class status by birth. While most of the characters enjoy lavish wealth, one character typically figures the working class, as in the mysteries of the city. Sometimes, the wealthy female protagonist finds herself destitute. The rich hero's defenses of the working woman character are common, as they would be in the working-girl formula. This passage, in which a wealthy brother defends his attraction to a working woman to his sister, became a stock speech for Libbey's heroes:

> Your ideas of aristocracy are very discriminating, Helen, and you have yet to learn the true meaning of the word. . . . Cecile, in the midst of her poverty, while toiling for her bread, was an aristocrat in a truer sense of the word than you, with thousands at your command.[65]

In Denning's terms, these novels could be read with working-class "accents" even as they offered a fantasy of wealth and opulence.

The category of dime novel romances, including those with both wealthy and working-class heroines, should not be confused with middle-class women's domestic fiction, despite shared qualities. In general, middle-class readers considered dime novel romances far beneath the level of domestic fiction because of their sensational plots.[66] Domestic fiction emerged from narratives in religious and middle-class advice literature, as well as earlier novel conventions. It celebrated women's moral authority and purity in the home and in personal relations. Through emotional scenes of transportive piety and purity, the domestic heroine often sacrificed her life for the moral transformation of others. However, as Jane Tompkins argues, the domestic novel was far from only concerned with personal relationships. The kinds of transformations women could effect were portrayed as central to the redemption of the country and the world.[67] Domestic fiction bore structural resemblances to the dime novel romances, but middle-class women insisted that their fiction, like their fashion, differed from commodities consumed primarily by the working class because of its moral value. Nevertheless, domestic women's novels emerged from the same technological advances as dime novel fiction, and like dime novels became a highly successful set of commodities. In addition, domestic fiction, like the dime novel romances, was highly melodramatic.

Peter Brooks argues that melodrama represents a Manichaeistic battle between good and evil, and requires the protagonist, symbolizing a larger group, to encounter forces and conflicts beyond her/his control. Indeed, both domestic and dime novel fiction were melodramatic because they raised questions of morality, albeit differently. Brooks argues that after the French and American revolutions and the secularization of the state, melodrama became an arena in which people could explore issues of morality in a changing society, and could thus raise potentially radical critiques.[68] Domestic fiction such as Uncle Tom's Cabin, then, could serve as an indictment of race relations while still promoting white, middle-class power, just as dime novel fiction pitted good against evil, indicting oppressive elements of industrial production even as it carried middle-class influences. But middle-class women insisted that dime novels, like working women's fashion, lacked morality and taste. Thus, they could defend their own commodity consumption as driven by values rather than by a selfish or corrupt interaction with the market.[69]

When Laura Jean Libbey wrote her first working-girl dime novel, she had already proven herself as a writer of the other dime novel romances. Her first serialized romances featured wealthy heroines in convoluted plots of adventure and romance, often with working-class "accents." Her first working-girl dime novel was entitled *Leonie Locke; or The Romance of a Beautiful New York Working-Girl*, directly referencing Whittaker's successful Larry Locke. (Another of Libbey's heroines, Ione, is described in one passage as "the lovely daughter of a Knight of Labor," though her father dies by page 2 of the novel.) Like Larry, Leonie encounters a series of contests in the style of the adventure romance. However, like Bertha, the Sewing Machine Girl, Leonie also has to defend her virtue from numerous villains; indeed, this is her primary site of contests and challenges, rather than the political arena of strikes and elections in which Larry engages his foes. Also in contrast to Larry, the character of Leonie does not develop or advance in a job. Rather, as in both the working-girl stage melodramas and the earlier dime novel romances, Leonie's secret inheritance liberates her from labor. Finally, while Bertha marries a working-class man who has worked his way to the top (a man much like Larry Locke), Leonie marries the son of the boss.[70]

Laura Jean Libbey successfully copied and creatively combined elements from the three established and popular formulas. She made a great hit with *Leonie Locke* and immediately was copied by a host of other dime novel fiction writers including Geraldine Fleming, Lillian Drayton, Charlotte M. Stanley, and, of course, herself. Libbey produced more than sixty novels in the 1880s and 1890s, which reportedly had aggregate sales of ten to fifteen million copies.[71] Indeed, Libbey's working-girl formula became one of the most popular, filling the story papers and cheap libraries; along with the other dime novel romances, it continued to be rewritten and reprinted into the 1920s. While Denning dates the end of the dime novel heyday at 1890, the working-girl formula had just hit its peak in the 1890s. In addition, publishers translated the working-girl dime novel formula into the inexpensive pulp magazines of the turn of the century, and later into serial motion pictures. Together, they formed a body of commodities that became uniquely interwoven with working-class women's culture.

The market niche of the dime novel romances ensured that working women would not read about politics directly. The dime novels did not portray women engaging in strikes or any other kind of political action. This at first seems strange, because two of their major sources of plot mechanisms, the stage dramas like "Bertha, the Sewing Machine Girl" and honest mechanic stories like "Larry Locke, Man of Iron," represented strikes in positive terms. The lack of politics may have been because Libbey did not see public political action on the part of working women, without male counterparts, as appropriate. Bertha's actions were always represented in tandem with honorable working-class men, who led the strikes; in Libbey's novels there are rarely any working-class men at all. However, by the 1870s such overt representation of labor conflict as Whittaker's were already becoming rare; Libbey was conforming to the new standard in excluding overt political content. As the fiction industry developed, it increasingly aimed to please the many and offend the few. William Wallace Cook, a dime novel author who wrote at least one romance of the "Laura Jean Libbey type," said one editor instructed him: "SHUN POLITICS AND RELIGION in any form, direct or indirect, as you would shun the devil."[72]

Perhaps more importantly, the middle-class campaign against dime novels further stifled overt political content. The Comstock Law of 1873 prohibited the mailing of obscene or vulgar material and partly targeted dime novels because of their "stories of bloodshed and crime." This crackdown greatly affected publishers of "outlaw" dime novels, in which the outlaw hero represented a political critique of the status quo. It also put the entire industry on the defensive, because virtually all dime novels contained sensational stories, including representations of bloodshed and crime. In response, dime novel publishers claimed they published "wholesome" and "good" literature, and editors configured narratives more carefully to avoid middle-class attacks of any sort.[73]

The dime novel romances that became such a common aspect of working women's culture, then, were greatly shaped and limited by the market. Rationalization of the labor process meant that women readers would find a set formula that had pleased women before them, a formula packed with thrills and adventures stemming from the sensational newspapers and decades of popular story development. Because this fiction was categorized as "cheap" by the middle class, it did not need to answer to middle-class notions of taste or moral value, as did middle-class women's domestic fiction.

Though the novels bore the traces of the economic and cultural forces of their production, critics have been mistaken in dismissing them as merely sending oppressive messages to working women, or juxtaposing them with "free expression" in other print sources. Joyce Shaw Peterson argues that the dime novel romances often replicated middle-class ideologies that could be found in advice books about manners. The romances, she asserts, could serve to train women in the ideals of middle-class ladyhood, and thus undermine class-consciousness. Indeed, the dime novel heroines *look* like the ideal of the lady: they are naturally dainty, with small hands and feet and innocent faces. Further, the secret inheritance could send a message that ladyhood is an inherited trait after all, and the working girl is triumphant only because she is not really a working girl.[74] Historian Joanne Meyerowitz argues that the dime novels present heroines that seem to her to be "utterly helpless." Meyerowitz sees the twists and turns of plot, the endless and various attacks on the heroine, as communicating a sense of female powerlessness in the world. She argues that these qualities, combined with occasional rescues by male heroes and the marriage at the end of the book, could teach women their correct role in patriarchy.[75]

Both of these critiques are based on a middle-class style of reading for character development, rather than on a style of reading that anticipates melodramatic adventures and a dramatic reward. The dime novel plots were not based on character development; thus, the pleasure of reading them did not come from vicarious empowerment through identification with the heroine. When the dime novels are read as melodrama, the heroine confronts an array of attacks and adventures but is not made powerless; on the contrary, her actions secure her position as a virtuous and laudable worker and woman. Readers know this because she gains two rewards: an inheritance that affirms her inner and unchanging worth, and marriage to a millionaire, which provides widespread social recognition of that worth. While the dime novels certainly contained contradictions and possibilities for multiple interpretations, they did not simply convey oppressive and patriarchal meanings to working women readers.

Likewise, the fact that cheap fiction typically avoided overtly political subject matter does not mean that it held only conservative meanings for working women. Certainly, it would be a mistake to contrast this limitation with "free expression" in print directed to a middle-class audience. Dime novel fiction, like fashion, emerged as part of the same large profit-directed industry that produced commodities for the middle class. While the categorization of this fiction as cheap and without moral value did indeed shape its content, scholars have too often accepted the middle-class myth that its own commodities were not equally, if differently, affected by their market niche.[76]

To illustrate, let us return briefly to the example of James Oppenheim's very different literary products written for *American Magazine*, a muckraking journal targeted largely to a middle-class audience, and *The Ladies' World*, a cheap magazine targeted largely to working- or lower middle-class women. Oppenheim, trying to make a living from his writing, could not escape the firmly entrenched market divisions in 1910s publishing.[77] Though he was paid by both magazines, he could publish his political writing only in the magazine that working women were unlikely to see. Despite his radical politics, Oppenheim participated in the class-differentiated access to ideas and the means of their distribution that capitalism promoted.

Writers of fiction targeting the middle class gained publication only when their stories matched editors' expectations, just as did writers of fiction targeting working-class readers. However, the middle-class attachment to culture with value meant that the rationalization of writing had to be limited and obscured in middle-class journals, while it could continue unabated in the commodities labeled part of working-class culture. Editorial control was unabashedly strong in the story papers and intended to enforce a formula that was proven to sell, but editorial control in middle-class journals operated more often through the veto power of the rejection slip than through a dictated narrative or style. Of course, writers also learned and participated in the cultural values that shaped middle-class formulas, and often conformed to them without direct editorial feedback.

Oppenheim's experience with *The Ladies' World* is instructive on this count. Editors undoubtedly dictated the plot of "Peg O' the Movies." This was common practice, but we can be sure of it in this case because *The Ladies' World* linked the plot of "Peg" to an earlier serial they published. "What Happened to Mary" was a monthly serialized working-girl story that was released at the same time in film serial form by the Edison company, starring Mary Fuller as Mary. Oppenheim wrote some of the scenarios for the film version of *What Happened to Mary*. The unprecedented collaboration, translating the working-girl formula into motion picture form, made a great profit for both the film and magazine companies. *The Ladies' World* wanted to further capitalize on their success: in "Peg O' the Movies" Peg acts in a movie whose plot matches that of "What Happened to Mary." In a sense, the fictional Peg plays Mary Fuller, playing the fictional Mary. Because the plot of "Peg" is tied so closely to the plot of "What Happened to Mary," we can be confident that it was not Oppenheim's autonomous creation. At least two other writers worked on the Mary story, and they responded both to editorial direction and to contests in which consumers competed to suggest the best next episode. Like the dime novel romances that preceded it, "Peg O' the Movies" was devoid of overt political content.

In contrast, when Oppenheim wrote for the *American Magazine* he likely experienced no direct editorial intervention. However, the topic of working women was a timely one, and much of the poetry that Oppenheim wrote on other topics did not get published in such a format. Indeed, writers John S. Phillips and Lincoln Steffens, along with several others, started the *American Magazine* in 1906 as a journal meant to be more free from editorial control than the muckraking journal, *McClure's*, for which they had been working. S. S. McClure tightly monitored writers and the content of articles to maximize sales. However, Steffens recalled in his autobiography that as soon as the writers were in charge of the business, they exerted a similar editorial control over themselves. He was advised by his colleagues to "go easy" in his reporting so as not to offend anyone. "And I noticed," wrote Steffens, "with some pain, shame and lying denials to myself, that I was going easy." He soon left the magazine.[78] Oppenheim similarly felt constrained writing for publications like the *American Magazine*. In order to freely express and publish his poetry, Oppenheim and Waldo Frank started the *Seven Arts* in 1916, a patron-sponsored little magazine that claimed to be entirely free from market influence. Yet because of its limited distribution and high cost, the *Seven Arts* was even less likely to reach the hands of working women than the *American Magazine*.[79]

While "Peg O' the Movies" was a formulaic narrative that occluded Oppenheim's political perspective, it should not be dismissed. Both middle-class and working-class literary arenas were impoverished by market forces, but both likewise offered imaginative possibilities for readers. Middle-class literature could include political discussion, but tended to censor attitudes and subjects that did not conform to middle-class values, variously conceived. Literature aimed at the working class had no need to profess middle-class values, except to keep Comstock at bay; it could maintain allegorical narrative structures with rich potential for imaginative readings. We are left with two historical sources related to working women of the 1910s: a poem about them written for a middle-class audience, and a story about them written for a working-class audience. Ironically, "Bread and Roses" has regularly, if unreflectingly, been included as source material in labor histories, particularly of the Lawrence Strike of 1912. "Peg O' the Movies," in contrast, has never been mentioned in scholarly work. Many working women read and thrilled to such stories every day, yet they seldom receive analysis.

Highly contradictory in content, the fiction and fashion commodities so central to working women's lives at the turn of the century emerged from the imperatives of the capitalist marketplace. When women consumed them, they developed particular habits and practices that were in part directed by the highly ephemeral nature of the products: clothing that quickly wore out or fell apart, and serial fiction whose cliffhanger chapter endings prompted readers to buy the next installment. At the same time, the nature of these commodities was contradictory:

they were richly laden with cultural connotations and available for a variety of readings and uses in working women's daily lives. How did working-class women utilize these commodities? To close in classic cliffhanger style: Please continue to the next chapter to find out.

CHAPTER TWO

LADIES OF LABOR

Fashion, Fiction, and Working Women's Culture

Did you ever go down to one of our city settlements full of the desire to help and lift up the poor shop girl? Do you remember the chill that came over you[?] ...There must be some mistake, you thought. These could not be poor girls, earning five or six dollars a week. They looked better dressed than you did! Plumes on their hats, a rustle of silk petticoats, everything about them in the latest style. You went home thoughtful about those girls who wasted their hard-earned money on cheap imitation, who dressed beyond their station, and you failed to see what enjoyment they got out of it.

—Bertha Richardson, 1904[1]

The task here is not to celebrate each and every new possibility qua possibility, but to redescribe those possibilities that *already* exist, but which exist within cultural domains designated as culturally unintelligible and impossible. —Judith Butler[2]

Lillian Wald, founder of the Henry Street Settlement House on the Lower East Side of New York City, described in her memoirs her frustration with one young working woman who longed for fine clothes. The woman lived in a crowded tenement, had begun working at age eleven, and failed to demonstrate the interest in self-improvement that Wald attempted to foster through Settlement work. Despite her long, tedious work hours and her bleak tenement apartment, Wald wrote, "her most conscious desire was for silk underwear; at least it was the only one she seemed able to formulate!" Wald decried "this trivial desire" for fashion in the young women she served, as she felt it deflected them from more serious pursuits: education in English, the arts, work skills, and union organizing.[3] For others, like Bertha Richardson quoted above, working women who wore the latest fashions and perhaps exceeded them "dressed beyond their station," and thus confounded her efforts to bestow charity on a class of women unambiguously "lower" than herself.

Reformers and union leaders also despaired at some working women's habit of dime novel romance reading, which they found as trivial as the pursuit of fashion, particularly because it offered a fantasy of magnificent wealth bestowed on the working-girl heroine through a secret inheritance and marriage to a millionaire. Journalist Rose Pastor admonished women workers:

> With our free circulating libraries what excuse is there other than ignorance for any girl who reads the crazy phantasies from the imbecile brains of Laura Jean Libbey, The Duchess, and others of their ilk! ... I appeal to you— if you read those books— stop! stop![4]

Critics feared that the books instilled in readers a vague "hope that some man or some chance will come to change the monotony of their lot" and would therefore deflect women from union activity.[5] Perhaps most disturbing was that working women incorporated their consumption of fashion and fiction into a social practice of calling and presenting themselves as ladies, complete with an affected style of speech, walk, and manners.[6]

But Wald was mistaken when she dismissed the desire for silk underwear as entirely trivial. There was a system of meaning at work that was incomprehensible to her, bent as she was on extending bourgeois values of self-improvement to the working class. Judith Butler argues that some kinds of agency are, in fact, unrecognizable as such when they operate outside of the epistemology of those trying to understand them.[7] Whereas Wald looked for the kind of subjectivity that *to her* meant empowerment and improvement, working women exhibited subjectivities based on a variety of consumer practices with their own cultural configurations of gender, class and ethnicity and did not exhibit the "self-interest" Wald expected. Working women's use of consumer goods was intensely invested with meanings, but they were unintelligible to Wald.

In order to understand this arena of meaning rooted in commodities, we first need to recognize that commodity consumption is not a single, discrete event. Film critic Jane Gaines has recently noted that the word "consumption" refers to many events, not just one, so cultural critics should distinguish among buying, having, and using as aspects of the meaning-making process.[8] Likewise, Janice Radway has called for a distinction between the activity of reading within a particular social context, and the actual meaning readers make from the narrative itself. Exploring when and where people read, argues Radway, makes us better prepared to use textual interpretation to understand how people might read to gratify needs, perhaps those that prompted their choice of texts.[9] This chapter therefore looks at three aspects of working women's consumption of fashion and fiction: the act of purchasing or otherwise acquiring the products, the acts of reading the dime novels and wearing the clothing, and the imaginative interactions with a narrative or an outfit. The first two aspects, the acts of purchasing, and reading/wearing, occurred in a social context and became part of working women's collective culture. Women's memoirs, reformers' and union records, and periodicals reveal these aspects of women's consumption. The imaginative experience of a narrative or an outfit, while shaped by the workplace culture, was necessarily more internal and idiosyncratic. "Textual" analysis of the stories and clothing, embedded in this social context, reveals the ways products could support the practice of "ladyhood." The meanings that women created through all three of these aspects of consumption operated together to imbue the commodities with significance.

Specifically, working women's consumption of fiction and fashion engaged their identities as workers, as women, and as immigrants. Through their purchases, women used the money they had earned, thus participating in consumption *as workers*. They bought fashion products and books written in English in part to mark themselves as "American." They used both types of products at their workplaces in ways that refused the terms of subordination they experienced on the job and created another, imaginative reality in which they were highly valued. In addition, some quite literally appropriated work skills, and sometimes materials and time, in order to make their own clothes, and in this way avoided being entirely subordinated to the needs of capital.

Finally, women could use the narratives and the specific clothing to create themselves as "ladies," a signifying practice that allowed them to occupy a creative space of cultural contradiction and to affirm their lived experiences as workers, as women, and as immigrants. The practice of working ladyhood engaged gender, class, and ethnic exclusions that working women daily experienced in a society that saw the heroic worker as male, the heroic woman as middle class, and the heroic American as a native-born Anglo-Saxon. Working ladyhood was a set of consumption-based conventions and practices through which individuals variously constructed particular subjectivities. Thus, the practice of working ladyhood created a site of multiplicity, a shifting identity which played off a range of cultural contradictions and instabilities in turn-of-the-century society.

The practice of working ladyhood built on a shared firsthand knowledge of the daily injustices of women's labor, but it was not a self-conscious political strategy and it did not contain a specific, articulated political critique. The phenomenon did have ramifications for organized labor politics, which will be explored in chapters 3 and 4. But I do not argue that these practices necessarily functioned as a step along the path to organized political activism. Rather, I argue that working women could *use* the cultural resources of ladyhood to construct formal political subjectivities. Furthermore, working ladyhood had political significance in itself because when working-class women made themselves into ladies, they rejected the denigration they experienced at work and in public and replaced it with pride and dignity. As Robin D. G. Kelley writes, "Still missing from most examinations of workers are the ways in which unorganized working people resisted the conditions of work, tried to control the pace and amount of work, and carved out a modicum of dignity at the workplace."[10] A broader examination of politics requires understanding the systems of meanings that sustained workers on a day-to-day level. In particular, bringing into view working ladies' particular cultural configurations of gender, class, and ethnicity reveals a key terrain of subjectivity formation that was in some ways connected to, and certainly as important as, the subjectivity formation of women who became labor leaders. Working women's subjectivities, however, were rendered invisible by contemporary organized politics and historical analyses, both of which searched for political actors who matched preconceived cultural ideals.

Because working ladyhood was rooted in both fashion and fiction consumption, the two forms of popular culture must be studied in tandem. Popular culture activities exist in isolation only in academic studies. For historical actors, the fashion they wore was related to the dime novel they read in the same day or evening, creating a weave of meanings. To isolate products based on academic distinctions between "literature" and "clothing" would analytically sever the meanings working women themselves created from both. Conversely, intertextuality, or looking across different kinds of "texts," guided by the lived experience of working women, allows greater insight into the meanings of both types of consumer products.

The consumption of fiction and fashion products also operated as what Colin Campbell calls "imaginative" events in the lives of working women. Fashion is commonly seen as a way that an individual "sends a message" about themselves to the larger society. However, as Fred Davis has argued, this reduces a complex process to a simplistic single meaning. While at times people wear clothing to publicly communicate membership in a particular group, pleasure in clothing also stems from the personal and imaginative process of creating oneself within a range of recognizable social meanings.[11] Similarly, the reading of dime novels is best understood not simply as the reception of messages by the reader from the text, but as the creation of meaning imaginatively by the reader via the text. Contradictions within the text and the various cultural contexts that the reader brings to the reading process make reading as much an imaginative event as fashion. Indeed, the reader may *consume* a book, in that she purchases and uses it, but she *produces* a text as she reads, through her interaction with the book's narrative.[12]

For analytical purposes, this chapter separates three aspects of consumption: purchasing, wearing/reading, and imaginative interactions with the products. However, these three aspects are intricately related. For example, the imaginative experience of both fiction and fashion can exceed the boundaries of the physical interaction with the goods themselves through daydreaming and conversations about the products with others. Thus, the meanings women made with the texts themselves became closely related to the meanings created collectively in their uses of the products. In this way, working ladies formed what literary critics call an "interpretive community," partly within what historians call "workplace culture."[13] To borrow Walter Benjamin's language, women experienced and shaped an imaginative "dream world" through the collective imaginative acts of purchasing and using dime novels and clothing.[14] Thus, the concept of the "dream world of commodities" should be broad enough to encompass all three aspects of consumption.

Women of different ethnicities necessarily had different relationships to consumer culture. Young Jewish women enjoyed relative freedom compared to Italian women; they tended to have more control over their paychecks and could attend dance halls and amusement parks. These public amusements served, as Kathy Peiss argues, as sites for the development of new styles and sexual mores. Italian parents usually expected daughters to help out at home after work and required them to be chaperoned in public places. As Miriam Cohen argues, young Italian women had relatively few opportunities for independent social lives and more rarely participated in the public life of amusements. However, Cohen argues that Italian women did attend motion pictures, read romance novels, and dress "in style"—engaging in the very aspects of mass-produced popular culture studied here.[15] Thus, while the cultural experiences of Jewish and Italian women were not identical, they did intersect.

Working women could purchase dime novels extremely easily in working-class neighborhoods from pushcart and newsstand vendors. Indeed, this shopping served as entertainment in itself. Pushcarts became prevalent in New York in the mid-1880s, transforming the way goods were sold in the city (fig. 2.1).[16] About 2,500 pushcarts were on the

2.1 Working women bought dime novels, cloth remnants, and inexpensive ready-made clothing from pushcarts on New York's Lower East Side.

Lower East Side in 1906, and the mostly Jewish, Italian, and Greek peddlers sold nearly everything: "Dried fruits, fresh fruit, pickles, preserves, vegetables, meat and fish alternate with household utensils, boots and shoes, jewelry and clothing, books and stationery."[17] As the secretary of the New York Commission Appointed to Investigate the Pushcart Problem reported, "When our list of goods sold was complete, we felt it would have been easier to make a list of things that were not sold." The pushcarts catered to the hours of a working-class population and remained on the streets in the evenings, when the lights hung on the carts made the streets "look as if a carnival were in progress."[18] Working women, particularly Jewish women who enjoyed more freedom of movement, regularly walked together down Grand Street or other main business streets in the evenings, looking at pushcarts and in shop windows and conversing with friends.

It may seem strange that a largely immigrant population made English-language romances a key part of its culture. Obviously, the dime novels could only be read by women who were literate in English. Young immigrant women often went to work immediately after arriving in the United States, without even a speaking knowledge of the language. However, many working women could read English. Immigrants who arrived in the United States as children usually attended public school for a number of years, though many left before the legal age of fourteen to take jobs. Those born to immigrant parents also went to school. And many women, particularly Jewish women, who lacked an English-language education attended night schools.[19] These women purchased dime novels because they were readily accessible and because they felt "American" buying and reading an English-language book.

Dime novels were accessible for working women partly because of their low price. The romances cost ten cents each, which was not an insignificant amount of money for young women who earned as little as $3.50 per week while learning a job, and typically five or six dollars per week as regular pay. Very few women had much spending money. Many turned their pay over to their mothers as their needed contribution to the family economy; others supported themselves, living as boarders or in furnished rooms. Some saved to bring other relatives over to America. Nevertheless, as Kathy Peiss argues, women saved money by walking to work rather than taking the streetcar, and by skimping on lunches.[20] Rose Schneiderman made extra money to purchase dime novels while working at Ridley's department store on Grand Street on the Lower East Side:

> I began reading English [-language] novels in the ten-cent paper-back editions of the day that I somehow managed to buy. The only money I ever had was six cents Mother gave me every day for my lunch—a sandwich and a piece of fruit. But the saleswomen would send me out to buy their lunches, paying me a penny each. I saved those pennies until I had enough for a book . . . I devoured everything I could lay my hands on.[21]

New York newsstands and soda water stands loaned romance novels for a lower price, allowing purchasers to read more novels for their money and the proprietor to sell the same book multiple times.[22] Working women probably also traded already-read novels among themselves.

Working women also purchased dime novels because they were available. As chapter 1 argued, only some kinds of literature were both inexpensive enough for women to buy and available for purchase in working-class neighborhoods. This accessibility was crucial, particularly for immigrants who might not have been familiar with stores and institutions off their beaten path from neighborhood to workplace. While Rose Pastor asked why women did not use "our free, circulating libraries" in making their choice of reading material, Rose Schneiderman explained in her memoir that dime novels, despite their cost, were more accessible to her than books available free of charge from the library:

> I knew nothing about going to a public library and taking out any book my heart desired . . . I did not even know about the College Settlement House which was only a block away.[23]

Pushcarts and newsstands put dime novels into the hands of working women without first requiring other cultural competencies.

Women bought English-language novels so eagerly in part because they signified Americanization. To purchase and read one was seen as a great accomplishment. Immigrant Rose Cohen recalled in her memoir her unflagging efforts to learn English, and the first English-language book she read: a romance. That book, besides containing a story, became a badge of her American status. Cohen said, "I felt so proud that I could read an English book that I carried it about with me in the street. I took it along to the shop. I became quite vain."[24] Sadie Frowne reported in 1902 that she had attended night school in the winters after work for two years, and she also proudly applied her skills to dime novel reading:

> I can read quite well in English now and I look at the newspapers every day. I read English books, too, sometimes. The last one that I read was "A Mad Marriage," by Charlotte Braeme. She's a grand writer and makes things just like real to you. You feel as if you were the poor girl yourself going to get married to the rich duke.[25]

As late as 1924, one dime novel publisher explained to the *New York Times* that dime novel romances sold on stands in northeastern and midwestern cities as part of Americanization. As the *Times* reporter wrote, "the American-born generation, eager to learn all about this America of which they are told so much, come with their ten cents in change and buy the books as they would buy a magazine."[26] Interwoven in their melodramatic plots, dime novels contained local references and place names, and promised to give readers information about America.

Jewish women's willingness to pick up English dime novels may have been influenced by the popularity of similar narratives available in Yiddish. Since its inception in the 1840s, the dime novel industry had thrived free of an international copyright: nearly identical novels existed in German, French, English, and, by the late nineteenth century, Yiddish. One of the most popular Yiddish writers, Shomer, copied from French romances, adapting places and names to the United States. Immigrants used even these Yiddish novels for information on America. And as Michael Denning notes, Shomer's plots bore a strong resemblance to those of Laura Jean Libbey.[27] The prevalence of such Yiddish cheap novels potentially increased Jewish women's likelihood to pick up English versions of these stories when they learned English. Indeed, Rose Cohen, whose first English book was a romance, had earlier read the Yiddish romances aloud to her mother.[28]

Despite the barrier of English literacy to many, then, English-language dime novels did gain currency among first- and second-generation immigrants. According to a contemporary study of working women's amusements at the turn of the century, 12.5 percent of Jewish women surveyed reported that reading was their favorite pastime, *despite* the fact that reading was not one of the choices listed.[29] And knowledge of dime novel plots was by no means limited to those literate in English. Dime novel romances were popular topics of conversation among women at the workplace, extending their range of influence. As Natalie Zemon Davis argues about sixteenth-century France, printing and literacy affected more than those individuals who owned books and could read them; reading also affected the oral culture for those who lived "on the margins of literacy."[30] Many women read at work, on their lunch hours, and often discussed the novels throughout the day. As Dorothy Richardson recalled,

> Promptly at half-past twelve the awakening machinery called us back to the workaday world. Story books were tucked away, and their entranced readers dragged themselves back to the machines and steaming paste-pots, to dream and to talk as they worked, not of their own fellows of last night's masquerade, but of bankers and mill owners who in fiction have wooed and won and honorably wedded just such poor toilers as they themselves.[31]

Richardson reported that readers recounted entire plot lines to co-workers. The work group discussed the particular qualities of heroes and heroines and exchanged opinions about preferred novels and authors. In doing so, they became an "interpretive community," creating collective meanings and experiences in relation to their commodity consumption.

Dime novels were so common a part of workplace discussions that women expected co-workers to have at least a cursory familiarity with the narratives. Dorothy Richardson recounted one conversation about dime novel romances in which her unfamiliarity with the novels became a point of ridicule. Richardson worked in factories but had a middle-class background. She wrote about her experiences in 1905, and it is unclear whether she had to work or whether she worked, like many middle-class women, to gain material for a book. When the fact that she had never read a dime novel romance was revealed one worker cried in surprise and disgust, "Oh, mama! Carry me out and let me die!" Another clutched her throat and cried, "Water! Water! . . . I'm going to faint!" At this point both workers gave way to laughter at Richardson's expense. They later hastened to help her overcome her deficiency by including her in their discussions of plots and heroes, and recounted the story of one Laura Jean Libbey novel.[32] Dime novels were so important in working women's collective experience of daily life and work itself that they were part of the process of *becoming* a working woman. That is, the romances, as valued objects, played a role in subjectivity formation.

Working women's act of reading at work, during their thirty- to forty-minute lunch hours, was a rejection of the relentless tedium of the workplace. Factory workers usually labored at highly repetitive tasks that required concentration, dexterity, and physical endurance. Because of the rationalization of the production process, creativity or intelligence was largely irrelevant, and after one mastered the task at hand, learning ceased. Employers paid women by the piece, which meant that only great speed ensured an adequate wage. Women regularly reported that the repetitive yet demanding piecework left them exhausted in mind and body. In this context, reading allowed women to engage another, fictitious world in which working-girl heroines embarked on sensational adventures. As Janice Radway has argued, the "act of picking up a book is a form of social behavior that permits the reader to suspend momentarily all connection with the outside world."[33] Because of time constraints, workers often physically could not leave the factories or shops for lunch, and employers rarely provided lunchrooms. Workers stayed at their benches or sat on the floor among the work materials scattered about, sharing sandwiches and pickles. Reformer Gertrude Barnum remarked upon the readers' intense absorption in the novels: "A pale little paper box maker will sit on the floor of her factory at the noon hour lost to the world behind the cover of her book."[34] Dorothy Richardson recalled that in her workplace, "Although we had a half-hour, luncheon was swallowed quickly by most of the girls, eager to steal away to a sequestered bower among the boxes, there to lose themselves in paper-backed romances."[35] By reading at work, women literally changed the shop itself during the lunch hour to a place that could provide relief from labor. In addition, by reading women refused to act like machines. They engaged their minds with thrilling adventures, and some simultaneously practiced their English literacy skills. Indeed, the narratives in which working heroines were ladies offered a counterpoint to the real-life devaluation of the workers. The practice of reading and discussing the novels, then, actively rejected the terms of women's subordination through the piecework system.

Working women also read dime novel romances at home, after the workday was completed. Sources suggest that this reading, too, stood as a counterpoint to the tedium of piecework and devalued labor. Rose Pastor, writing as "Zelda" for *Yiddishes Tageblatt (Jewish Daily News)*, castigated readers of dime novel romances in her column for working girls. She offered to provide any woman a list of "good" literature. Several women responded to Zelda's offer, and their letters requesting "good books" reveal some of their attitudes toward reading. While clearly on the defensive, these women conveyed their investment in the novels and their value of material that was not "dry." Sarah Cohen asked for reading that was "educational, and at the same time entertaining; I have not the patience to get interested in dry reading, for I have only the evenings to read in, as by day I work in a dry goods store as a sales girl."[36] A worker echoed these priorities in a complaint to the editors of *Life and Labor*, the Women's Trade Union League's journal. She said:

> I am sorry, but I'm too tired when I get home at night to read things like that article on Industrial Education. I'm sure I ought to know about it and think about it, but I'm too tired. We work longer than ten hours a day standing all the time and it does affect your brains.[37]

Tony Getz also worried that a new course of reading would be "dry":

> I am a girl of fifteen years of age and I have already read a good many books which you don't like: most of them are by Mrs. Bertha M. Clay, Georgie Sheldon, Mrs. Southworth, etc. I like instructive books quite well, but I think them a little dry, but as you say I ought to read them, I will try my best to do so.

Two respondents to Zelda's offer reveal a deep and pleasurable engagement with the melodramatic language of dime novel romances.

One seemed less interested in hearing Zelda's advice than in sharing her own, rather sophisticated, creative product. She wrote her letter in melodramatic language and cleverly made fun of Zelda's alarm:

> Your heart to heart talk with the girls about good books has saved a girl from misery and misfortune. She was quavering on the brink of an abyss, its dark fathomless waters anxious to swallow her and increase the numbers of victims already fallen low by second class literature. She was insane from imbibing the injurious stuff from cheap novel reading . . .

Another respondent clearly saw her dime novels as "good books." Indeed, her conviction was so strong that she failed to understand what Zelda meant by "good" literature. Addressing the columnist as "My dear Zelda," she proudly listed the books she read—all dime novel romances:

> I read many books, and especially novels, such as: *Beatrice, Lena Rivers, Claire, A Broken Wedding Ring, A Heart's Bitterness* and so on. I think all these very interesting, and wish that you would advise me as to whether these are the proper kinds of books to read or not. I would give up all other enjoyments to read good books—I love to read.[38]

For some women, identification with the working-girl heroine who became a lady was so strong that, according to Dorothy Richardson, they took on aristocratic names from the dime novels. Richardson recounted one worker trying to convince her to adopt a new name:

> All the girls do it when they come to the factory to work. It don't cost no more to have a high-sounding name. . . . Georgiana Trevelyan and Goldy Courtleigh and Gladys Carringford and Angelina Lancaster and Phoebe Arlington—them girls all got [their names] out of stories.[39]

By taking on new names, women moved the internal imaginative process that occurred while reading into the collective space of workplace culture. Furthermore, when workers changed their names they shed their family names and the ethnic and class associations that went with them. Experience had taught them that such associations were liabilities in the United States, and they adopted aristocratic-sounding English names instead. This practice certainly reveals that the dime novels encouraged women to obscure their race and ethnic identities and to identify with the dominant culture. At the same time, however, when women adopted "rich"-sounding names from dime novels they resisted the depersonalization that occurred at the workplace. Because piecework, as a method of labor control, reduced the skill and creativity required for jobs, workers were rather interchangeable. Bosses and supervisors reflected this fact in the ways that they treated and addressed them. In some factories, supervisors assigned and called workers by numbers to keep track of their piecework production. Elizabeth Hasanovitz remembers her forelady often calling, "*Hundred and twelve*, what happened to you?" Supervisors also regularly used derogatory names, such as "stupid animal," as Sadie Frowne was called.[40] Women used the dime novel fantasies to insist on their own worth when they took on names like "Rose Fortune," the name given Richardson by her co-worker.

Just as "high-sounding" names countered the implicit message of piecework production that women were merely stupid cogs in a machine, the elaborate fashion women wore asserted their worth in a context that denied it. Through fashion, women borrowed from the cultural values placed on objects they produced to dignify their own devalued labor. Working women knew from daily experience that owners subjugated workers' health and welfare to the needs of industry in exchange for a wage that was usually inadequate. Whatever their view of unions, workers in factories, sweatshops, and laundries complained of long hours and unpaid overtime, unfair fines for lateness and botched work, sexual harassment, work speedups, and unventilated, unhealthy, and unsafe working conditions. Women workers lost a great deal of time to illness, and after years of factory work many suffered from malnutrition, exhaustion, and sometimes serious chronic diseases. Working-class immigrant women daily learned what United States society had to teach them: the clothes they made, laundered, or sold were more important than they were themselves. When they borrowed the signifying logic of the display window to increase their own worth, they claimed a cultural franchise they would otherwise lack. This act held particular resonance for the many women who labored to produce, maintain, or sell fashion commodities.[41]

Just as work experiences taught women that they held less value than the products they made, their social interactions taught them that, in the United States, appearance mattered more than character. Working women's encounters with bosses, wealthier Americans, and men in general shaped their understanding of the ethnic, class, and sexual economies in which they had to find a place, all of which involved clothing. Many historical accounts record this generation of urban immigrants' embrace of American fashion as a sign of Americanization. Historians have focused primarily on the differences between customs in the United States, where ready-made clothing made it possible for most to dress with style, and in the "old country," where fine dress often still signaled nobility. Indeed, in parts of Eastern Europe only women of the upper class could wear hats, coding a rigid caste system.[42] When both Jewish and Italian immigrants embraced American fashions, they imbued them with meanings rooted in a collective memory of oppression. But the social meanings of clothing also came from day-to-day practices and hierarchies in the United States.

Immigrants soon learned of these hierarchies. One candy manufacturer, who primarily employed Italian women, admitted that he would not hire a woman who did not wear a hat when she applied for a job, but arrived bareheaded or wearing a shawl in the tradition of Italy. He claimed "Americanized" women were easier to work with. An investigator reported that Italian women encountered prejudice in hiring unless they "dressed like [their] fellow-workers and spoke their language."[43] Lillian Wald similarly reported that many Lower East Side working women wore "paint" on their faces, not first out of a love for makeup, but because "employers did not like to have jaded-looking girls working for them."[44] Perhaps employers did not like to see the daily effects of labor on their young, female workers. Whatever the logic of individual employers, however, they sent a consistent message that appearance, rather than experience, skill, aptitude, or attitude, was what mattered when applying for a job. In addition, they made it clear that appearance, rather than contribution to the nation's wealth as a worker or participation in the United States' culture, was at the heart of Americanization.

Working women also regularly encountered members of the middle and upper classes who drew stark class distinctions on the basis of dress. Working women widely understood and resented that many people saw them as "unrefined," and therefore less womanly, because of their labor and their income. When they did not put on style (and of course some did not, out of both choice and necessity), they encountered harsh judgment. Elizabeth Hasanovitz recounted attending the opera with a general admission ticket, which meant she would stand through the performance. She was quite ill at the time, and one man who left his seat early offered her his ticket. However, two "ladies" called the usher and had Hasanovitz removed, despite the ticket, because she was not dressed properly. Hasanovitz recorded the anger, as well as a fantasy of wealth, that she experienced after this event:

My heart was bubbling with anger and feeling of injustice. Why had I not a right to the music I liked so much? . . . And while I stood leaning on the rail, I was seized with a new ambition—an ambition to get rich and buy up a number of seats among the richest, and place on those chairs people with shabby clothes. And to show that "shabbiness" perhaps understands and feels music more than "gold embroidered chiffons."[45]

Finally, women quickly learned that clothes played an important role in the sexual economy as well. As one garment worker, who spent 25 percent of her wage of four dollars a week on clothing, said, "A girl who does not dress well is stuck in a corner, even if she is pretty."[46] Two other working women bought nice clothes on the installment plan, and upon wearing them secured dates for supper and a motion picture. A reformer narrated their later conversation:

You see . . . what a difference a few good clothes make! If you want to get any notion took of you, you gotta have some style about you. And anyway! Them clothes has saved us some money a'ready—got us free dinners an' free shows—an'll save us more.[47]

As Kathy Peiss has argued, working women took part in a leisure economy in which they relied on male "treating" to make up for insufficient wages.[48] Clothing was often seen as the investment one had to make to participate in this system. Another working woman noted the effort women put into making nice clothes before their long-saved-for summer vacation at a country house:

For weeks ahead they sit up late into the night making dresses, petticoats, and other useless cheap fineries; for they must appear "swell" at those expensive country homes. And who knows? Fate may bring them together with a decent fellow in an expensive boarding-house; and there are chances of marrying and getting rid of the hated shop and eternal anxiety for a living. So the long, exhausting deprivations, the investment in good clothes, may after all prove profitable.[49]

Women knew the cultural value of clothing in a job market which systematically kept their wages lower than men's.

Given the value of commodities in United States culture, specifically the currency of clothing in the formation of ethnic, class, and gender hierarchies, it is not surprising that fashionable clothing became important to working-class women. Dressing with style was a tradition for white working-class women before and after the time period and context studied here, and it has been key to African Americans as well. Nevertheless, the specific meanings that clothing held for working-class women in the late nineteenth and early twentieth centuries took root in their particular circumstances. As with dime novels, clothing took on collective meaning from women's practices of acquiring it, discussing and wearing it at work, and the specific ways they altered established styles, or the "content" of their fashion.

Most of working women's clothing was purchased ready-made from pushcarts, small stores in working-class neighborhoods, or department stores, particularly the bargain basements.[50] Ready-made clothing particularly appealed to working women because of their limited time; a contemporary study revealed that most working women did little sewing beyond mending, or sewing underwear and shirtwaists.[51] Women purchased the majority of their clothing much as they purchased dime novels: by saving and skimping on other expenditures. However, the higher price for clothing meant that some women had to resort to additional measures as well, including compensating for their small amount of expendable income by buying on the installment plan in small neighborhood shops. In Chicago, peddlers or "agents" went door-to-door offering clothing on this system.[52]

When working women purchased clothing, they exercised their new entitlement as workers. As females, women had traditionally worked to maintain the household; when they worked for pay, they owed the whole of their wages to the family economy. Parents expected daughters to hand over pay envelopes to the household financial manager, which in Italian and Jewish households was usually the mother. In return, most received a small allowance. Fathers and sons, however, could justly open their own envelopes before returning home and extract sums for their own leisure. Many sons simply paid "board" to their mothers and kept the remaining money for themselves. Breadwinning was still associated with a male role, and male breadwinning earned this right.[53]

Turn-of-the-century sources are filled with accounts of working women struggling to change this system and lay full and equal claim to the name of "worker" in their families. They did so in part through demanding more of their paychecks for their own use. In one case, a Jewish immigrant named Jean found a blouse she wished to buy for three dollars on Grand Street on New York's Lower East Side. However, her mother only allowed her a two-dollar allowance from her wages of eleven dollars per week. Her mother suggested she choose a cheaper blouse; Jean refused. Jean kept her pay envelope unopened for four weeks, withholding it from the family economy. Finally, her father suggested a solution usually reserved for sons: Jean was to pay one dollar per day for room and board and keep the remaining four dollars per week for her own use. Jean's later fashion purchases doubtlessly were symbolic of the status that she had won as a breadwinner. "I used to go out on Clinton Street and get a hat for twenty-five dollars . . . and my mother used to say, 'What's on this hat, gold?' "[54] Filomena Moresco also dismissed the allowance system and kept money from her pay envelope. She spent twenty-five dollars, nearly a month's wages, on a "pretty party dress, a beaver hat and a willowed plume."[55] When women claimed their pay envelopes to purchase clothing they laid claim to the status of "worker," enjoyed by their brothers but often denied to them, and made clothing a badge of their own labor (see fig. 2.2).

While purchasing clothing could serve as an enactment of women's identities as workers, women also drew upon the skills and the knowledge of styles they gained at work to make and alter clothing. As stated earlier, working women could rarely do *all* of their own sewing: a tailored suit, jacket, or dress was complicated and laborious, demanding more time, and often more skill, than the women possessed. Nevertheless, working women often made shirtwaists and underwear and applied trimmings, lace, feathers, and other decorations to dresses and hats.[56] Thus, they rescued from their labor additional personal value, and inflected their consumer practices with an element of their

2.2 Stylish working women gather outside their workplaces during the lunch hour.

own creative production. As one journalist wrote in 1900, "In the matter of dresses it is natural that the East Side should be strictly up to date, for does it not furnish clothes for the rest of the town?"[57]

The New York pushcarts provided Lower East Side women a rich trove of cheap and ever-changing materials with which to make or alter clothing. Some pushcart peddlers carried complete ready-made clothing. One reformer noted that Italian women bought ready-made clothes "in department stores, in small shops in the neighborhood, or even from pushcarts." Other peddlers carried fabric "remnants, odd pieces and samples" from nearby garment shops and wholesale warehouses, and would daily carry different kinds of items. In short, they functioned as a sort of flea market for cheap materials and goods of all kinds, even "goods left over thirty days in the laundry."[58] Angela McRobbie argues that most post–World War II subcultures utilized the secondhand market in clothing to create distinctive styles.[59] Similarly, working-class women could utilize the pushcart economy to extend their abilities to put on style. According to a *New York Tribune* reporter, large pieces of lace, worth twenty dollars or more, could be bought on Hester Street for fifty cents. Women could make the articles of clothing listed by this reporter easily and quickly:

> From bits of lace, bought for a trifle from the pedlers [sic], other women have made fichus [scarflike triangles of fine cloth arranged around neck and shoulders], capes, overskirts, etc. Pieces of fine cloth, in sizes from half a yard to several yards, are often sold at low rates.[60]

Women could thus acquire expensive materials at low prices in their own neighborhoods. If they could sew a petticoat, for example, they could fulfill the wish for "silk underwear" for under a dollar.

Equipped with inexpensive materials, women drew upon workplace skills to assemble a wardrobe. While owners did not reward learning, women turned their education about style to their own advantage. The high turnover rate of jobs meant that the majority of women garment workers, like Elizabeth Hasanovitz, had worked in different kinds of shops, on various "grades" of goods. These women learned the difference between "good quality" products and cheaper versions. Hasanovitz recorded the efforts of her co-workers:

> It made one wonder to watch with what endeavor they tried to piece out waists of the smallest remnants, copying the styles from our shop. Seldom could a girl (unless she was a "swell") afford to buy a waist in our shop, for though we made them, they were too expensive for us, and we had to find satisfaction in cheaper imitations.[61]

Department store workers were infamous for learning the styles from the clothing that they sold, and laundry workers saw a continual stream of fashionable clothing go through their machines. While some critics saw working women's knowledge of style as morally threatening, giving women a taste for what they could not afford and potentially leading to prostitution, others saw a version of populism in the practice of wearing the styles one worked on during the day. As one commentator said, "If my lady wears a velvet gown, put together for her in an East Side sweat shop, may not the girl whose tired fingers fashioned it rejoice her soul by astonishing Grand-st. [sic] with a copy of it on the next Sunday?"[62] Paid little for their labor, working women elevated their own cultural value by wearing what they produced.

Women not only used their knowledge of styles gained from their jobs, they also sometimes acquired materials, and actually made the clothing, while at work. The *New York Tribune* reported that one garment worker made her shirtwaist from fine, thin material bought from a Hester Street pushcart for twenty cents. But she used her skills as a neckwear worker, and materials from the shop, to give her shirtwaist distinction:

> Its "style" came from the really handsome neck arrangement, which she had made herself; she worked at neckwear and the "boss" had allowed her to take the odds and ends from which she had fashioned the pretty thing.[63]

This neckwear maker had used her skills and workplace materials not for her boss's profit but for her own. Though this worker was reportedly "allowed" to take remnants from the shop, bosses regularly accused garment workers of stealing materials. Besides the obvious opportunity to liberate some supplies while at the shop, garment workers had additional opportunities to keep some materials for themselves: they often took piecework home at night to complete before the next morning, in a frantic attempt to raise their wages. The written record registers women's outrage at being falsely accused, and it is undeniable that many were. However, women's sense of their right to the styles they made can be seen as part of a "moral economy"—a way to recover unpaid wages or long hours lost to labor—and might have included directly absconding with remnants or whole pieces of fabric.[64]

Some workers also used the workplace itself to make their own clothing. One woman reported that when the dull season hit their shop in May, workers would sit and wait for work that might come in, as was typical in the small garment shops. They used this time to make their own clothes on the shop's machines:

While waiting, the girls busied themselves in making their own clothes. They would buy up all the remnants left in the shop, or hunt up bargains in the various department-store basements, and prepare their own summer outfits.[65]

Garment workers were paid by the piece in the vast majority of shops. This meant that bosses paid workers less when there was less work, transferring much of the risk and cost of a seasonal industry to the workers. In order to work at all, these women had to sit and wait for the small amount of labor they would get to perform. Their wages typically dropped by half during such slow periods. When workers made their own clothes, they were not literally taking time back from the owner, since they were not being paid at those moments. However, they did turn the oppressive piecework system to some value to themselves. As Michel de Certeau argues, such activities diverted work resources toward labor that was free, creative, and not directed toward profit. Such activities signaled workers' capabilities and their solidarity with others, with whom they created their own products.[66] Indeed, for these few hours, workers labored for themselves. They were not overtly challenging the labor system, but they were recapturing some of the value of their labor from its appropriation by capital.

When women bought or made clothing, then, their consumption was already infused with work-related meanings. The second aspect of consumption—the act of wearing the clothes—was also related to their workplace experiences. To be sure, women wore their fine clothes to dances, amusement parks, weddings, the movies, or to walk about in the evenings, activities that could build upon and augment the workplace culture. But women also wore their fine clothes to work. Sometimes they did so because they planned to go directly to dance halls or other amusements afterward. Dorothy Richardson recorded the array of stylish clothes assembled for this purpose:

> Hanging from rows of nails on all sides were their street garments—a collection of covert-cloth jackets, light tan automobile coats ... and every other style of fashionable wrap that might be cheaply imitated. Sandwiched among the street garments were the trained skirts and evening bodices of the "Moonlight Maids." ... Along the walls were ranged the high-heeled shoes and slippers, a bewildering display of gilt buckles and velvet bows; each pair waiting patiently for the swollen, tired feet of their owner to carry them away to the ball.[67]

Some women wore their stylish clothes to work because they had no others, having invested the whole of their budget into one outfit.[68] Finally, women wore fine clothes to work because they wanted to look well when traveling to and from their jobs. When Richardson's "learner" at a box factory found she did not have an apron, she instructed her to turn her skirt inside out to protect it from the glue. When Richardson balked, her learner insisted, "The *ladies* I'm used to working with likes to walk home looking decent and respectable, no difference what they're like other times."[69] As Angela McRobbie has argued, the highly structured, monotonous, and sometimes dirty nature of their labor produced a desire among many working-class people to "mark out distance from the factory floor" once work was completed for the day.[70] Robin D. G. Kelley further notes that when African Americans dressed up after work in the mid-twentieth century, they presented a "public challenge to the dominant stereotype of the black body, and reinforce[d] a sense of dignity that was perpetually being assaulted."[71] When working women shed aprons and donned fine clothes for the trip home, they asserted that their labor did not lower their dignity or worth.

Whatever the reason women wore their fine clothes to work, one result was that they shared, and showed off, their clothes to each other, making dress a central part of workplace culture. Additionally, as with the dime novels, the importance of "fashion" went beyond the products themselves, because women dreamed and talked about them, imagining future purchases and styles seen in shop windows.[72] When women discussed "swell evening pumps and lace petticoats," they shared information, developed collective "tastes" in clothing, and a created a collective dream world centered in commodities.[73]

The consumption of dime novels and fashion, then, consisted of a number of related social practices of buying and having that shaped the place of particular texts and clothing items in women's lives. These practices all had imaginative elements in themselves. Purchasing a fashionable dress from a brightly lit pushcart, dreaming together of dime novel heroes or a coveted outfit, and taking on "rich" names from dime novel heroines all served to create a collective dream world of consumption that was rooted in the painful limitations of daily life and labor. Women's imaginative experiences of reading the narratives and putting on the articles of clothing articulated to these social practices. While individual idiosyncrasies and the multiple possibilities for interpretation meant that not all women "read" the fashions or the novels in exactly the same ways, a close look at the texts of the dime novel formula and the typical clothing worn by working women can reveal more about the contours of their collective dream world.

When working women dressed with "gentility" and read about working-girl heroines who became "ladies," they engaged the "wish images" embedded in the products—a term Walter Benjamin used to describe the utopian element present in much of popular culture. For Benjamin, products such as fashion pleased because they offered a fleeting fulfillment that anticipated a potential, emancipatory reality. While such products could not emancipate people from oppressive labor or class structures, as wish images they engaged a potentially revolutionary or egalitarian impulse within the imagination. Benjamin argued that wish images were spurred by the new but rooted in the old, in culturally sedimented images remaining from unfulfilled desires. Fictional figures of gentility operated in this way: the "ladies" of the dime novels evoked a past era of nobility even as they referenced middle-class privilege from which working-class women were excluded in daily life. The elaborate fashion worn by working women likewise evoked a fairy-tale princess's grace and status even as it was spurred by the latest signifiers of glamour. (Indeed, a popular style worn by working women at the turn of the century was the "princess dress.") While Benjamin did not see wish images as radical in themselves, he did see a utopian imagination as a necessary component of social change.[74]

Working women, however, did not simply *imbibe* wish images embedded in the dime novel narratives and the fashion products; they *enacted* wish images when they made themselves into ladies. In this way, the wish images of the commodities became part of a much larger, socially materialized practice. Women acted as ladies through "aristocratic pretensions" similar to those played out by African Americans of the same time period when competing in the cake walk.[75] They adopted an exaggerated walk, mocked by Dorothy Richardson as "nervous, jerky, [and] heavy-footed," along with elaborate manners.[76] Working women bowed hello or good-bye with "grace put on," and "fine flourishes" of the arms.[77] Taking a seat could be a "fine art," a "great, grand effort to sit down with all ease and grace."[78] This "vulgar vanity," as the middle class saw it, was matched by aristocratic speech. The working woman, complained Gertrude Barnum, "will search her brain for long words and high-sounding phrases, and use them in a grandiloquent style which expresses nothing but ignorance and affectation."[79] Middle-class judgments notwithstanding, working women clearly enacted a commodity display that wove the wish image of the lady in dime novels and fashion into a social practice. But what kind of wish image was available in those products themselves?

Working women who already participated in some of the social practices related to ladyhood would bring particular cultural competencies, or what Radway has called "social grammars," to their dime novel reading experience.[80] Chapter 1 acknowledged that the texts themselves offer a multitude of potential readings. However, the cultural competencies of working women learning to be ladies could promote certain readings over others. Specifically, working ladies could read the dime novel romances as melodramatic defenses of women's position as wage earners. The novels offered narrative fantasies of social recognition that allowed them to briefly bridge painful cultural contradictions that assigned heroic worker status to men and heroic "lady" status only to middle- and upper-class white women.

The structure of the dime novel narrative prompted a different mode of reading than did that of the bourgeois novel. The narrative formula begins with the working girl becoming orphaned, homeless, and jobless, usually within the first ten pages of the novel. The long series of adventures and calamities that follow comprise the bulk of the narrative. The working girl gains a secret inheritance near the middle of the book, and finally marries the rich hero at the end. The novels followed the "adventure-romance" (or aristomilitary romance) tradition, in which the protagonist must survive a series of contests that prove her/his worth and grant her/him a valorized position in the group as well as a reward.[81] As in the adventure-romance, heroines in dime novels did not change through the stories: they were already perfect. But their worth had to be proven to the outside world to become recognized as valid. Dime novels invited a highly visceral identification with heroines who met rapid successions of suspenseful adventures.

The bourgeois novel, in contrast, centered around personal growth through education or inner struggle, often to solve a problem or gain mastery over an external situation. Therefore, it relied narratively on character development, while the dime novel romance did not. Chance also played a very different role in the two types of books. In the bourgeois novel, a character often must find a way to grow and gain mastery over a problem in spite of the vagaries of chance. For example, in *Little Women*, the government required the father to leave home and serve in the Civil War. This element outside of personal control sets up the premise of the book: the "little women" have to grow up and become virtuous, caring women without a male authority figure. They must try all the harder to master themselves and be good because father is absent; they must develop in spite of circumstances. The orphaned dime novel heroine is similarly without a father, but she hardly has time to notice that before she loses her job, is abducted, poisoned, trapped in a building that is on fire, etc. The dime novels are not about the exertion of will over chance but about meeting a string of challenges and responding to each one.

Thus, the dime novel heroine changes in a very different way than do protagonists of bourgeois novels. Gaining a secret inheritance makes the dime novel heroine magically a "lady," which she unknowingly has been all along. Her change is dramatic and sudden, yet merely a manifestation of what was already true. Both types of novels validated the protagonists' selves in the social world, but according to quite different narrative mechanisms.

Dime novels solicit readers' identification largely by first prompting indignation on the heroine's behalf or a suspenseful anxiety for the heroine. Film critic Elizabeth Cowie has argued that readers identify with characters not when they share specific characteristics with them, but when they have common "structural relations of desire." That is, readers do not identify simply because they are "like" a character, but because they can associate the desire of the character with one of their own—so they come to desire with, or on behalf of, the character.[82] The dime novels entice such correspondence first by regularly making readers privy to conversations about the heroine that she herself does not hear, or by making readers the witnesses to grossly unfair treatment. For example, the romances routinely include a conversation between members of the hero's wealthy family about the working heroine, in which someone invariably voices common middle- and upper-class pretensions and prejudices. As one rich villainess put it, "Can he, who is the patrician through and through, care for a girl who actually works with her hands?" Another says, "How horribly ill-bred she must be!"[83] These conversations set up a key theme of the dime novel while inviting readers to align their resentment of class distinctions—or other distinctions—with the heroine's.

Dime novels also enticed an anxious identification with heroines through the use of suspense. Readers often know more than the heroine does about a plot that is about to ensnare her. By being able to see the danger that the heroine cannot, the readers might wish to warn the heroine, urge a particular action on her behalf, and thus align their good will with her welfare. For example, readers repeatedly are told the actions and thoughts of the villains as they plot the heroine's demise. This narrative mechanism did not intend to prompt an identification with the villains, but to inform the readers of the heroine's new and present danger. The readers then know roughly what is going to happen, but they do not know how it will turn out. As Cowie notes, this tactic prompts an especially emotional experience as readers anxiously fear for the heroine's safety.[84] If working women readers did indeed respond to narrative invitations and in some way align their interests to the heroine's, they would likewise feel a vicarious thrill and vindication when the heroine successfully evaded harm or heroically saved others as well as themselves.

The different narrative structures of dime novel romances and bourgeois novels thus could promote quite different experiences and pleasures of reading, and understanding them can help explain why some critics could find the dime novels so disempowering to women, while many working women loved them. Someone reading the dime novels for character development and the expectation that the heroine would grow might well find the heroines "weak" or "vapid," as have some scholars and contemporary critics. This is not to argue that the character traits of the heroine are irrelevant, but rather that working women might take different narrative cues and form different impressions.[85] In fact, the formula introduces the heroines as both vulnerable and strong. One heroine is described as at once physically small and courageous:" 'I don't care *who* hears me!' she cried, snapping her little white fingers and stamping a mite of a foot. 'I'll stick up for my rights. No one shall run over *me!*' "[86] Readers could feel anxious or indignant on behalf of the vulnerable heroine *and* thrill to her successful adventures and thus her power.

The first thing that happens to every dime novel heroine is that her established identity is suspended when she becomes an orphan. In the first chapter of almost every novel, the working girl labors to support a sick sister or father, who invariably immediately dies. The heroine then loses her job, perhaps because she misses work when she attends her sister's funeral or because the boss wants to make her his mistress. Here, the novels always invoked some injustice that working women typically experienced: unfair fines for botched work (or work claimed by the boss to be botched), sexual harassment, no time off to care for family members. Readers are privvy to the whole story of the innocent heroine's calamity, while the other characters often blame her for her misfortunes. Libbey's *The Heiress of Cameron Hall* overtly solicited working women's identification:

> Only those who know what "discharged" means can pity poor
> Helena. Only those who have had a page of just such an experi-
> ence in their own past lives can understand what Helena suffered,
> and an answering chord will thrill in their hearts for her.[87]

The heroine then loses her home, perhaps because she does not have rent money due to her boss' unfairness, or perhaps because someone falsely reports to the landlady that she has compromised her virtue. Orphaned, jobless and homeless, the heroine finds herself cast into the city, the epitome of vulnerability, with villains and seducers hot on her trail.

The heroine's extreme vulnerability was crucial to the adventure element of the novels, but her orphan status served other functions as well. Heroines who were orphaned were not only vulnerable, but also free of the class and ethnic associations that accompanied their family identity, and free of the patriarchal or paternal supervision working-class women typically experienced in their parents' homes, some boarding houses, and at work. Women's class identity derived not solely from their labor, but also from the class status of the male producers (fathers or husbands) in their families. In order to provide a fantasy of a new class identity, the dime novel romances had to rid the heroine of her old family connection and provide her with a freedom to move about the city that most women could not claim.

The orphaned working girl heroine also could signal freedom to women who experienced a paternalism at work that overtly capitalized on women's subservient place in the family. Employers baldly denied women a living wage because they assumed them to be secondary wage earners, in part supported by their parents. Some employers went so far as to refuse to employ women who did not live with parents, because their wages could not support someone even at barest subsistence.[88] Employers often supported building boarding homes for working women, to keep them from being driven to "vice," but would not raise wages. Such paternalistic authority drew the ire of working-class women. One complained of an employer's interest in working-girl "homes":

> What the employer has got to learn and learn quickly is that women are going to have a living wage, enough to let them live where and how they like. There has been too much of this father idea to working women. We would like the freedom of being orphans for a while.[89]

Even unions sometimes dismissed women's actual struggles on the basis that their "ideal" role was in the home. They often countered women's pleas for attention by telling them to go back home, an impossibility for most.[90] Thus, when the fictional working-girl heroine became orphaned, she embarked on a new social world of possibility, symbolically freed from the definitions of gender, class, and ethnicity that had constrained her.

To a working-class reader, the heroine could epitomize a familiar vulnerability and oppression, but also an exhilarating freedom from the oppressive and intertwined constraints of work and family. The romances barely mention work or the workplace after these first ten to twenty pages. However, the novels were about *being* a female worker throughout. The attacks the heroine encounters are always in the context of her status as worker. Key to the dime novel plot is the question: Can a worker be a lady? That is, does work indeed degrade, spoil one's virtue, make one coarse and masculine? The heroine's adventures make her the victim of male villains who believe her status as worker makes her "lower" and therefore available for their pleasure. They usually try to force her into marriage with them. The hero, of course, thinks that "a woman may work with her hands and yet have a soul like snow," because he can see her inner, unchanging worth.[91] The hero and heroine, however, are torn apart through misunderstanding, usually plotted by the villains, and the hero goes away, often to Europe, for most of the book. When heroines fend off villains, they demonstrate their own worth as workers, without the aid of the hero, though occasionally they are rescued by others.

The dime novel heroine's challenges and contests are varied, but often put her in a position of extreme peril. Heroines are regularly abducted, bound and gagged, drugged, locked in remote caves, and forced to sign marriage licenses committing them to lives with villains. Evil, rich women attack their virtue and tell them lies about their rich heroes. Sexual vulnerability was a key narrative element, but dime novels handled this theme much differently than did stories about working women aimed at a middle-class audience. Such middle-class tales often portrayed heroines as "weakening" and "succumbing to temptation," and often ended with the working woman's death. These stories offered middle-class women very different fantasies of freedom from bourgeois social restraint. The dime novel heroines did not struggle with inner temptation but with outer attack. Their virtue was falsely questioned by boarding-house matrons, bosses, and wealthy villainesses. In one romance, even the trade union refuses to help the heroine because of a rumor of her sexual dishonor.[92] However, the actual possibility of rape or willful sexual relations was very understated, particularly in comparison with middle-class novels. Heroines had to extricate themselves from compromising situations, but villains rarely got away with more, sexually, than a stolen kiss. The issue was the working girl's ever-assailed *reputation*, rather than her actual sexual honor.

When working-girl heroines encountered challenges, their task was not simply to endure, or to wait to be rescued by someone. On the contrary, they proved their bravery as much as their virtue, and often saved themselves. Indeed, heroines showed that they were "really" ladies by accomplishing dramatic and daring physical feats. They escaped from compromised positions by breaking glass windows with their fists, untying their own bound wrists, and physically fighting with villains. One abducted heroine rebukes a stolen kiss "with a stinging blow, just as she had done once before for the same offense, straight upon his aristocratic face with her little clinched white hand." When he persists, this heroine struggles with the villain "with almost superhuman strength" until he (accidentally) falls off the bridge on which they have been standing.[93] These scenarios celebrated the powerless overcoming the powerful, much as people cheered Houdini for his masteries of escape during the same time period. Furthermore, dime novel heroines did not simply react to peril: they also actively sought challenges. Another heroine discovered that her kidnappers ran a counterfeiting ring in a tunnel that connected to the room where she was kept: "For a moment, Gay stood as if rooted to the spot, but she was a brave, daring girl, and in a trice she had quickly recovered her composure, the love of adventure which was keen within her, leading her on."[94] While heroines exhibited great vulnerability, their success in adventures signaled their bravery and physical strength.

The most powerful demonstrations of bravery and strength occurred when the heroine saved *others*. The dime novel formula extended heroic narrative forms particularly associated with masculinity and usually reserved for male characters to the working-girl heroine. In one novel, Gaynell literally interrupts a traditionally masculine heroic narrative: the duel. The hero challenges the villain because he has insulted the heroine's honor. Gaynell learns of the duel moments before it is to begin. She dashes to the scene in a carriage and darts between the two men just as they fire their shots. The horse takes both bullets, and the working-girl heroine upstages the duel by saving both men.[95]

Another heroine completely replaces the traditional male hero. Helena saves an opera singer trapped in a runaway carriage:

> Helena was brave and daring by nature and in an instant she had decided what course to pursue. "Jump" she cried out springing to the edge of the pavement, "jump, and I will catch you!" . . . the next moment the . . . [carriage] lay dashed into pieces against an adjacent lamppost, and the young lady, through sheer terror, lay in a deep swoon in Helena's arms.

Helena is versatile in her abilities: she goes on stage for the stricken opera star that same night and is a smash hit.[96] This heroine not only replaces the typical male hero, but by sheer force of narrative convention, the lady's swoon in Helena's arms carries an element of homoeroticism. Helena is not only the "hero"; she is also the "lady," literally taking the opera star's place on stage that night. For working women readers, the heroine's status as worker was profoundly validated. She was accorded male privileges of heroism, just as working women often claimed male privileges of wage earning, yet she also excelled at ladyhood. Indeed, in the dime novels, true ladies exhibited bravery and strength, as well as beauty and charm—that is, ladyhood included a transgression of gender norms.

About one third to one half of the way through the book, the heroine discovers that she is really an heiress. This discovery narratively highlights the heroine's virtue and bravery, recognizing that she is a lady. As Peter Brooks argues, in melodrama, the recognition of virtue is more important than the reward, which is usually a secondary manifestation of the recognition.[97] Narratively, this also allowed the heroine to run about in stylish dresses, attending balls and meeting dangerous adventures in the glamorous world of society *before* marrying the rich hero. With marriage, the final reward is granted, adventures cease, and the story ends. The secret inheritance and life as a lady could operate as a powerful wish image for women readers, figuring as a utopian world of plenty. As Jane Gaines argues, the display of luxury in popular culture does not so much *erase* class differences as it "*figures* social inequities."[98] This is particularly the case in the dime novels, because the heroine retains her identity as worker even as she is revealed to be lady. As one heroine says, "I am only a working girl. . . . I shall never feel above them; my heart will always be with them."[99]

The secret inheritance certainly is among the most contradictory narrative features of the dime novels. It proclaims that the heroine is and always was a lady, despite her status as worker, effectively destabilizing and inverting class definitions. At the same time, the narrative potentially re-essentializes class by suggesting that the heroine's consistent beauty, grace, and charm have all along been possible simply because she isn't really a worker. This narrative instability could partially explain readers' desire to repeat the experience of the dime novel romance, to see the working-girl heroine become a lady again and again and again.

Finally, the heroine is reunited with the hero, misunderstandings melt away, and they marry. Marriage to the wealthy hero is the ultimate reward, overcoming the forces of evil and deprivation and restoring moral, heterosexual order. Despite the importance of this closure, the element of romance does not entirely structure the narrative. Indeed, the millionaire hero himself only makes rare appearances into the busy adventures of the heroine after their tragic misunderstanding at the beginning of the novel. The two reconcile when they realize they have misunderstood each other. A twist of fate, not virtue, usually makes this realization possible.

The dime novel romance differs in key respects from other popular romance formulas. The element of misunderstanding bears some resemblance to Harlequin romances, but unlike the Harlequin hero, the dime novel hero does not change, soften, or show another side of himself. He is perfect, beginning to end. Nor does he attempt to change, or even affect, the heroine in any way, unlike in classic Hollywood melodrama, in which heroines often have to negotiate male power and will in a romance.[100] The romance instead provides crucial narrative tension while the heroine goes about her adventures. While the traditional, heterosexual closure recontains the heroine's adventurousness within the confines of marriage, this is likely a closure that does not fully close. As film critics have argued, the utopian potentials within a narrative cannot often be negated by, or contained within, the closure. In contrast to middle-class narratives about working women or many melodramas in classic Hollywood cinema, the heroine was not punished for her adventures. Unlike Jo in *Little Women*, the dime novel heroine did not have to renounce her adventures in order to become a grown woman and marry. On the contrary, the marriage functioned as a reward for daring adventure.

The dime novel formula clearly held powerful resonances for working-class women who dressed and acted as ladies. The heroines not only encountered the kinds of oppression with which working women were familiar, they also enacted a transformation to ladyhood that provided continued adventures, lavish fashion, and the opportunity to attend upscale balls. As Kathy Peiss has noted, many working women considered dances one of their primary means of amusement. In addition, various institutions in working-class neighborhoods, including settlement houses, put on dances annually to raise money.[101] For young Italian women, weddings were big social occasions, usually offering an opportunity to dance and socialize. Working-class female readers could easily see the dime novel heroine as engaging in activities similar to their own. Furthermore, just as the women who wore encumbering fashions to work demonstrated that labor did not masculinize them or lower their status, the heroine could, to these women, show that someone could be physically active and yet deserving of the highest valuation. The heroine's inherent virtue and physical strength in fighting off villains could be read as validating women's labor, while the secret inheritance could affirm an unassailable, *inner* worth of women workers.

A close look at the content of working women's fashion choices reveals a parallel utopian impulse to the dime novels. Working women dressed in fashion, but they exaggerated elements of style that specifically coded femininity: high-heeled shoes, large or highly decorated hats, exceedingly long trains (if trains were in style), and fine undergarments. In addition, they used more color than was considered tasteful by the middle class to dress up their garments and heighten the element of display in their clothing. As one headline stated: EAST SIDE FASHIONS. THEY KEEP PACE WITH THOSE OF FIFTH AVENUE, AND PERHAPS OUTRUN THEM A LITTLE. The reporter explained that on the East Side, styles were:

> allowed to expand at their own sweet will. Does Broadway don a feather? Grand-st. dons two, without loss of time. Are trailing skirts seen in Fifth ave? Grand-st. trails its yards with a dignity all its own. Are daring color effects sent over from Paris? The rainbow hides its diminished head before Grand-st. on a Sunday afternoon. Grand-st. is Broadway plus Fifth-ave., only very much "more so."[102]

By appropriating and exaggerating the accoutrements of ladyhood, working women invested the category of lady with great imaginative value, implicitly challenging dominant meanings and filling the category with their own flamboyant practices. Working women created a cultural style similar to gay camp or drag, in that they appropriated an overdetermined style of femininity from which they were excluded by the dominant culture. Like gay men in drag, working-class ladies seemed more absorbed in the element of display than in verisimilitude.[103] They created their own distinctive style that implicitly denied that labor made them masculine, degraded or alien.

Working ladies may have dressed in fashion, but they did not dress with "taste" in the middle-class sense of the word. As Fred Davis argues, most studies do not differentiate clearly between "fashion" and accepted, "tasteful" dress, so that both are regularly called "dressing in fashion." Davis states that "fashion" is the new mode of dress introduced at the beginning of the cycle, the style that surprises or even shocks. Once a style becomes established, it is "part of the common visual parlance" and represents good taste.[104] Working women dressed with fashion, and thus circumvented middle-class taste altogether; they did not aspire to be tasteful but to surprise or shock. This can explain why women were accused of at once being "imitative" and lacking any taste. According to a writer for the Yiddish press,

> The very latest style of hat, or cloak, or gown, is just as likely to be worn on Grand Street as on Fifth Avenue. The great middle class does not put on the newest styles until they have been thoroughly exploited by Madam Millionaire of Fifth Avenue and Miss Operator of Essex Street.[105]

2.3 Fashionable young workers share a popular newspaper. The woman on the right has decorated her hat with large, artificial flowers.

Without the guidance of middle-class taste, which since the nineteenth century had served to imbue clothing with simplicity and morality, working women emphasized rather than denied the element of display that played a part in all clothing (see fig. 2.3).

Many working women incorporated elements of stylish dress even when they could not afford a fully fashionable wardrobe. Among a group of striking shirtwaist workers in 1909, fashion ranged from plain to ornate (fig. 2.4). While overcoats cover some women's suits, we can see that the striker third from the left in the first row wears a "picture turban," the new style of the season. The young woman in the front row and farthest to the right displays ornamental buttons on a stylish coat and a hat decorated with plumes. In this posed picture, she partially blocks our view of the striker directly behind her, but leaves a gap to her right, allowing us to admire a sister striker's outrageously large, white muff.

Hats and hair offered an arena for feminine invention at the turn of the century. Large hats and piled pompadours, often created with the aid of false hair "puffs" or "rats," rose quite a distance from stylish women's heads. Working women favored what one journalist named "three story hats," adorned with what Jane Addams called a "wilderness of feathers."[106] Because it was quite inexpensive to buy extra trimmings for a hat to dress it up further or change its style, women often wore hats with "plume[s] four inches too long" and "two dozen feathers, instead of merely a paltry ten or

2.4 Striking shirtwaist workers incorporate stylish elements into their wardrobes in a variety of ways.

twelve."[107] One observer noted with humor a similarity between this practice and working-class ethics of generosity: "Whatever a hat may lack in quality, there is never anything to be desired in the matter of quantity. The East Side, though poor enough in all truth, is ever generous. So far as the people can afford there is no stint in hospitality or charity, and the same rule is applied to hats."[108] Whether they spent a dime or twenty-five dollars, working women could endow their hats with the feel of ladyhood. Anzia Yezierska's novel of immigrant life narrates a character's enthusiasm: "Give a look only on these roses for my hat [cried Mashah]. . . . Like a lady from Fifth Avenue I look, and for only ten cents, from a pushcart of Hester Street."[109]

French heels also became popular with working women. These high heels received a mixed reception in the United States and never gained wide acceptance among the middle class. Rose Pastor rhetorically queried working women:

> If common sense bids one wear a low-heeled shoe and, fashion, a shoe with French heels that come about three inches high and makes one look like a trained dog walking on its hind legs—the body aslant forward and very expressive of a longing to drop on all fours and make walking easier, which ought one to choose?[110]

French heels were often among the first purchases newly arrived immigrants made in America. One middle-class "lady in disguise," who performed wage labor to gain material for a book, reported that some newly arrived "Slavic" immigrants admired her muff greatly, but explained through an interpreter that they could not understand why she wore such unfashionable shoes. They stuck their French heels out from under their dresses for her approval.[111]

Finally, working women used color to emphasize the element of display in dress. Turn-of-the-century middle-class clothing was predominantly dark, with tasteful highlights of color in trim, neckwear, or the hat. Working women far exceeded this. Lillian Wald upbraided one working women for wearing a yellow waist that looked "tough."[112] She offered to buy the offensive shirt from the young woman for five dollars to keep her from wearing it. Rose Pastor likewise tried (in vain) to convince women to use less color in their clothes:

> Now, you cannot deny, girls, that some of you wear a combination of dress that equals Joseph's coat of many colors in variety.... It is not the gay color in itself that I object to, it is how much of it you wear. ...Is red becoming to you, my dear! Then wear it! But only WEAR it; don't make a big display of it. One can wear red without looking like a danger signal and making an (UN) "holy show" of one's self.

Women not only used an excessive amount of bright color, they also used many different colors on the same garment. Pastor wrote, "It is surprising to note what a host of colors some girls will put on in one single dressing—several colors on the hat and some on the dress. It is always a ridiculous sight."[113] But of course, her urgings were bound to fail, because making "a big display of it" was exactly the point. Women's fashion operated as a wish image, claiming the cultural value associated with ladyhood that working women usually were denied. Working ladies capitalized on the contradiction between middle-class assertion that "character" was an essence of being and their practice of marking character through dress. As such, working ladies' fashion contributed to an alternative class identity. They claimed ladyhood through their own practices, that is, without following middle- or upper-class prescriptions or rules.

Let us return, finally, to the young woman who, to Lillian Wald's dismay, desired only silk underwear. While it might be difficult to wholly celebrate this desire, it is possible to understand it. Silk petticoats were a key element, albeit hidden, in the creation of oneself as lady because of the distinctive sound that they made when one walked. This sound was in itself a very fashionable "frou frou," marking wealth that could not be seen. Notice that Bertha Richardson, cited in the epigraph to this chapter, was offended in part by a "rustle of silk petticoats" among the working girls she wished to "uplift." Thus, "silk underwear" signaled the invisible, interior ladyhood, similar to that promised by the dime novels, to which working women laid claim.

As part of the subculture of working ladies, the woman who desired silk underwear participated in a series of cultural practices that constituted a highly utopian commodity display. Ladyhood created a space for a differently gendered class identity, a counterpoint to the masculine versions women typically encountered in labor unions and to the classist assumptions of some well-meaning reformers. Imagined through the dream world of fashion and fiction commodities, and played out in the daily lives of working women, it offered a gratifying image of emancipation from oppression, which was fundamentally populist. Expressed through commodities, ladyhood was itself a wish image. Within the social practices of working women's daily lives it became an identity category that allowed them to negotiate the exclusive categories of "worker," "American," and "woman."

Working ladyhood thus operated within a semi-autonomous subculture. It cannot be seen as fully autonomous, because women formed it in relation to the larger society and the ways it addressed working women. In particular, this subculture created *public* identities for women as workers and consumers that rejected both middle-class native-born definitions and some Old World proscriptions. Yet working women's culture was regulated from within, by working women themselves, rather than from without. Dorothy Richardson was repeatedly schooled when co-workers pressed her to turn her skirt inside out to keep it clean and to adopt an aristocratic walk—indeed, she faced exclusion if she failed to do so. In addition, ladyhood was not widely understood outside the subculture of women who practiced it. Even Lillian Wald, who lived on New York's Lower East Side in the Henry Street Settlement House, did not understand its basic principles. As part of a semi-autonomous subculture, ladyhood thus had its own "politics," its own rules and values governing inclusion.

But ladyhood served political functions in another respect: it provided for solidarity, resistance, and identity formation in relation to the larger society. It was part of how working women maintained dignity and self-worth in a highly exploitative and degrading context of selling their labor and their time. But precisely because most people did not understand the system of meaning inherent in ladyhood, few recognized its cultural practices as political in nature. Like Wald, most found the flamboyant display bewildering, epistemologically unintelligible. And since they did not see the sense of such practices, like Wald most declared them nonsensical.[114]

When more than 20,000 New York shirtwaist makers walked off their jobs in November 1909, they engaged in an action that the wider society *did* recognize as political. Of course, many of the strikers visibly did so as *ladies*; they could not do otherwise. The practices of ladyhood had shaped who they were and had centrally formed their public identities. The dramatic shirtwaist strike captured public attention in New York City and the nation at large. For the majority of observers, however, it did not appear to be an extension of working women's already-formed public identities, but a surprising, almost inexplicable emergence of working women onto the public stage. Chapter 3 explores how women's subcultural styles became part of the public debate about the validity of the shirtwaist strike, and why leaders chose to obscure working ladies' participation in the strike.

CHAPTER THREE

FASHIONING POLITICAL SUBJECTIVITIES
The 1909 Shirtwaist Strike and the "Rational Girl Striker"

I had come to observe the Crisis of a Social Condition; but apparently this was a Festive Occasion. Lingerie waists were elaborate, puffs towered; there were picture turbans and di'mont pendants. . . . This was a scene of gaiety and flirtation. My preconceived idea of a strike was a somber meeting where somber resolutions were made, and there was always a background of mothers wiping their eyes with their aprons vowing that they would still endure for the Great Cause, and of babes who wept bitterly for a soup bone to suck. . . . "But they don't look as if they had any grievance," I objected. It is always painful to renounce a preconceived picture.—Sarah Comstock, *Collier's* (1909)[1]

On November 23, 1909, 20,000 shirtwaist makers, 85–90 percent of them women, walked off their jobs in hundreds of factories across New York City. The dramatic strike captured the public eye as popular magazines and the city's many newspapers scrambled to cover the most salient events of this female-dominated conflict. The popular press focused on the elaborate fashions and festivity of many of the strikers, bearing witness to the visible participation of working "ladies" in the strike. They printed police reports about strikers' violence on the picket lines and represented the strikers as fashionably dressed hell-raisers. This coverage served in part to undermine working women's claims as political actors, because such ladies did not meet middle-class expectations for the proper demeanor of public participants. To Sarah Comstock, reporter for *Collier's* magazine, well-dressed and smiling strikers did not seem to have the seriousness of rational, political actors, nor the visible poverty that would legitimate their claims of low wages. Thus, they did not "look as if they had any grievance." Comstock could not see women with identities based in working ladyhood as political subjects, even when they enacted the recognized political script of a strike.

It should not be surprising that public discussion of the mass strike recurrently focused on women's styles. Fashion already carried a diverse range of cultural meanings that would have political valences in the context of a strike. For Enlightenment thinkers, democratic political exchange depended on the capacity of participants to act *rationally*. The nineteenth-century middle class built upon these ideas and created the notion of a "public sphere" in which rational white men could engage in such exchange. They defined the public in opposition to the concept of a "private," feminine, and irrational realm. These concepts did not describe the reality of nineteenth-century politics, which consistently defied such boundaries, but they did shape normative expectations about the nature of political subjectivity as well as legal barriers to political participation.[2] Note that Comstock did not exclude women or clothing entirely from her picture of an ideal strike. But she imagined women as *mothers*, wiping tears from their eyes with their aprons— private beings who constituted a domestic and emotional "background" rather than rational political participants in their own right. To many, like Comstock, the elaborate dress of shirtwaist strikers signaled femininity and irrationality: two qualities that disqualified a person from being a political subject. In addition, many saw elaborate fashion on working-class women as evidence of wealth and desires "beyond their station," invalidating their claims that wages were too low. Women's flamboyant fashion thus would become a lightning rod for political debate about the central contests of the strike: women's right to act politically and the legitimacy of their claims about workplace conditions.

Labor leaders responded to this publicity and tried to make the mass strike of young, working women intelligible and favorable to a largely middle-class public. They portrayed the strikers as serious, "thinly clad," nonviolent victims of police abuse, constructing an ideal political subjectivity that countered the damaging publicity. The leaders represented women as political subjects despite their gender, class, and ethnicity by declaring that the strikers *acted* like political participants recognized by the wider culture. Specifically, labor leaders combined Enlightenment ideals about rational political participation with quite different, charity-based notions of "needs." They depicted striking women as bringing rational claims to unionization, but bolstered their worthiness by emphasizing their abject poverty and exceptional physical need. In so doing leaders erased the participation of working ladies in the strike, and promoted strikers in ways that ran counter to many working-class women's proud identities rooted in consumer culture. Working lady-hood, as we have seen, expressly rejected the condescension and the stigma of impoverishment so often associated with the "poor working girl." Leaders' representations were calculated to counter damaging portrayals of women as irrational or greedy, but also tried to reform working women's appearance and cultural practices to more closely resemble this ideal image.

This chapter argues that the public debate about the strike, including labor leaders' contributions, constricted the intelligibility of working ladies' own attempts to claim formal political subjectivities. That is, existing ideals of what a political subject looked like obscured working ladies' identities. While labor leaders rendered crucial assistance and legitimation to the strikers and their cause, their efforts to cast the women in the most "positive" light contributed to a widespread failure to recognize the diversity of political subjectivities. Historians, drawing principally on labor union records, have replicated this failure. As strikers thronged the public streets of New York City, demonstrated in parades and mass meetings, and picketed in front of factories, they challenged established assumptions about the identity and appearance of political actors and access to public space. These working-class, largely immigrant women comprised a subordinated group long denied an active voice in recognized political forums. By occupying the arena of labor politics through a mass strike, they demanded a voice. But the strike was not an arena of free will or total agency. Women did not magically transcend the structures that had limited their political participation in the past and enter a space of free expression when they walked off their jobs.[3] Rather, they worked within and against oppressive structures even as they struck. Indeed, even as the strike challenged certain hierarchies in U.S. society, the public debate and striking women's limited ability to influence print media replicated existing inequalities, and curtailed the degree to which these women achieved a recognized public voice in the union and in the society at large. This chapter analyzes the strike terrain upon which women developed formal political subjectivities to reveal the limitations and challenges striking women faced; chapter four will explore how women fashioned political subjectivities within these limits, using available cultural resources, including the practices of ladyhood.

Even as striking women laid a claim to formal political participation, they did not gain full access to the public debate about them. In part, this debate occurred in the popular press. Jürgen Habermas argues that the ideal nineteenth-century "public sphere" encompassed not only public space but also the media, including newspapers and periodicals in the early 1900s. The ideal held that democratic and objective news would allow for a broad-based debate of rational citizens, too many in number to meet in person.[4] But newspapers themselves were far from a democratic and open medium. The historic subordination of working-class women's voices meant that they could purchase the papers with their wages, but could not directly affect their contents or use them as a means of promoting their own perspectives. Newspapers were first and foremost capitalist enterprises: they published stories about the shirtwaist strike because it had sensational and novel elements that would entice customers to buy. While newspapers did not operate according to the noble principles of free exchange championed by Habermas, their desire to print stories of widespread interest to capture the market prompted them to print nearly daily accounts of strike events and picket line skirmishes. Thus, they kept striking women's political actions and demands in the public eye, albeit without representation of all sides, and are important sources into the public debate and its exclusions.

Newspapers did respond to efforts by some people to influence coverage, particularly those who seemed to operate in "official" capacities in the strike, including employers, court magistrates, and the loose alliance of pro-union forces—the International Ladies' Garment Workers Union (ILGWU), the Women's Trade Union League (WTUL), the Socialist Party (SP), the American Federation of Labor (AFL), and local suffragists.[5] The popular press quoted labor leaders, employers, and court magistrates regularly and at length, and printed articles and letters written by labor leaders, suffragists, and employers. In contrast, striking women themselves did not gain direct influence. I have found only one article authored by a striking worker in the popular press, and quotes of striking workers were very brief—usually one to two sentences.

We cannot assume that the ILGWU, the WTUL, or the SP represented the striking women in the popular or the Socialist press as the strikers would have represented themselves, for the job of these leaders was not so much to serve as conduits for women's voices as to strategically intervene in the public debate. If public opinion deemed the striking women to be legitimate political actors with grievances, owners would be greatly pressured to bow to union demands or risk losing sales. Therefore, strike leaders needed to *politicize* striking women's grievances. Political theorist Nancy Fraser argues that what is considered "political" is usually defined in contrast to what is "economic" or "personal." In the nineteenth-century bourgeois public sphere, economic decisions were ideally the exclusive responsibility of business, not issues of general concern. Fraser argues that the "economic" and "personal" are used to "enclave" or shield certain matters from "generalized contestation" in the wider society.[6] Strikers and leaders sought to make women's workplace grievances an issue of general concern. Conversely, anti-union forces sought to delegitimate women as political actors and to enclave workplace conditions as the business only of owners. Thus, leaders' priority was not to facilitate striking women's expression but to advocate effectively on their behalf. Indeed, leaders often believed that they were better prepared to present the striking women's case than the "inexperienced girls" themselves. Ironically, working women's historical exclusion from the arena of formal political exchange amplified leaders' willingness to speak *for* them. The Socialist press did not include articles written by striking workers and, like the popular press, quoted them only briefly. Thus, the experiences and understandings of striking women themselves were not directly expressed in the popular or the Socialist press. As a result, striking women were largely excluded from the debate in print about them.

Historians of this strike have taken leaders' strategic representations of striking women to be factual descriptions. The strikers appear in historical accounts much as they did in labor leaders' strategic but partial representations: serious, thinly clad, nonviolent. This is partly because none of the existing histories closely examined the public debate about the strike, the context in which leaders formed their representations. Indeed, no historical account makes systematic use of the newspapers in which this debate was largely waged. As a result, fashion does not figure in any of the strike histories, despite its centrality to the public debate and the visible participation of working ladies in the strike. Historians have based their accounts primarily or exclusively on labor leaders' records and dismissed the popular press coverage as "biased."

I surmise two reasons for this choice. First, women's labor historians writing in the 1970s and 1980s sought to re-dress the male-centered heroic narrative of working-class activism that had emerged with the "new social history." They sought out working-class heroines who stood as tall and proud as their brothers in strikes and protests. Operating out of assumptions about the nature of heroic political action that were similar to those made by the *Collier's* reporter decades earlier, they found the labor leaders' strategic constructions of serious, plainly-dressed working women believable and highly appealing. Academic history had long participated in the construction of a normative—and heroic—political subjectivity based in nineteenth century divisions between public and private. When women's labor historians discovered leaders' representations of striking women, they mistook them for "fact" partly because these very heroic terms were the key to inclusion in the larger historical narrative.

Second, women's labor historians accepted leaders' accounts because they sought the "facts" of the strike, and believed that newspapers, as "biased" sources, would reveal only the "representations" of the strikers rather than the truth. Historians have been correct to see the newspapers as biased. Popular papers sought to make money in a highly competitive market; they printed any story quite willingly if they believed it would make for good copy, and regularly printed "facts" without verification. In addition, even a casual glance at the daily papers reveals their reliance on clothing advertisements: the papers had oblique business ties to the garment industry. The dailies thus contained multiple and contradictory perspectives, including virulently anti-union ones. However, *all* historical sources are representations emerging from particular cultural locations—labor leaders' accounts no less than newspapers—and thus can serve as evidence of the broad contest over meanings of the strike. Both leaders' and newspaper accounts were more than mere "images of women strikers," they were acts and interventions into the course of the strike,[7] but historians took the labor leaders' accounts of strikers to be reliable reportage rather than tactical manuevers. As a result, the contours of the debate about women's political subjectivities, and the diversity and range of political styles evidenced by working women, were buried in the historical record. Ironically, labor historians seeking to recover working women's experiences replicated labor leaders' erasure of working ladies' political participation.

When newspaper records and leaders' accounts are viewed together, they provide considerably more evidence about the strike debate than when seen in isolation. This chapter first examines available sources to reveal a dramatic public debate over whether the striking women were legitimate political actors with sound grievances, and the ways the strike itself was a terrain of limited agency for the women. After a brief outline of strike events, it explores popular press coverage and leaders' strategic responses. Chapter 4 will read the same documentation of the strike against the grain, to discern as much as possible how women themselves created political subjectivities in the strike.

The broad contours of the strike were as follows: conflicts began several months before the 1909 general strike in the Triangle and Leiserson factories. Employers claimed a slack season and laid off women workers who had been organizing with local 25 of the ILGWU, but then advertised for new workers, effectively locking out the pro-union women. The workers began picketing to persuade others not to take their places. The picketers met great resistance from police and thugs hired by the employers; many were arrested, and the WTUL began to assist them. The conflict hit the popular press on November 5, after the police arrested a wealthy WTUL member, Mary Dreier, while she walked the picket line. On November 22, the ILGWU held a mass meeting to discuss a general strike. Clara Lemlich, a striking worker from the Triangle factory, interrupted to make a speech that would become famous in labor history, moving that the shirtwaist workers go out on general strike. The motion passed unanimously, and the next day thousands of workers walked off their jobs. The numbers overwhelmed even the most optimistic of the ILGWU and WTUL leaders: the union was unprepared to handle workers from so many shops. Each shop had to organize picketing, decide on specific grievances and demands, and settle individually through discussions with employers. SP members and suffragists stepped in to help the ILGWU and WTUL manage the thousands of workers needing to join the union, form picketing brigades, decide upon grievances, and petition for strike benefits. The AFL sent a representative to assist them. Because police and thugs severely challenged women's picketing, many leaders also supervised picket lines and attended night court, where magistrates tried arrested picketers. Leaders produced a great deal of publicity about the strike by writing articles and creating promotional events calculated to capture the attention of the press. Meanwhile, manufacturers formed their own association to fight the strike collectively.

In mid-January, the strike committee and manufacturers' association agreed to a compromise to end the strike; it granted workers better wages and working conditions, but did not include union recognition. The striking workers overwhelmingly rejected this compromise. Their insistence on union representation, rather than simply improvements in workplace conditions, fractured the uneasy alliance of leaders. The AFL representative and many prominent suffragists broke ranks with the strikers and claimed that the workers were swayed by the Socialists. By mid-February, ILGWU leaders officially declared the strike over, and strikers from 150 shops went back without agreements. Because the improvements experienced by many did not include a change in the structure of power or decision-making, conditions soon deteriorated. Despite the strike's mixed results for the shirtwaist workers, it inaugurated a chain of large strikes in garment industries that established women as important members in the ILGWU.[8]

The strike debate soon focused on the dramatic, gendered conflicts over public space on the picket lines. Striking women experienced daily challenges to their right to act politically as picketers. Employers hired thugs to harass and attack picketing workers, police readily arrested them, and city magistrates imposed harsh fines and jail sentences on those arrested. Leaders reported that thugs initiated physical confrontations with picketers, and police would then arrest women strikers for disorderly conduct. Police also arrested strikers for using the word "scab" and for congregating in groups rather than maintaining lines. Police even arrested one group of strikers on the request of an employer because "they were standing in front of my factory."[9] The terms and tactics used by employers, police, and court magistrates to oppose picketing merged typical and time-honored strike-breaking techniques with particularly gendered attacks designed to undermine women's basic claim to political subjectivity. Police violence, mass arrests, and harsh sentences were standard fare for workers who sought a political voice through strikes. Because the striking women were working class and mostly immigrants, police and thugs did not feel compelled to treat them with the deference due to white, middle-class women. The women also faced tactics that capitalized on the historic association of unescorted women in public space with disorder, including sexual disorder.

Shirtwaist picketers regularly encountered accusations or insinuations that they were prostitutes; their public activity called into question their sexual respectability. This began during the conflict at the Triangle and Leiserson shops that preceded the general strike, when manufacturers hired female prostitutes as well as male thugs to harass the picketers. Employers knew that women who occupied public space without male escorts already jeopardized their sexual reputations. Regulatory norms originating in bourgeois conceptions of public and private deemed women sexually virtuous only when they were contained in the private realm. Indeed, in the nineteenth century, prostitutes were commonly referred to as "public women." For this reason, some middle-class people believed that working women were, or soon would be, compromised in virtue.[10] When these women picketed, their overtly political action challenged the normative definition of public space even more intensely. Manufacturers knew that hiring prostitutes to stand on the same corners as the pickets would intensify the association between female picketing and disreputable behavior. This tactic apparently drew too much protest from observers and neighborhood businesses and did not persist into the general strike. However, Mary Brown

Sumner, in an article for *The Survey*, noted that in the general strike, " 'Streetwalker' is one of the terms that the police and the thugs apply daily to the strikers, in fact it has become in their vocabulary almost synonymous with striker."[11] By calling picketing women "street-walkers," police and thugs repeated the discourse that had historically served to keep women from public life,[12] not only insulting picketers by associating them with a stigmatized group, but also resolutely denying them a political subjectivity. To the police, women in public were not political actors, but "public women."

Successful picketing was crucial to the strike effort, and it was on the picket lines that striking women most visibly enacted political subjectivities. The first function of picketing was to bring work in shops to a halt by preventing scabs from taking strikers' places. This alone would pressure owners to deal with them through union agreements. Picketing also effectively brought shop floor struggles out from behind the closed doors of the factory and into the public space of the street. The second function of picketing, then, was to demand public recognition of workplace struggles and insist that control of labor conditions was not the private prerogative of owners but a political matter in which the larger community had an interest. Thus, the opposition from thugs and the police had potentially grave consequences. Striking women had to picket, because it was imperative that they stop production and make the strike a public issue.

Ironically, the extreme repression that striking women encountered on the picket lines functioned to increase debate about women's political subjectivities. The cumulative effect of the violence and arrests by thugs and police was to recognize that striking women did indeed act politically. In addition, a direct outcome of the pitched battle over the picket lines was increased public attention to, and press coverage of, the strike. As police arrested hundreds of young women, the newspapers scrambled for stories of recent skirmishes. Their representations of these events became central to the public debate about women's right to be political actors and the legitimacy of their grievances. Newspapers sensationalized the conflict and selectively reported daily arrests and magistrates' decisions, making some courtroom proceedings part of public knowledge about the strike. Leaders responded to both the repression and the newspaper coverage by launching a concerted public relations campaign to promote their view of the strikers.

Identifying a singular meaning or effect of newspaper coverage on the strike is impossible. First, the papers were not all alike. Some, like the *New York Times* and the *New York Tribune*, targeted a more middle-class audience and tended to foreground business interests. Others, such as the

New York Evening Journal and the *New York World,* catered to a wide audience that included many working-class people and had reputations as "sensational rags." The various papers covered the strike somewhat differently. Editorials and letters to the editor introduced multiple perspectives and gave certain papers "pro-union" tones, while others clearly espoused "anti-union" positions.[13] Second, we cannot determine a single effect of newspaper coverage because the same stories often portrayed the striking women in multiple or even contradictory terms. In addition, the same stories could be read in different ways, depending on the social positions and cultural competencies of readers (chapter 4 will explore this idea further). While some coverage was definitely negative, the papers did include some prostrike letters and editorials, report divergent court decisions on the legalities of picketing, and regularly quote strike leaders at length.

Nevertheless, leaders' objections to newspaper coverage of strike events were justified. Because newspapers were market-driven, news reports hinged on the novelty of the events. Intense competition for readers prompted all of the papers to foreground those aspects of the strike that were most surprising, dramatic or titillating. As they did so, despite their diversity and differences, *all* of the papers utilized tropes emerging from dominant middle-class views on gender, class, and order which precluded taking striking women seriously as political actors. Specifically, the city newspapers represented striking women as constituting a feminine, irrational disorder: fashion-oriented, interested only in fun, and violent on the picket lines.

Much of the popular press' emphasis on dress and demeanor may not have sprung from a conscious anti-union sentiment, but simply from a desire to write "good copy." Among the novel elements of the strike the papers emphasized, the most fundamental was that the strikers were predominantly female. Newspapers rarely mentioned male strikers or leaders, despite the fact that men comprised up to 15 percent of the striking workers, and nearly all of the ILGWU leadership. Rather, they focused on the transgressive element of working-class women acting politically in the public sphere. The battle as represented in the press was primarily between young, female strikers and the combined forces of young, female scabs and male authorities: police, magistrates, and employers. The focus on the female-dominated nature of the strike did not in itself damage the cause. However, the ways newspapers emphasized this fact directed readers' interests to the alleged disorderly conduct of women on the lines, rather than to a consideration of their claims.

For example, newspapers disproportionally listed names and addresses of arrested female strikers at the ends of articles. Comparison with similar reporting in the *New York Call*, the Socialist daily paper, suggests that the popular press omitted the names of many of the male strikers and almost all of the scabs or thugs arrested. This could give an impression that striking women were the only ones arrested. The *New York Evening Journal* singled out one woman for such exposure in an article headlined HOSE TURNED ON FIGHTING GIRL STRIKERS. A fight reportedly broke out between pickets and strike breakers at the Acme Shirt Waist shop, which "was quelled by turning water on the crowd from a fire hose in the factory." (The passive voice hides the actor wielding the fire hose: it may have been a hired thug, a police officer, a manufacturer, or a strike breaker.) The *Evening Journal* reported that "the police arrested six men and one girl, Florence Brodas, sixteen years old, of No. 1930 Prospect place."[14] Readers' interest was directed toward "girl strikers" and the named female "lawbreaker," rather than toward the nameless arrested men or the invisible fire hose handler. In addition, by stating the age of the striker, which was typical in strike coverage, the article provided another marker that would signal dependency and irrationality to many middle-class people.

Some articles mentioned clothing in seemingly neutral descriptions that had a similar effect. For example, a *New York Sun* reporter described the fashions of women in public space: "In the streets outside [strike] headquarters young women in furs and feathered hats gathered in groups."[15] While refraining from negative comment, this article nevertheless suggested that women's appearance was somehow significant to their political claims, inviting readers to evaluate striking women's actions in different terms than they did men's in similar situations.

Newspapers regularly reported on the proceedings in night court, where magistrates heard the cases of arrested women. Those reports both prompted public discussion of women's right to picket, and promoted a view of women as violent on the picket lines. Papers particularly printed widely variant decisions that revealed disagreements among magistrates on the definition of peaceful picketing. Magistrate Krotel upheld women's right to picket early in the strike when he dismissed women arrested for standing in front of a factory. However, the very same night Magistrate Corrigan sentenced a striker to five days in the workhouse for a similar offense and publicly declared that he would "deal severely with any strikers brought before him." Most of the strikers were charged with "disorderly conduct," a sufficiently loose charge that could bend to fit the occasion. Magistrate Butts dismissed a case in which the striker was charged with disorderly conduct for "shouting and causing a crowd to collect." His comments criticized the police and other magistrates for their ready use of the charge: "These strikers have the right by fair and peaceable means, by reason of argument to win over to their cause those who are working, in order to obtain better conditions in their manner of livelihood. I hold that in order to constitute disorderly conduct it must be shown that the defendant was liable to provoke a breach of the peace under the existing conditions." In contrast, Magistrate Barlow reportedly said, "If these girls continue to rush around and cry 'scab' I shall convict them of disorderly conduct. There is no word in the English language so irritating as the word scab."[16] The papers thus made courtroom battles a matter of public concern, and raised the question of what constituted acceptable behavior on the lines.

At the same time, however, papers printed magistrates' most dramatic or extreme statements, most of which chastised the strikers for (alleged) unlawful or immoral behavior. Collectively, these comments represented young striking women as "girls" who were out of control. Magistrate Cornell revealed his association between the strike and female, even sexual, disorder when he verbally harangued a picketer, saying, "Why do you paint your face?" The newspapers all picked up this story and reported somewhat different versions of it. In some, the magistrate sent an officer to rub his finger on the young woman's face to see if she wore makeup; in others, the young woman herself wiped her finger on her face to prove that she did not.[17] Certainly, whether the striker wore makeup or not should not have been an issue in deciding her innocence or guilt. But the fact that Magistrate Cornell seized upon this is revealing. Many people in 1909 associated makeup with prostitution or the theater, both of which offered women less than virtuous means to make money. (Both also featured women in public.) Among many working-class women, however, the practice of wearing makeup was acceptable and widespread, and did not carry such overtones. The magistrate's question insinuated that the picketer lacked sexual respectability. The incident occurred in night court, and Magistrate Cornell knew that most of the women present who were not connected to the strike were arrested prostitutes, or as one strike commentator put it, "the painted street girl."[18] Like the employer who hired prostitutes to harass the pickets, Cornell disparaged the picketers' public actions by associating them with "public women," calling into question the legitimacy of their political subjectivity.

Some newspaper articles abandoned the tone of neutrality, and explicitly focused on the dress and demeanor of striking women in ways likely to delegitimate working women's claims to political subjectivity, particularly for a middle-class readership schooled in Enlightenment ideals of rational political participation. Articles characterized striking women not as producers making political claims, but as consumers having fun. Under the headline 40,000 WORK GIRLS AT EASE, one *New York Sun* article described the strikers as an "unwonted leisure class of 40,000, all in holiday attire, all excitedly gossiping, visiting, shopping."[19] Striking workers undoubtedly did feel an exhilaration from successfully walking off their jobs, being momentarily released from the drudgery of monotonous toil, and joining with other workers at strike headquarters. Labor history is replete with examples of workers creating a holiday atmosphere in a strike, complete with wearing their very best clothes.[20] However, this article obscured women's identities as workers when it called them a "leisure class" and emphasized socializing and shopping, rather than their workplace grievances. Some accounts represented the walkout itself as a frolic: "The girls went out with a whoop. . . . Laughing and shouting, the girls dropped their work and ran for their hats and coats." One announced a mass meeting to be held two weeks into the strike as a "party," noting that it "was going to be a whopper." Another article claimed that at strike headquarters, "All were in the highest of spirits, though many of them admitted that they had no grievances, but said they did not want to remain at work when the others struck."[21]

Reporters described employers, in contrast, as rational men attending to the crisis in meetings. A particularly damaging *New York Times* headline at the beginning of the strike read GIRL STRIKERS DANCE AS EMPLOYERS MEET: THE WAISTMAKERS ARE HOLDING IMPROMPTU PARTIES IN THEIR HEADQUARTERS. The article reported the creation of the Association of Waist and Dress Manufacturers, an organization formed to oppose the strike, as well as the many resolutions passed at the first meeting, including a resolution against the closed shop. In contrast, the *Times* stated that strikers "seemed to be in good spirits yesterday and held impromptu dances in several of the halls where they met."[22] Clearly, in this story manufacturers, not strikers, hold "somber meetings" and pass "somber resolutions" in order to rationally promote their interests. Indeed, one reporter noted that a middle-class WTUL leader "seems to take the matter much more seriously than the many thousands of women who look to her for direction and information." This coverage provided support for some manufacturers' strategic interpretation of the strike, represented well in one owner's statement: "The strike is altogether silly."[23]

The popular press also undermined women's legitimacy as political actors by representing them as an irrational mob, emotionally under the sway of union leaders. One reporter claimed that on the first day of the strike, "the excited girls created the din of a howling mob, setting the entire neighborhood in an uproar." Strikers formed "stampede[s]" and "hysterical swarms," and went "wild with excitement" whenever addressed by leaders. Yet another claimed the strikers acted with "hysterical optimism," and that strike headquarters were a "clamorous jam." Newspapers also regularly reported that women attacked police in direct inversions of public order. In the most dramatic article, the *New York World* reported that one hundred "petticoated antagonists" mobbed two policemen, ripping and ruining their uniforms.[24] Of course, we must maintain skepticism about the accuracy of such stories. But the overall picture painted by this coverage was of young women irrationally out of control in public, rather than of citizens making political claims.

Popular descriptions of picketing particularly associated fashion with a distinctively feminine irrational disorder. Comstock, the *Collier's* reporter, provided an image of ruined clothing to sensationalize her description of picketing:

> Picketing and its results have furnished more excitement than any other phase of this spectacular strike. . . . But although the instructions run "moral suasion," somehow other elements have crept in: witness the hurling of pie and the kicking of shins as example. Just where the trouble begins it is hard for an outsider to say; but girl has met girl, and presently there have been a torn plume, a bedraggled bow, a detached cluster of puffs, and an officer on the spot, then a patrol wagon and a group of strikers whirled off to the station, thence to Jefferson Market Court.[25]

On November 26, only three days into the strike, the *New York World* reported a "riot" between strikers and strike breakers in front of a large shop on Greene Street on the Lower East Side. The paper described the picketing women as an "army of Amazons" who fought the equally aggressive scabs in an "Amazonian melee," throughout which witnesses could reportedly hear "steady grinding and ripping sounds produced by tearing clothing and scratching faces." The next day, similar stories of the event appeared in the other papers. A *New York Tribune* article claimed that picketers and scabs used "the most approved feminine tactics" in their fight: "Hair was pulled out of heads by the handful, hats and coiffures were torn, tresses were disarranged, and many received marks of the fight from the nails of their antagonists." The *New York Times* claimed that the "riot" continued for two hours "while dresses were torn, faces

scratched and the headgear of many girls on both sides were wrecked."
Newspaper articles reported later altercations in similar terms. One
described a "riot" in which "the girls kicked, scratched and pummelled
each other until the street was littered with torn and tattered millinery.
Bleeding faces and blackened eyes were the general rule."[26]

Torn and disheveled clothing in these descriptions probably signified
irrationality and disorder, as well as gender deviance, to middle-class
readers. Certainly, women were expected to keep their clothing intact.
In addition, such details could be titillating for an audience that was
primed to see working women in public—that is, "streetwalkers"—in
sexual terms. Finally, such coverage served to erase strikers' individuality
and cast them as a mob of virtually indistinguishable puffs, furs, and
feathers, or as one article said, "shirtwaist whirlpools."[27] The press's
coverage of the picket line battles then, whatever its intentions, undermined women as political subjects: it implied that women were not
really producers but consumers; they were not rational; indeed, they
were hardly individuals. Representations of ethnicity also reinforced
these ideas. The *New York Tribune* covered a courtroom exchange by
noting that "The proceedings immediately became clogged with
patronymics. It seemed hard for the magistrate and court officers to
remember that Miss Rothnagle was not Miss Kate Mokovsky and that
Pauline Rankus was distinct from Ida Scholinsky. But the proceedings
finally narrowed down to Miss Mokovsky. . . ."[28] By repeating the
names of the picketers, which would sound "foreign" to many Euro-
American readers, the paper drew on nativist representations of immigrants as "swarms" of humanity, odd and indistinguishable, but fundamentally different from American citizens. Strike leaders thus had a great
deal to counter in the public debate from the beginning of the strike.

Newspapers also represented women's fashion in terms that could
suggest that strikers' claims for higher wages were unfounded. A *New
York Evening Journal* article noted that the women, dressed "in their best
gowns and hats, were picturesque enough, and looked far from starving
or downtrodden." A *New York Sun* article claimed that strikers in a
parade "all looked prosperous." Another article described a group of four
strikers as "well dressed," and reported that the strikers themselves,
when pressed, did not think union demands were justified.[29] Such articles tapped an existing discourse about "the woman's wage" that
excluded women from a notion of citizenship based in a producer
identity. Historian Alice Kessler-Harris has explained that while unions
and reformers worked for a living wage for men, they also advocated a
separate "woman's wage." This ideal wage should be enough for a

woman's individual subsistence but no more; specifically, it need not provide for "extras" such as fashionable clothing. Such a wage could augment a family's income, but would not threaten men's primary position in the workplace or the home.[30]

The idea of the woman's wage had roots in nineteenth-century notions of "free labor" and the "American Standard," which defined citizenship for working-class men. In the early nineteenth century, white male artisans advanced the idea of "free labor" which, they argued, endowed them with independent judgment and made them men, capable of independent, political participation. Wage labor, they argued, made one dependent, like a slave. Later in the century, as the artisanal system gave way increasingly to factories, working-class activists advanced the concept of a wage that could sustain manly independence and citizenship: the "living wage." This ideal overtly excluded all female workers and people of color. A living wage was high enough to allow a white man to support himself and his family in moderate comfort, with a modicum of leisure. As Lawrence Glickman has shown, by the turn of the century this included "needs" beyond subsistence and justified a certain degree of consumption as a right. The American Standard of a living wage provided for "higher" needs of the white male worker and claimed that, *as citizens*, they deserved a comfortable existence.[31]

The woman's wage, conversely, marked women's exclusion from this definition of "worker." To proponents of the American Standard, women workers' consumption did not signal their higher needs as citizens, but their dangerous independence from the family economy and thus their threat to the living wage for men. Many feared that if women's wages rose, competition between male and female laborers could cause the higher wages paid to white men to fall. Working-class leaders and their middle-class allies thus worked to maintain and extend the American Standard for white men, and supported the woman's wage for women. As Kessler-Harris notes, this excluded women from established means that white working-class men used to claim a citizenship based in labor.[32] Most notably, it denied them the independence through labor deemed necessary for rational political action. Thus, newspapers' assertions that striking women "all looked prosperous" or "looked far from starving or downtrodden" had extended and potentially devastating ramifications for how readers would see the strikers—even readers who might support men's strikes.

Newspaper coverage of women's fashion also tapped middle-class fears of disorder. For the white middle class, striking women's consumption of fashion, unbridled by middle-class values, held decisively sexual overtones. Middle-class contemporaries worried that desires for higher wages and clothing would escalate uncontrollably, until they could only be satisfied by a prostitute's income. The deserving poor, in middle-class eyes, should not dress "above their station." Newspaper articles focused on whether women had too much or not enough, rather than on their participation, as political actors, in decision-making processes. The articles in general did not treat striking women as political actors making claims but rather invoked the limits of their citizenship by focusing attention on their consumption as women.

These news articles were not the newspapers' only contribution to the public debate. Several female columnists countered the representation of striking women's fashion in newspaper reports with their own, prostrike editorials. This provided readers with a diversity of representations that could indicate that the meaning of the fashionable, striking women was more a matter of debate than a matter of fact. The columnists were middle-class suffragists, and they understood how damaging portrayals of striking women as fashionable and frivolous would be to middle-class readers' opinions. They provided a counterpoint to the predominant image of the strikers, but their defense did not represent them as political actors but as impoverished women in need of uplift.

Female columnists accepted the idea that fashionable dress signaled frivolousness and lack of need; they therefore categorically denied charges that working women dressed fashionably. Beatrice Fairfax, reporting on one parade, insisted that the strikers "were all quietly and suitably dressed, there was no attempt at finery. Some of them were hatless."[33] Dorothy Dix went further and reported that the strikers were

> young girls who had no pleasure, no amusements, who never had a full meal, or a pretty dress—girls to whom the buying of a new pair of cheap shoes is a matter of saving and scraping, and self-denial and economy, and the acquiring of one of the hundreds of dainty shirt-waists, that passes through their hands, an utter impossibility.[34]

Many shirtwaist workers certainly were impoverished, but their meager incomes did not prevent them from experiencing pleasure or obtaining pretty dresses. However, an image of young women who had "no pleasure" and who made "no attempt at finery" fit nicely the preconception of the "deserving poor," consistent with an image of the strike in which, in the Collier's reporter's words, "mothers [wiped] their eyes with their aprons . . . [and] babes . . . wept bitterly for a soup bone to suck." Such representations assured middle-class readers that striking women challenged poor working conditions but not the class structure itself. Middle-class journalists who supported the strikers thus represented them less as political actors than as the needy poor, and they ignored the participation of working ladies in the strike.

Prosuffrage supporters regularly used charity language when advocating for working women, voyeuristically exposing hardships by delineating the women's budgets and describing their homes to demonstrate that they lived below subsistence. One article, headlined GIRL BARES DIRE POVERTY OF A WAIST-MAKER, recounted a story of the journalist visiting a worker's overcrowded tenement home. The author, Ethel Wren, invited the reader to

> use your imagination, and you can fill in the tragic background—
> a background of squalor, poverty, and want, and more want; want
> that goes to bed with them at night, and gets up with them in the
> morning, and stands behind their shoulders all through the long
> day, and spurs the aching back and eyes and tired fingers, and
> makes tender young girls look like hard women.[35]

While these articles did not exaggerate the degree of hardship experienced by the working-poor immigrants, they left out the women's own ways of making meaning within that poverty. Thus, striking women's lives appeared pathetic, and their labor demands the meager and humble requests of the proper charitable subjects. Dorothy Dix wrote:

> These women asked so little of life, so little of their employers—
> just a fair wage for the work, just the simple human right to
> work under conditions that were not a menace to health and
> morality. No wonder their cry struck a responsive chord in the
> breasts of all who have hearts that can feel and pity and be touched
> by the sight of poverty and distress . . . .[36]

Dix did not mention strikers' demand for union recognition and the right to participate in decision making.

The hardship of the strike itself offered proponents additional opportunity to represent striking women as proper charitable subjects. Because most shirtwaist workers made so little money, few could afford to go weeks without income, and many dedicated strikers went hungry during the conflict. Representations of their want, however, often bolstered the image of them as in need primarily of charity, rather than union participation. One headline read: FACING STARVATION TO KEEP UP STRIKE: MANY GIRL SHIRTWAIST MAKERS EVEN NOW IN WANT, THEIR LEADERS REPORT. FREE LUNCHES FOR THEM. The article quoted Eva McDonald Valesh of the American Federation of Labor as saying, "In this charitable city every homeless man may have a turkey on Christmas Day but there will be no turkey tomorrow for most of the striking shirtwaist makers. There is no charitable organization to provide a Christmas meal for poor women."[37] Prostrike newspaper coverage thus often represented strikers as "poor women" analogous not to male strikers, but to homeless men without property or successful productive labor. They were not citizens but clients.

Strike leaders in the ILGWU, WTUL, and SP sought to impact the public debate. They launched an extensive public relations campaign designed to extend striking women's occupation of public space and to promote a positive view of strikers as political actors. For example, on December 3, leaders and over five thousand strikers marched through the Bowery to the mayor's office at City Hall to protest police violence and unfair arrests. On December 29, striking workers sold special issues of the *New York Call* that contained articles about the strike from the perspective of the union, particularly decrying the obstruction of picketing. Traveling all over Manhattan, including to Wall Street, and into the boroughs, the women expanded their occupation of public space as strikers and themselves spread the union perspective. Leaders also organized a large meeting of strikers in Carnegie Hall on January 2 to address the same issue. Banners hung around the hall defended women's right to picket: A STRIKE IS NOT A CRIME, A STRIKER IS NOT A CRIMINAL, and PEACEFUL PICKETING IS THE RIGHT OF EVERY WORKER. The event honored arrested women by placing them on the stage in public view: the twenty women who had served time in the workhouse wore placards reading WORKHOUSE PRISONER. Three hundred and fifty sat behind them with placards that read ARRESTED.[38] The events increased striking women's public presence and created additional forums for public debate. These staged dramatic events also drew media attention and increased coverage of the union's position in the popular papers.

The special issue of the *New York Call* was the leaders' attempt to publish their own "popular" newspaper. Because strikers sold the *Call* on streets across Manhattan, the Socialist paper gained a much wider readership than usual. The special issue makes it clear that the leaders' representations were not the same as the voices of the strikers. No articles by strikers appeared in the special issue, nor did any article quote strikers at length. WTUL volunteers who put the December 29th issue together were apologetic about this, but confident in their ability to speak for the strikers:

> We regret that more of the stories are not from the pens of the girls themselves, but Christmas and Sunday intervened and made it practically impossible for us to get at the girls in time to get

them to write much for the paper. Of course, every line in it deals with the strike from the viewpoint of the strikers.[39]

Perhaps Christmas and Sunday proved a more serious impediment to the WTUL members than to the mostly Jewish strikers. Despite the volunteers' insistence that they presented the "viewpoints" of the strikers, leaders' representations in the special issue were consistent with other strike coverage in the *Call*, magazine articles by leaders, and popular press coverage that presented leaders' views. In these forums, leaders countered the popular press' common depiction of striking women as fashionably dressed hell-raisers by representing them as thinly clad, downtrodden, and powerless, yet rational in their actions and capable of political participation.

Strike leaders had little choice but to deal with the issue of clothing: the extensive press coverage of striking women's fashion carried powerful and potentially damaging associations. Like the middle- and upper-class suffragists, strike leaders understood this, but their claims differed significantly from the suffragists as well. No leader in the SP, WTUL, or ILGWU claimed that the strikers had never had any pleasure or a "pretty dress." Perhaps they feared such a statement would ring false for anyone who had seen the strikers and would undermine leaders' credibility. Instead, they emphasized the poor *quality* of the clothing and avoided the issue of fashionable or "pretty" styles. This emphasis contained an important element of truth. As chapter 1 argued, inexpensive, mass-produced clothing that working women could purchase was decidedly substandard in quality: while the *styles* were similar to those available for middle- and even upper-class women, the garments were cheaply made. Additionally, working women often spent the whole of their available income for a suit (skirt and jacket), shirtwaist, petticoats, shoes, and hat, and did not have the considerable sum of money necessary for a functional winter overcoat. Picketing in December and January was indeed a hardship for such inadequately dressed women. Typical articles by strike leaders ignored the style of clothing and portrayed the strikers as "thin, pale-faced, ill-clad" or as "insufficiently clad and fed." Others described their "scanty clothes" and their "thin and poorly nourished bodies and insufficient clothing," helping create an overall picture of women as impoverished and on the "verge of starvation."[40]

A drawing in the *New York Call* provided readers with a visual image of strikers. Entitled "Two Phases of Yuletide" (fig. 3.1), the two-part drawing contrasted shirtwaist strikers, above, with middle-class women shoppers, below.[41] The shirtwaist strikers appear haggard, dressed plainly; most wear

THE STRUGGLE FOR BREAD AND BARGAINS.

3.1 Cartoon printed in the *New York Call*, December 24, 1909.

shawls over their heads, and the few that wear hats wear very plain ones decorated with a lone feather. The drawing of middle-class women depicted them likewise in a mass, and showed them shopping for shirt-waists, surrounded by signs offering discounts. In contrast to the strikers, they are dressed with great ornamentation: they all wear hats with elaborate plumes and wear furs about their necks. None wears a shawl. The drawing implied that one class of women sought "bargains," driving prices down, and depriving another class of women of "bread." However, like the verbal descriptions of striking women, it erased the participation of working ladies and their language of entitlement related to dress.

Labor leaders catered to the middle class when they obscured strikers' elaborate fashions and emphasized impoverishment, but they also represented women as serious political participants. To do so, they promoted an image of the strikers as rational subjects in keeping with Enlightenment ideals and excluded aspects of working women's culture that did not fit such an image. Theresa Malkiel reflected this concern when writing for the *New York Call*'s special strike issue:

> An uprising of women, a girls' strike! The average reader smiled as he read the first news of it. The average reader still thought that girls are flippy, flighty little things, working for pin money and more interested in the style of hairdressing for the coming season than they would be in any organization, let alone a trade union.

Malkiel reassured readers that "It is not for riches or luxuries" that women struck, but simply for "a living wage, a little more freedom, the right to co-operate with each other for their common defense." Unlike Dix, who wrote for the popular press, Malkiel included political participation in the list of women's demands. The popular press tended to represent the strikers as having feminine fun on strike; in direct contrast, Malkiel showed the strikers rationally taking personal risks, not partying or "whooping" when they walked off their jobs. "Of the 47,000 workers employed in the industry 35,000 laid down their scissors, shook the threads off their clothes and calmly left the place that stood between them and starvation."[42]

Leaders countered popular press representations of women's violence on the picket lines by representing them as peaceful and powerless victims of thugs, police, and magistrates. They described the striking women as "frail" or "tiny" strikers falling victim to "great big scabs," a "huge henchman," or a "burly" and "six-footed [sic] policeman."[43] The *New York Call* printed two artists' drawings that emphasized striking women's vulnerability. "Saving Society: How the Police Are Protecting the Public From the Terrible Shirtwaist Strikers" (fig. 3.2)[44] positioned a lone shirtwaist striker dressed in a dowdy short skirt and plain coat and hat, in front of a crowd of cross-eyed policemen. This drawing caricatured police aggression against the strikers: the police were ridiculous and cruel to harass such clearly harmless "little girls," as source after source called them. However, it also portrayed the strikers as powerless and extremely plainly dressed: a far cry from the ornamented styles of working ladies. Another drawing represented a diminutive working girl (Rebecca Taylor) before a looming magistrate and a huge male scab

How the Police Are Protecting the Public From the Terrible Shirtwaist Strikers.

3.2 Cartoon printed in the *New York Call*, January 3, 1910.

whom she reportedly threatened to assault. "Please Protect me, Mr. Judge! She threatened to Beat Me Up!" (fig. 3.3)[45] served to dramatize the opposition women faced on the picket lines and the injustice of the courts, but it painted a picture of the strikers themselves as vulnerable victims rather than able and heroic picketers.

These two drawings qualified claims to political subjectivity by emphasizing women's frailty and need for protection. Such "feminine" traits historically functioned as signs of women's "dependence" and were integral to women's consignment to the "private" sphere. Leaders thus created a contradictory representation of striking women as rational and thinly clad, yet frail and powerless victims. As they challenged women's historic exclusion from public life, they also replicated notions

"Please Protect Me, Mr. Judge!
She Threatened To Beat Me Up!"

INCIDENT IN THE SHIRTWAIST STRIKE.

REBECCA TAYLOR, A STRIKER, WAS FINED $3 ON THE STATEMENT OF JOSEPH
LILLIE, A SCAB OF SOLOMON & LEFFLER 117 WEST 17TH STREET, THAT SHE HAD
THREATENED TO ASSAULT HIM—NOTWITHSTANDING THAT MISS TAYLOR HAD A
BLACK EYE HERSELF!

3.3 Cartoon printed in the *New York Call,* December 29, 1909.

rooted in class and gender hierarchies. They depicted striking women in terms consistent with the historical political subject, yet they also incorporated gendered images of powerlessness that mollified the middle class and built upon a history of working women as charity subjects. Thus, they represented striking women *both* as citizens and as clients. In each aspect of this representation, however, they found it necessary to obscure women's fashionable dress.

Strike leaders' strategic representations of working women as powerless *were* effective in garnering a positive response from some white middle-class people. Working women who claimed political subjectivities profoundly challenged class, gender and race hierarchies; but *as clients* striking women's political claims directly threatened shop owners' interests without appearing to threaten the class position of those who pitied them or took up their cause. Casting striking women as supplicants, leaders tacitly placed middle-class observers in the powerful position of judge and, potentially, benefactor. Indeed, the strategic representation of striking women as helpless not only garnered support for the shirtwaist strike, it culminated in a wave of protective legislation in the 1910s that limited women's work hours but not men's. The coalition of reformers and unions argued that women workers were frail "future mothers," powerless and oppressed and therefore in need of state protection. In this way, working women gained "a voice," that is, a recognized identity in relation to public and state power, partly via claims of utter defenselessness. Leaders' strategies thus inflected the development of a welfare system as well as union ideologies.[46]

There were two main problems with the labor leaders' strategy. First, it stood in uneasy relationship to the structure of unions, which ideally demanded for workers an ongoing voice in the decision-making process. Some supporters did not pay much attention to this and believed the strikers would be satisfied if their demands for higher wages and improved conditions were met. This limitation in the strategy was revealed when the workers turned down the January compromise agreed to by the strike committee and manufacturers. The compromise would meet the strikers' demands concerning wages, hours, and conditions—in Dix's terms, the "little [they asked] of their employers." However, it would not recognize the union, and thus would not grant women a voice in grievance procedures or in future contracts. The strikers rejected it unanimously, revealing an insistence on democratic participation that exceeded that of their leaders and prompting a split in the fragile alliance of strike supporters. Many of the middle- and upper-class suffragists, along with Eva McDonald Valesh, the AFL representative, withdrew their support and charged that the strike was controlled by Socialists. For them, strikers were now stepping beyond their place.[47] For the suffragists, striking women now challenged the class system; for the AFL representative, they challenged the skilled craft union basis of the AFL, which reserved full union membership and the living wage for men.

The second problem with the leaders' strategic representation of the strikers as thinly clad, rational, and powerless was that it did not match the way many working women saw themselves. The intervention of leaders in the popular debate about the strike is understandable. The visible culture of working ladies could undermine women's already shaky claims to a political voice in the eyes of many working- and middle-class people. Middle-class columnists' defense served to position strikers as charity cases who needed *only* philanthropy and pity rather than as political actors who deserved to participate in workplace decisions. Labor leaders thus faced entrenched assumptions and formidable foes. However, by erasing women's subcultural practices rather than building upon their meanings, they represented women in terms that striking ladies might find conflicted at best, insulting at worst. This would prove to have an ongoing impact on the ways labor leaders addressed working women.

An understanding of the relationship between working ladies and the web of social actors in the strike requires additional attention to the process of subject formation. Chapter 2 focused on women's own social relations within the semi-autonomous group and the ways that they enacted subjectivities through daily cultural practices. However, when analyzing the position of this group in a web of larger social relations, we require a theory of subjectivity that can draw lines of influence and impact. Louis Althusser's notion of "interpellation" argues that individuals become "subjects" within a particular culture or ideological system when they are addressed or "hailed" in a particular way. For Althusser, a person is interpellated when she or he recognizes her or himself in that address. At the moment of recognition, the subject is constituted and becomes recognizable to others within the same ideological system or culture. In these terms, the labor leaders "hailed" women as rational political subjects, literally trying to change who working women were by interpellating them into a union discourse.

Althusser's notion of interpellation helps to explain the way individual subjectivities are formed in and through ideology, but cannot explain the sources or qualities of human agency.[48] Judith Butler revises Althusser's theory by arguing that it is interpellation that makes a limited agency possible. Interpellation calls subjects into being, providing both the capacity for speech and the limits of that speech. An individual thus becomes recognizable, part of the culture, and gains ability to act in intelligible ways within it, even though this same interpellation forecloses other options and is oppressive. In addition, because language is limited in its ability to define and constrain, subjects always exceed the boundaries of their definitions. Interpellation must therefore be repeated. Through this necessary repetition, variation may occur. Butler does not place as much emphasis on the *recognition* of the hail as Althusser, but sees interpellation as a chain of signification, a ritual of repetition that individuals need not overtly endorse in order to be shaped and affected by it. Butler does not locate agency outside ideology, as a sovereign assertion of mind or will, but as an *effect* of power within culture, resulting from interpellation and its inevitable failures.[49]

This theory can illuminate aspects of working ladyhood. A particular subject is hailed in numerous ways over time that inevitably conflict with and contradict each other. The subjectivity called into being when a working woman was hailed by employers, for example, was contingent upon her history of interpellation, the other ways in which she had been called into social being, and the dissonances that this new hailing might produce. In short, her resulting subjectivity depended on the cultural resources available to her as she shaped and interpreted this new interpellation. Thus, ladyhood can be seen as a site of agency that emerged from a matrix of conflicting interpellations of working women: as coarse, degraded women in need of uplift (and undeserving of the title "lady"), as cogs in a machine, and as immigrants undeserving of the title "American." Each interpellation endowed working women with a social visibility, even as each sought to define and contain them. The women gained agency not only because the interpellations inevitably failed but because they creatively built upon the contradictions among interpellations, fashioning a subjectivity out of the very language and tropes that had been marshalled to control them. The resultant subjectivity was necessarily not identical for all women, and it was multiple and contradictory. In this view, agency is not defined as unified, willful action to consciously or freely shape one's world, but as the contingent, creative force that arises from the history of the subject. It is necessarily limited, but nevertheless powerful.[50]

Working women collectively created the cultural practices of ladyhood from the addresses of the fashion industry, employers, native-born Americans, and middle-class women. Indeed, as ladyhood became established and shared, working women interpellated others into it. Thus, ladyhood was both an arena of agency and creativity and a limiting discourse. Once working women became ladies, ladyhood was part of their subjectivities, part of who they were. It engaged their histories and their present placement in the web of power relations. When these women walked off their jobs, they inevitably carried the subjectivities formed through consumer practices into the context of the strike.

When labor leaders obscured working ladyhood, then, they implicitly (and sometimes explicitly) asked working women to change fundamentally in order to take part in the labor union. While they represented strikers strategically to win public favor, many leaders believed that the ideal of a serious and rational subjectivity was indeed necessary for sustained political participation. In fact, some sought to reform working women's cultural practices of ladyhood—fashion and dime novel reading—because they believed such practices prevented the women both from being accepted as political actors and from attaining the requisite ability for rational thinking. Leaders did not simply describe actual women strikers, rather they called the "rational girl striker" into being. As Judith Butler writes, "The mark interpellation makes is not descriptive, but inaugurative. It seeks to introduce a reality rather than report on an existing one; it accomplishes this introduction through a citation of existing convention."[51] Of course, working women did not necessarily recognize the leaders' address as fitting them, even if they were union members. Nevertheless, they certainly recognized that the address was meant for them; for those who participated in ladyhood it could make union discourse contradictory rather than simply emancipatory. A closer look at how leaders addressed working women reveals a link between an antagonism toward popular culture and the ideal of the rational girl striker.

Working women "heard" the leaders hail the rational girl striker in three forums: in the print material already examined here, which leaders created first and foremost for public relations, in large and small strike meetings or rallies, and in later labor publications created to influence working women. Strike leaders did not write articles or give quotes to newspapers in an attempt to shape women's identities. Nevertheless, working women did look at the daily papers, particularly during the strike. Though many of the immigrants did not read English, workers passed copies of papers around picket lines and shop meetings, and surely found ready translators.[52] In the newspapers, striking women found a plethora of competing representations of them in photos and verbal descriptions.

Discerning the ways in which leaders verbally addressed striking women is more difficult, because no transcripts of the innumerable formal and informal speeches and conversations between leaders and strikers exist. We can reason that leaders at large rallies expected media presence and addressed striking women as "rational girl strikers," consistent with the ways they promoted them elsewhere. Leaders probably addressed the women in more diverse ways at informal meetings, however. Leaders traveled from shop meeting to shop meeting (there were hundreds of shops on strike) on a nightly basis to speak to the strikers. It is possible, indeed likely, that they would modify their addresses to be appealing to the strikers, while still promoting identities and behaviors that they believed necessary for union participation. Released from the necessity to present a somewhat united front to the press and entirely unsupervised by their peers, individual leaders from the WTUL, SP, and ILGWU could address the strikers in whatever ways they believed most beneficial to the cause. Thus, while leaders certainly addressed striking women as rational girl strikers at times, they may have varied this in more diverse ways than the historical record reveals.

Labor publications aimed at working women, however, actively promoted the ideal of the rational girl striker and not only erased but attacked women's popular culture activities, particularly the primary components of ladyhood: fashion and dime novels. Such articles and stories appeared in the WTUL journal *Life and Labor* and the ILGWU journal *Ladies Garment Worker*.[53] Both of these publications originated within a year of the shirtwaist strike, and most of the articles and stories attempted to foster attitudes and identities that leaders believed were conducive to long-term union participation. Some working women did read these publications, especially those quite active in union activities, such as shop chairladies. These sources provide hints about how strike leaders and organizers may have addressed working women verbally during and after the strike.

This is not to suggest that the two publications offered identical ideals of working women as union members. While the ILGWU's *Ladies Garment Worker* occasionally referred to working women as "frail" or drew attention to their "insufficient clothing," it also regularly published heroic pictures of strikers and clearly advocated women's participation in unions.[54] The WTUL, in contrast, portrayed working women primarily as defenseless. Historian Pamela Gaddy argues that *Life and Labor* "constructed a subject position for working women . . . that was romantically honorable but also naively childlike—in need of pity, protection, maternal guidance and uplift."[55] The two publications were quite distinct in mission and content, but both contained attacks on dime novels and fashion that assumed these forms of popular culture were incompatible with unionization.

A year after the shirtwaist strike, Charlotte Barnum put forward an extreme proposal in *Life and Labor.* She argued that because the general public believed that working women dress too well, the union should set a maximum amount of money (two dollars) that each member would spend on dress per week. She wrote that "public opinion will never demand a living wage for women until these two excuses are removed: 1. Girls usually pay nothing for board and room because they live at home. 2. Girls spend nearly all their money on dress." While Barnum argued that both statements were untrue, they contained "enough truth" to warrant action. Going one step beyond proposing a limit for expenditure, she also envisioned "experts" in fabrics and the art of shopping to counsel the working women in "tasteful" dress, who would naturally "soon realize the importance of studying durability and of avoiding extreme and transient styles and colors."[56] By thus attacking working women's cultural practices, the WTUL signaled to working women that it was part of the middle-class opposition trying to keep them in their place. When Charlotte Barnum recommended a limit to women's expenditures and schooling in "taste," she demanded both that working women not dress "above their station," and that they assimilate and demonstrate middle-class values. As chapter 1 argued, this notion of "taste" was central to middle-class identity and had long worked to maintain class distinction.[57]

Stories and articles in the *Ladies Garment Worker* did not promote "tasteful" dress, but they did portray fashionable working women who read dime novels as irrational, the opposite of the ideal political subject. Gertrude Barnum's didactic stories positioned wise workers who belonged to the union against dreamy, empty-headed, and weak-willed women who were interested in fashion and fiction. In one story, "This Style—Six Twenty Nine," Barnum equated working women with the cheap clothing they wore, and implied that such women were as easily manipulated as a store-window mannequin:

> The window wax-lady maintained a fixed smile in spite of the ignominy of her position as she turned on her pivot to exhibit a cheap hat and the fit of a cheap gown . . . her outstretched arms seemed to appeal to be taken at any price. "She is the dead image of Rose, in our shop," Edna continued. "The forelady could unscrew Rose's head and she'd just smile on, making goo-goo eyes. There's Mollie, too. Mollie wobbles her hips and pokes her elbow out for all the world like that. Mollie's a sign! She thinks all New York goes outdoors for the purpose of getting a look at her.[58]

For Barnum, fashion made women dupes. By wearing consumer products, she seems to suggest, working women *become* consumer products. But Barnum's critique of commodities misses the meanings women themselves made with those commodities.

Gertrude Barnum also attacked dime novels as incompatible with political subjectivity. In one story in *Ladies Garment Worker*, a working woman named Edna takes a dime novel from Beatrice, a "dressy blonde," and reads a passage that clearly states Barnum's interpretation of the meaning of dime novel romances:

> Edna opened [the book] at the following passage: "The piteous appeal in the soft blue eyes of the helpless orphan maid touched the heart of the stern young man before her, deeply. In a flash, the cold, politic non-comcittal [sic], business man was changed to an ardent, trembling lover." "Gee!" said Edna, "That's a fairy tale! I wish you *could* get around cold, politic, non-committal business men that easy; but I've never seen it done."

Edna proceeds to take Beatrice to the boss and demand another "checker" (the person who punched time cards so workers would not be fined for being late when waiting in line to punch in). After the boss grants this practical demand, Edna says:

> "Beatrice has learned something. Page one, lesson one, for helpless orphan maids: 'Stop being helpless!' Page two, 'cut out appealing with soft blue eyes, and talk United States, with your tongue, fair and square.' Page three, 'Business men are alright, but you gotta talk business to 'em.' "[59]

The condescending tone of this story reinforces its didactic juxtaposition of dime novel reading with union participation.

Likewise, Pauline Newman regularly admonished women who read dime novels to read "GOOD fiction, fiction that is to an extent a reflection of life" In one issue of *Ladies Garment Worker* she wrote, "Don't read books that take you into a fairy land and introduce you to a Prince who falls in love with you. You are wasting your time reading such books." Newman, a garment worker who began working for the union during the shirtwaist strike, specifically suggested the novel *Comrade Yetta* and the history *Women in Industry* for women workers, the latter despite the fact that, as she warned, "this is not a novel," and some readers would find it "dry." "But if you want to know something about women in industry you will have to put up with it," she wrote.[60] As historian Annelise Orleck notes, "the didactic tone of [Newman's] columns reflected the gap that had opened up between her and the average shop floor worker."[61] Leaders also sent the message that working ladies needed to change in order to be good union members.[62] They thus failed to recognize the ways popular practices served some political purposes, articulating entitlement and fostering solidarity among working women; instead they waged a war against those practices.

Charlotte Barnum's suggested programmatic reform for women's dress did not go unchallenged. Mary Anderson, who organized boot and shoe workers in Chicago, wrote an angry letter in reply to Barnum's proposal to limit women's fashion expenditures:

> It is almost wicked to speak of dress when one remembers the thousands that sit up at night making their own clothes, and if the girls dress fairly, well, why not? Have they not worked hard enough? It is not so much a question of spending money wisely as how to procure a living wage and have some to spend. When we think of the girls at piecework and the hard training how to make the most of the time, we may well trust them to spend the money wisely.[63]

Anderson countered the way that Charlotte Barnum interpellated women as workers by repeating a producer-based rhetoric formally reserved for men: working women earned the right to spend their money as they pleased because they worked hard for it. Barnum's ideas, clearly steeped in middle-class values, may have sent a strong message to working women readers of *Life and Labor*, but they did not become a practiced reform program. Nevertheless, they reveal that for some, the image of the plainly dressed striker carried an implicit attack on working women's distinctive culture.

Efforts by Pauline Newman and Gertrude Barnum to reform working women's cultural practices undoubtedly had more far-reaching effects than did Charlotte Barnum's proposal. Both women not only wrote regularly for the ILGWU, WTUL, and SP publications, but also served as full-time organizers of working women in the years of the most intense strike activity. Gertrude Barnum, who came from a prominent middle-class family, began organizing laundry workers for the WTUL in 1905 and worked with many different strikes over the next decade, including the 1910 garment workers' strike in Chicago, and the Iowa button workers' strike and the great Cleveland garment workers' strike, both in 1911. Newman joined the Socialist Party in 1906 at age 15, and organized while working over 52 hours per week as a shirtwaist worker until the 1909 strike, when the ILGWU hired her as an organizer. She worked for the ILGWU for four years, traveled to fourteen states, and took part in many strikes, including the 1911 Cleveland strike and the 1912 Kalamazoo corset makers' strike. She met with countless groups of female garment workers over the years. Barnum and Newman, then, were among the handful of full-time union organizers in the field in these years, and had the ability to reach large numbers of women and to influence the union culture. Their pronouncements on working women's culture in labor publications, even when didactic or harsh, went unchallenged.[64] They reveal that overt critiques of working women's cultural practices undergirded their erasure in the publicity about the strike.

Leaders' representations of the rational girl striker thus were both strategic efforts to shape public perceptions, and evidence of a larger campaign to hail working women as political subjects. Labor leaders understood the threat of women's fashion to the public image of the strikers. They combined elements of the Enlightenment subject with charity-based ideals to paint strikers as poor and needy, wearing thin and tattered clothing, and bringing rational grievances to public attention in a serious and calm way. They then worked to get striking women to resemble this image.

Leaders thus obscured ladyhood and the fashion of the strikers, with four ramifications. First, they failed to build upon the indigenous practices and resistance of working women and urged them to adopt an image and subjectivity based in tropes that the women had already rejected. Most notably, they asked women to give up the bright and proud clothing of ladyhood and embrace an image of poverty and tatters. In other words, union leaders hailed women in terms that would likely be highly conflicted, rather than simply emancipatory, for many working women. If a striking woman wished to become an active union member, she would encounter and need to negotiate the figure of the girl striker and the ongoing address of union leaders. This would be no small task, for the practices of ladyhood were not simply *added on* to the social relationships in workplace culture, but for many *constituted* those relationships.[65] As such, ladyhood was the form that women's class, gender and ethnic identities had taken. At worst, leaders' efforts could serve to dissuade union participation. Indeed, a plethora of sources indicate leaders' frustration that women were willing to strike, but did not stay active in the union.[66] Certainly, there were a number of potential reasons for this, including that union leadership was male dominated and that women's help was often required at home after work, interfering with union meetings. However, many women also must have experienced a pull between gratifying cultural practices and union expectations, and thus between conflicting subjectivities.

Second, leaders' attempts to obscure or police working ladies' cultural practices replicated cultural norms that only recognized a political subjectivity that appeared rational and serious. Leaders extended it to women, but did not critique the gendered ideologies that defined rationality. They thus narrowed the public image of labor union resistance and types of political identities. In this way, the discourse of strike leaders "circumscribe[d] the domain of intelligibility" of working-class styles and subjectivities and promoted a narrowed sense of the diversity of working-class life.[67]

Third, leaders' strategic representations catered to middle-class desires to pity helpless and downtrodden (and unthreatening) working women, lacing the established notion of political subjectivity with the pathos associated with clients of social welfare. This left the matter of a democratic voice for working women somewhat clouded. Indeed, the WTUL gave up its original dedication to unionization for working women as the best means of empowerment after 1913 and emphasized instead protective legislation and a social welfare approach. It did so despite the fact that WTUL leaders regularly complained that bosses ignored *existing* labor laws when workers were not unionized.[68]

Finally, because the self-representation of working ladies did not become incorporated into union demands or rhetoric, it is largely hidden in the historical record. In the strike, working women claimed public space and a recognized and formal political identity in unprecedented numbers. While they could occupy public space, albeit at risk to life and limb, they could not directly influence public debate in newspapers and journals—even in the Socialist press. Thus their perspectives are not obvious in written records. Historians, drawing almost exclusively on union sources, have unwittingly mimicked union leaders' representation, taking it as self-evident "fact," and thus limited our understanding of the diversity of political subjectivities in history. Ironically, these historians who were motivated to restore stories of women's political activism—stories of possibility—to the historical narrative, also narrowed the historical understanding of the diversity of working-class culture and resistance, and foreclosed alternate political subjectivities by the ways they framed their subjects and sources. Judith Butler and Joan Scott call upon historians to explore how identities are constructed and how political subjectivities are formed through signifying practices. Rather than seeing identities as fixed aspects of already-constituted subjects, such critics suggest that we instead see the identities of historical actors as continually formed through signification, and thus unfixed and ever-changing.[69] By looking carefully at all sources as representations, it is possible to reveal the ways some identities became widely culturally intelligible, seen as natural and self-evident, while others receded into epistemological obscurity.

The more than 20,000 striking women thus faced a number of limitations and constraints as they walked off their jobs and claimed political voices. Their historic exclusion from public life meant that many working-class and middle-class observers did not see them as legitimate political actors. They faced gendered efforts by police and courts to obstruct picketing that built upon their questioned status as political actors. Additionally, they did not have access to the popular press in which the debate about them raged, nor did they have any direct influence over the Socialist *New York Call*. While the ILGWU, the WTUL and the SP joined forces to provide critical support for women in their political efforts, they also stepped forward to represent and advocate *for* them. These representations conflicted with the ways that the many working ladies in the strike presented themselves to the public.

Thus, the 1909 shirtwaist strike was not a moment of transcendent freedom in which strikers threw off their chains and acted out of free will. Rather, women workers found the strike itself to be a limited cultural terrain, much like other social arenas they occupied. Their agency came not from autonomy, but from their creative use of limited resources. They used these resources, including the cultural contradictions in the various ways they were addressed, to claim formal political identities as strikers. Indeed, the fact that the role of working ladies was *obscured* by strike leaders does not mean that they had *no* role. Leaders' attempts to control the workers or even to influence them were themselves greatly limited in the strike. The large number of strikers—tens of thousands—and the relatively unplanned nature of the strike meant that the alliance of leaders was often overwhelmed in its many duties. Women had considerable latitude to construct subjectivities as strikers from the available cultural resources, particularly leaders' interpellations and the established practices of ladyhood. Their very different story of the strike is buried in the historical record under the official version promoted strategically by leaders. Released from seeing the official record as equivalent to the strikers' stories, it is possible for us to unearth women's formal political subjectivities. Chapter 4 explores this hidden history of the shirtwaist strike of 1909.

LADIES AND ORPHANS
Women Invent Themselves as Strikers in 1909

We're human, all of us girls, and we're young. We like new hats as well as any other young women. Why shouldn't we?
   —Clara Lemlich, *New York Evening Journal*, November 26, 1909[1]

The boys and girls invented themselves how to give back what they got from the scab, with stones and what not, with sticks.   —Clara Lemlich, interview, 1974[2]

In being represented as a citizen within the political sphere ... the subject is "split off" from the unrepresentable histories of situated embodiment that contradict the abstract form of citizenship.   —Lisa Lowe, *Immigrant Acts* (1996)[3]

On November 22, 1909, an overflow crowd gathered at Cooper Union to hear a group of predominantly male union officials, including American Federation of Labor president Sam Gompers, discuss a general strike in New York City's shirtwaist industry.[4] No working women were scheduled to speak. After a number of men had spoken, worker and Socialist Clara Lemlich interrupted the proceedings, demanded access to the podium, and upstaged the union officials by moving that the assembly approve a general strike. The motion carried unanimously and the next day more than 20,000 shirtwaist workers walked off their jobs. Histories of the strike regularly celebrate Lemlich's motion, granting her the status of a political subject, but the fact that a female worker had to *interrupt* male political discourse to gain an audience has not been analyzed. During the strike, working women had to claim political subjectivities from limited resources and amid cultural contradictions between their own identities and abstract ideals of citizenship.

On November 26th, Lemlich again interrupted the political discourse surrounding the strike, this time with a unique article in the *New York Evening Journal*. Lemlich explained striking women's grievances and defended working women's fashion practices as part of a language of worth and entitlement. Her rhetoric in what was the only article in the popular press by a striking worker diverged starkly from the bulk of leaders' rhetoric about dress. Years later, Lemlich recalled that the strikers "invented themselves" how to behave on the picket lines. The stones, sticks, and "what not" that Lemlich remembered as part of picket line tactics likewise contrast markedly with strike leaders' and historians' picture of calm and rational strikers falling victim to strike breakers, thugs, and police. Historians have unwittingly split off Lemlich's celebrated strike call from these statements and have not analyzed them as part of the political discourse of the strike.[5]

When working women invented themselves as strikers, they drew upon what literary critic Lisa Lowe has called "unrepresentable histories of situated embodiment": cultural forms, daily practices, and enacted identities that seemed to contradict "citizenship" or "political subjectivity" as many middle-class people saw it. Specifically, for some working women the cultural practices of ladyhood proved to be an important resource as they enacted formally recognized political positions as strikers. Working ladyhood did not make them radical, but working women integrated elements of this identity, particularly utopian entitlement and a positive valuation of public display and physical aggression, into the terrain of political subjectivity in the strike. By a careful rereading of historical sources, this chapter maps the contours of that terrain.

Working ladyhood was not the only subculture that played a role in the shirtwaist strike. Historians universally attribute the strike to a specifically *radical* subculture, of which Lemlich was a part. Like many other young Jewish immigrants, Lemlich joined the Socialist Party as a teenager, regularly attended radical study groups, and actively sought to foment rebellion among her peers.[6] Though the radical activity of New York Italian women is less heralded by historians, they too took part in socialist and anarchist groups.[7] The radical subculture rewarded young women for intellectual critiques of society and passionate utopian visions for change. It introduced them to different cultural resources than they might otherwise have encountered, including radical theory and "serious" literature, and provided an arena in which they could build identities as political actors. Women in the radical subculture, like Lemlich and Pauline Newman, played instrumental roles in organizing and carrying out the shirtwaist strike. But when historians have focused nearly exclusively on such women, they have deflected attention away from the thousands of strikers who did *not* belong to the Socialist Party or identify themselves as radical, yet went out on strike. It is the motivations, experiences and subjectivities of these women that are the focus of this chapter's inquiry. While the rough categories of "radical subculture" and "working ladyhood" are necessary for analysis of the strike, they were not absolute or mutually exclusive. Indeed, Lemlich wove the language of ladyhood into her prostrike rhetoric.

My question is not whether popular culture "caused" working women to go on strike but whether women used popular culture as a resource when constructing political subjectivities. To ask whether popular culture caused women to go on strike would be to ascribe to popular culture *objects* a particular capacity for action and render working women passive. Instead, I suggest that working women could use popular culture for a number of ends. While many used the utopian entitlement inherent in ladyhood in creating identities as strikers, some used the same cultural resources to defend their choice to break the strike. The relationship between "ladyhood" and the strike is not one of simple causality. Rather, they are related in the historical processes of resistance and identity formation. That is, the ways in which people articulate demands and construct themselves as political subjects is a cultural process, related to the rest of their lives and to the discursive resources available to them. Even within a strike, resistance is cultural.

This chapter therefore traces the ways in which many working women marshalled available resources to claim a formal political identity that historically had been denied them. It does not celebrate the strike as a culmination or development of women's informal resistance into a radical consciousness. A strike should not be taken as an absolute indicator of the degree of workers' opposition. Certainly, the strike was a new experience for many and could change workers in various ways. But the metaphor of a strike as the "waking" of the workers reifies historically constructed notions of who and what can be recognized as political. It also obscures the various and interrelated means of social change by privileging resistance widely seen as formally political. As James Scott has argued, when subordinate groups are denied a public voice they maintain resistant subjectivities through "hidden transcripts," cultural practices and knowledge that are not visible to those in power. Labor historians also have shown convincingly that workers often maintain resistant identities even when not engaging in strikes or joining unions, so that an understanding of workers' consciousness requires attention not only to strikes but also to daily life on and off the shop floor.[8] Informal resistance not only maintained oppositional mindsets, it also often achieved social change and limited employers' power, which might otherwise remain unchecked.

In addition, as chapter 3 argued, who gains recognition as a political subject is historically constructed and socially enforced. To simply celebrate historical instances of formal protest as evidence of radical consciousness obscures the ways the line between "political" and "nonpolitical" existed precisely to limit access to formal political exchange to those with the greatest social power. When the shirtwaist workers went on strike, they challenged the existing definition of "political" actors and issues. Therefore, this chapter intends to challenge the culturally and historiographically constructed distinction between formal politics and not-politics in order to draw attention to how women constructed political subjectivities and articulated grievances in a context that did not automatically legitimate them, and explore the multifaceted and interrelated ways social change occurs.

Women did not create formal political subjectivities by adopting a particular idea or making a single decision; rather, they *enacted* those subjectivities through their daily practices as strikers. This complex process ensured that striking women would exhibit a diversity of subjectivities, rather than a singular consciousness or identity. Because the formation of subjectivity is an ongoing *process*, women's subjectivities as strikers were not unitary or unchanging, but were complex, heterogeneous and shifting in response to changing experiences. Thus, while chapter three could identify a somewhat unified, if internally contradicted, ideal of the "rational girl striker," this chapter traces no such clear outline of a specific figure. Instead, it maps the terrain of subjectivity in the strike by examining three central arenas in which striking women enacted political subjectivities—the walkout of November 23, the formulation of collective grievances, and the daily picketing on city streets—looking not only at the events involved, but also at the cultural resources women had at their disposal to "articulate" new identities in both words and actions. In short, it explores the strike as a cultural field, co-extensive with other cultural fields. Grassroots politics, in this view, is not conceptualized in Enlightenment terms as an arena of distinctive, unified, and willful action, but as one fraught with contradictions and cultural contestation, in which a variety of working women enacted identities in different ways.

As chapter 3 noted, however, this story about working ladies is buried in the documentation of the strike. Labor leaders obscured the participation of working ladies in attempts to effectively advocate for the strikers, while newspapers happily printed stories without verification and seldom printed the strikers' statements. Admittedly, some elements of the strikers' views and experiences are lost because of working women's limited access to print media. Nevertheless, it is possible to read the existing sources against the grain and discover a great deal about the strikers. Drawing on the example of the Subaltern Studies group of scholars focusing on India, this chapter will read fissures in the narratives that leaders or the newspapers promoted.[9] In particular, it will read differently situated sources against each other, paying particular attention to how the contrasting motivations of labor leaders and newspapers created different stories of the strike. The points of conflict, contradiction and congruence all provide clues to the unsaid. Crucially, it will also read with a knowledge of women's cultural practices of ladyhood and the range of cultural meanings they attached to clothing and the tropes of dime novels. By thus looking closely at women's political practices, including the walkout, the formation of grievances, and picket line strategies, this chapter will provide a new, more complete and worker-centered account of the strike.

The mass exodus from the shirtwaist factories on November 23, 1909 surprised union leaders and the general public alike. As one contemporary wrote, "None had guessed of this latent fire—neither the leaders, nor the Woman's Trade Union League, nor the girls themselves."[10] A delegate from the shirtwaist makers' union, the ILGWU, local 25, had hopefully predicted in the days before the strike that "a few thousand of them will quit the shops,"[11] but more than 20,000 strikers answered the strike call. While women workers had gone on strike since the 1830s, the Uprising of the 20,000 was at that time the largest strike ever in female- dominated industries. It was the first in a series of mass strikes in the early 1910s by predominantly female workers in the north-eastern and midwestern garment industry; it demonstrated that effective mass strikes *could* occur despite the number and dispersion of different shops. In aggregate, the large strikes of the 1910s organized the garment industry and brought working women into the center of unionization in the United States. But in November of 1909, such mass strikes by working women had not yet occurred; many believed the industry to be unorganizable because they saw women as more temporary workers than men and because the industry itself was so dispersed. How is it, then, that so many thousands of workers, the vast majority of them women with no union experience, answered the call to strike?

Some contemporary observers and historians have explained the preconditions for such a response by citing the workers' widespread shared experience and knowledge of demeaning working situations, including low pay, long hours, and unsafe working conditions. However, none has convincingly explained why so many workers believed they could change things at this historical moment. As Jeremy Brecher has argued, mass strikes cannot be explained simply by the existence of overtly oppressive conditions or even by a strike call. Brecher quoted the Interchurch World Movement Report on the mass steel strike of 1919:

> It cannot be too strongly emphasized that a strike does not consist of a plan and a call for a walkout. There has been many a call with no resultant walkout; there has been many a strike with no preceding plan or call at all. Strike conditions are conditions of mind.[12]

A mass strike is more than a logical response to bad working conditions; people who walk off their jobs en masse are also caught up in a utopian hope for a better situation and a refusal of existing conditions. In order for this hope to emerge, people must believe that change is not only just but attainable. They must be able to envision themselves as successful strikers. As Brecher argues, "people will try to adapt to even the most unpleasant situation if it seems stable and they feel unable to change it."[13] A walkout is in part an *imaginative* process of coming to identify oneself as a striker as one takes dramatic public action.

Some historians claim that it was the police brutality at the Triangle and Leiserson shops that moved shirtwaist workers to act. Recall that smaller strikes began in September at those shops, and police responded with great force and many arrests. Historians argue that this repression proved to be the last straw.[14] This is a valuable point. Working women certainly knew their work was oppressive. The subculture of radicals stated this overtly, and those who consumed fashion and dime novel fiction wove this knowledge into their daily enactment of ladyhood. In addition, police action has historically served as a catalyst for formal protest about ongoing oppressive conditions.[15] Indeed, a woman who went on strike one week after the general walkout explained that she felt guilty working while the police arrested her picketing co-workers.[16] But in this case, the worker was able to see her co-workers through the shop window. Women toiled in groups of ten to 350, in hundreds of garment shops across New York City. How could police brutality at the Triangle and Leiserson shops, affecting at most 450 of the more than 40,000 workers, impact women who never came into contact with the striking workers? Indeed, how would they even know about the arrests?

Other historians attribute the mass walkout to either a natural or a cultural tendency toward radicalism among Jewish women, who answered the strike call in greater proportion than did Italian women.[17] Some strike leaders explained this by claiming that Jews had particular racial characteristics, including a feisty militancy, while Italians were naturally more timid.[18] Later historians have distanced themselves from such explicit racial typography, but embraced an image of Jewish immigrant women as particularly intolerant of injustice and likely to take action, citing the very real forces of a history of racial oppression and resistance, including the growing Socialist movement on the Lower East Side. Most Jews immigrated to the United States in order to escape anti-Semitic persecution in Eastern Europe, including second-class citizenship, sporadic violence from gentiles, and organized pogroms. They incorporated this recent historical memory into a religious and cultural framework containing a long understanding of oppression and religious persecution. In addition, some Jewish workers had examples of resistance both in the "Old Country" and in the United States. Some had known of or participated in the Socialist Labor Bund in Eastern Europe, while others had watched their mothers or other female relatives fight for affordable living conditions in the 1902, 1904, and 1907–8 meat boycott and rent strikes. The growing Socialist movement on the Lower East Side spawned the *Forverts* (*Jewish Daily Forward*), a Yiddish, Socialist daily newspaper, and numerous radical discussion groups. Jewish daughters took part in radicalism and experienced relatively greater freedom of movement in the evenings than did women from other ethnic groups.[19] Many historians drew on this evidence to suggest that Jews, particularly on the Lower East Side, were radical as a group and that the thousands of Jewish workers who went on strike simply acted in accordance with their history and their culture.[20]

Historian Susan Glenn criticizes this celebration of a special Jewish propensity to militancy as an "ethnic myth" that "vastly oversimplifies the responses and outlook" of Jewish women. Glenn argues that there was a diversity of ethnic and working-class styles and ideologies among the shirtwaist workers, and that Jews did not unanimously or automatically answer the strike call or stand behind the union. Indeed, organizers described shirtwaist workers in general, before the fall of 1909, as generally apathetic about unionization.[21] Glenn also aptly argues that both Jewish and Italian workers had a historical memory of oppression and resistance and that both communities "contained diverse cultural and political constituencies." The lower level of Italian participation was due in part to the Jewish dominance of leadership, an explanation supported by the increased participation of Italians in later strikes involving more Italian organizers and leaders and Italian-only locals. To position Jewish workers as all already radicalized diminishes, for Glenn, our understanding of the range of ideologies that existed among working women. Her critique helps us understand how this ethnic myth has occluded a fuller understanding of the working-class culture from which the strikers emerged.[22]

Glenn's history of the strike, however, replaces the ethnic myth with a notion of an influential ethnic vanguard: she argues that women could strike in such great numbers in part because those who participated in the radical subculture, while few, carried great authority with their co-workers. Glenn maintains that a range of political positions correlated to a parallel range of style, with serious radicals (presumably plainly dressed) on one end, and "frivolous" women concerned with fashion at the other. Glenn condemns such women as abandoning the working class:

On one end of the Jewish spectrum stood the stalwart militants. . . . At the other end of the spectrum stood Jewish women who resembled those "Americans" whom union leaders viewed as "frivolous." . . . Some wage-earning daughters with aspirations to upward mobility more or less disassociated themselves from the struggles of the immigrant proletariat.

Glenn credits the "stalwart militants" with bringing the more ambivalent or indifferent 20,000 working women out on strike: "If many young workers knew little about politics themselves, they were inclined to pay attention to those who seemed more knowledgeable."[23] Historian Gerald Sorin also attributes the actions of the many to the political influence of the few. He argues that so many answered the strike call because "in many shops, young, unmarried women like [Clara Lemlich] influenced significant numbers of others. They did this through persistent discussion, by invoking a sense of sisterhood, and by example."[24] Historian Annelise Orleck similarly claims that so many women responded to the strike call because radical workers effectively organized the trade. Orleck argued that the strike was not surprising because Rose Schneiderman, Pauline Newman, Fania Cohn, and Clara Lemlich had been "organizing feverishly for almost three years." Many of the leaders whom the press often dubbed "inexperienced girls" actually were seasoned radicals who had their hopes and efforts staked on a general strike for months in advance. According to Orleck, the shirtwaist strike of 1909 was a well-organized endeavor built on hard, methodical work.[25]

Glenn's, Sorin's, and Orleck's explanations minimize the challenges of organizing in this industry. There were no full-time or paid organizers dedicated to the shirtwaist industry until after the strikes at the Triangle and Leiserson shops began. Rose Schneiderman began work as a paid organizer for the WTUL in 1908, but was focused on the white goods workers until the fall of 1909.[26] Women like Clara Lemlich and Pauline Newman labored to organize the shirtwaist trade while also working fifty-two hours per week or more in the shops for their own living.[27] They and other radical workers talked union wherever they worked (sometimes losing their jobs as a result), and organized after work as well. They could not enter other shops and could rarely speak openly in their own; much union talk occurred in the bathroom. This organization was central; the 1909 shirtwaist strike could not have happened without it. But it was not sufficient to explain the size of the walkout, given that there were more than 40,000 workers spread across New York City, many in small shops of ten to twenty workers. It was a labor organizer's nightmare. Even spreading the news of a meeting or the call for a strike would be a monumental task. The strike leaders knew this; that is why they were so surprised by the response.

When historians credit Jewish radicals with the walkout of over 20,000 workers they illuminate a crucial part of working-class immigrant experience, but also obscure its diversity. Jews' collective memory of oppression infused not only the radicals' lives but those of women exhibiting a variety of cultural styles; nevertheless, it is typically discussed only in connection to radicals' activities. Many labor historians depict Jewish collective memory as spurring critique and radicalism, juxtaposed to fashion and other cultural practices which are dubbed "Americanization." Radicals, in this view, carried the history of Jews into the future, while those who dressed "like Americans" were marginal to the main story and, by implication, to Jewish identity.[28] However, as chapter 2 noted, a collective memory of oppression could infuse the cultural practices of ladyhood for both Italians and Jews. George Lipsitz documents that collective memory has framed the production and reception of popular culture for a wide range of people in the twentieth century, including African Americans and Chicanos.[29] Collective memory is indeed an important element in understanding the shirtwaist strike, but must be traced in a diversity of ethnic cultural practices rather than simply attributed to the subculture of radicalism.

In addition, the argument that the majority of workers simply "followed" the radicals denies workers agency. Indeed, it bears remarkable resemblance to an *anti*-union argument made by a Jewish reformer of German descent in 1917. Bemoaning the cultural practices of young

Eastern European Jewish women, the author warned in *The American Hebrew* that such women would blindly follow labor radicals: "Out of touch with real American standards, [the Jewish Immigrant Girl] adopts in self-defense those pathetic symbols of the only standards she sees— the whitened nose and the high-heeled slipper. Without the language she cannot communicate directly with her employer and readily becomes the follower of foreign labor leaders and agitators."[30] Exploring such women's *choices* to strike, rather than rendering them passive followers, would provide a more complete analysis of the walkout and also enrich and diversify our understanding of Jewish immigrant culture, including the history of Jewish protest in which working ladies clearly played a part.

Historians' explanations of the walkout point to important elements but fail to capture the "condition of mind" of a wide range of women in November of 1909. The thousands who risked a great deal to walk off their jobs in 1909 could not simply have followed their radical sisters. How did women learn about the strike? How did they come to feel they could change the conditions that had oppressed them for years? What captured their imagination and prompted them to act? While it is impossible to pin down an individual's imaginative process of coming to identify with strikers, it is possible to trace a grid of cultural meaning that could support such a process. In order to identify with the strikers, women needed information about the strike, accessible and gratifying figures of identification, and optimism that the strike could be successful.

The popular press covered the events leading to the general strike call in ways likely to reach a large number of workers, provide them with pleasing images of strikers, and convince them that a strike could be successful. As historians have noted, the popular press began to print news of the conflicts at the Triangle and Leiserson shops when police arrested New York's WTUL president Mary Dreier as she picketed with the striking workers on November 4. Glenn argues that this got the "attention of the entire city," and Maxine Schwartz Seller asserts that the arrest of middle-class Dreier brought "respectability and publicity" to the strikers' plight.[31] However, the most significant impact of the newspaper publicity may have been that it spread the news of the strike to other shirtwaist workers, and did so in ways likely to capture their interest and fascination.

The newspaper functioned not only as "publicity," but as a popular culture form for working women. Those who read English regularly bought papers and shared them with co-workers, thrilling to sensational news stories about heiresses, murders, fires, and scandals, many of which closely resembled dime novel plots. Worker Sadie Frowne said, "I can read quite well in English now and I look at the newspapers every day." Journalist Clara Laughlin noted that the daily newspapers were "among the last things a working girl will deny herself."[32] Working women's familiarity with the highly accessible newspapers proved to be a link among them, as Helen Marot, secretary of the WTUL, reported in 1910:

> During the five weeks of the strike, previous to the publicity, the forty thousand waist makers employed in the several hundred shops in New York were with a few exceptions here and there unconscious of the struggle of their fellow workers in the Triangle. There was no means of communication among them, as the labor press reached comparatively few.

Marot argued that the publicity of the strike in the popular newspapers not only communicated the story to workers broadly, but aroused an interest that the leaders capitalized on with further union organizing:

> [The publicity] furnished the union its opportunity. It knew the temper of the workers and pushed the story still further through shop propaganda. After three weeks of newspaper publicity and shop propaganda the reports came back to the union that the workers were aroused.[33]

What exactly was "the story" in the popular newspapers that union organizers pushed further? What *was* the "temper of the workers"? The popular newspaper coverage after November 4 quickly shifted focus from Dreier and the involvement of "wealthy settlement workers" to the striking workers, providing readers a possibility for a gratifying identification with the strikers. Some published large photographs and sensational stories about the young heroines. As early as November 5, the *New York Evening World* printed a page three story headlined GIRL PICKETS BEG WORKERS TO GO ON STRIKE, accompanied by a large photograph of four picketers (fig. 4.1). The article's subheadline noted the "great excitement among workers around Washington Square" and described the strike's purpose, as well as Dreier's arrest. The large photograph placed the working-class women in the limelight. Two of the women pictured dressed with considerable ornamentation. Both wore hats, one with a number of plumes and the other with a large and elaborate design. The other two women pictured did not wear hats and dressed more plainly. While the article did not comment on the strike's likelihood of success, the picture would be likely to capture the attention of the city's shirtwaist makers, who were unaccustomed to seeing

Strike Pickets of the Girl Waist-Makers
Who Patrol Washington Place for Union

4.1 The *New York Evening World* provided citywide publicity of the Triangle and Leiserson strikes in a November 5 article and photograph.

pictures of ordinary working women in the papers.

The *New York Evening Journal* went further than the *Evening World* and printed articles declaring that a general strike was imminent and bound to be successful, and included pictures that celebrated strikers' heroism and solidarity. On November 10, less than a week after Dreier's arrest, a large headline on the top of page two of the *Evening Journal* read: 40,000 GIRLS TO JOIN GREAT STRIKE OF NEW YORK WAISTMAKERS. In this case, the popular press's willingness to publish stories without verification probably worked to the union's advantage. A general strike had been discussed in local 25 since October, but there had been no decision to issue a strike call. The paper cited that a "good authority" had assured the 140 members of local 25 that "by next week 40,000 girls and women would be with them in their strike for better wages and shorter hours." This story was clearly predictive and not a report on the facts, but the paper's wide distribution, confident tone, and assurance that "the girl strikers are now sure of victory" not only spread word of the impending general strike, but sent a message that change was possible—indeed, inevitable. The story continued, "With the array that they [the strikers] expect to join them, they would be able to tie up the shirtwaist making industry in New York, and thus force the employers to come to terms."[34]

Working women were likely to see and read this article because, in addition to the attention-grabbing headline, there was a large and stunning picture of the "girl strikers" who had been arrested at least five times (fig. 4.2). This picture, part photograph and part drawing, told a story of its own. At the top of the picture, eleven women pose for a photograph, several of them wearing hats decorated with ostrich plumes, bows, and lace. Two wear stylish fur pieces. The woman at the far left wears a smart suit with velvet trim at the neck and cuffs and an elaborate hat; all of the women who are fully visible in the picture wear suits with shirtwaists in the predominant style of the time. Some wear the "lingerie waists" noted by the Collier's reporter. These complex blouses featured a plethora of tucks, embroidery, and lace. The strikers display a range of styles, from those who are hatless and whose suits are more plain to those who sport feathers, fur, and trim. Most have confident expressions and at least two have a hand on another woman's shoulder in a gesture that conveys familiarity and warmth. Below, an artist's drawing shows the picketers in action. In the drawings, each woman wears a trimmed hat and struggles actively with a police officer. The police are drawn to appear bulkier than the women, but otherwise as much the same size, and the female figures seem to be putting up a good fight. The photograph and the drawing together present the strikers heroically in a posed photograph, even as they narrate their evenly matched battle with the police. Working women could see this composite picture as celebrating both the physical strength and the collectivity of the strikers. The pictured strikers had an experience that the vast majority of working women had not had: they had been arrested five times. Nevertheless, they looked and dressed much like working women all over the city.

Striking women made the New York Evening Journal's front page on November 16 in a picture and article that reinforced this "story." At the

4.2 The *New York Evening Journal* celebrated the Triangle and Leiserson strikers and confidently predicted a general strike in a November 10 article and photograph.

top and center of the front page, a group of eleven strikers pose under the headline GIRL STRIKERS FORM BAND TO FIGHT THUGS (fig. 4.3). The article reported that a "vigilance committee" or "flying wedge" of some of the most "capable and intrepid" strikers had formed to stand at strategic points and offer "effective help" to women pickets who were attacked by hired thugs. The article claimed that "The girls of the flying wedge are armed with short clubs, and their method of attack is to rush upon the thugs much as a football line gets into 'V' shape in a rush play."[35] As always with the sensational press, this report must be viewed with critical skepticism. Certainly, it contained elements of truth. As already noted, Clara Lemlich well remembered the physical fights on the picket lines; she herself was reportedly arrested seventeen times by November 22. But this story of an organized vigilante group is not corroborated by other sources and is probably a highly embellished rendition of picket line conflicts.

Whether true or not, this article would be likely to have a great impact on readers. Middle-class New Yorkers could be highly alarmed. The idea of women picketing in public and struggling with police and thugs was itself a challenge to standards of propriety. On top of this, the *Evening Journal* added a story of female vigilantes armed with clubs and executing football maneuvers. For the middle class, schooled in nineteenth-century ideologies of separate spheres, women were by nature passive and peaceful, while men were aggressive and tended toward violence. These readers could see vigilante strikers as abnormal, masculine women.

The impact of this picture and article, however, would likely be

Girl Strikers Form Band to Fight Thugs

VIGILANCE COMMITTEE OF STRIKING SHIRTWAIST MAKERS.

4.3 The *New York Evening Journal* gave front-page publicity to Triangle and Leiserson strikers on November 16, nine days before the general strike.

quite different for shirtwaist workers. Indeed, the front-page picture reinforced the earlier story established by the *Evening Journal*. The women appear strong and physically capable, though they are not as ornately dressed as some of the those in the earlier picture. Nevertheless, three wear fur pieces and several wear hats, one of which (second from the right, top row) is a picture-turban, a very popular style remarked upon by the *Collier's* reporter. The women are pictured together, signaling that this is not a story of a single heroine or "star" but of many "stars." Women waistmakers had a cultural repertoire that would allow them to read the story and picture as celebrating the strikers' strength, bravery, and ladyhood. Working women were familiar with female violence from their experiences in the factories and ethnic neighborhoods, and from reading about it in dime novels. In these contexts, some kinds of female violence were understandable and even admirable, especially if conducted in the name of loyalty, self-defense, or protest.

Violence between women workers occurred with some regularity in factories and sweatshops, particularly in disputes about "lady friends," which Dorothy Richardson described as strong, dedicated friendships between two women in the factories. Analogous to "smashing" relationships between middle-class college women (although never studied in detail), these relationships legitimated a form of homoeroticism and dedication in a largely female environment. Richardson reported that some employers refused to knowingly hire lady friends, because loyalty or jealousy regularly prompted physical fights.[36] Jewish women could also draw on a memory of female violence in the meat boycott of 1902, and the rent strikes of 1904 and 1907–8. Women's well-known militancy in these struggles revealed their distance from a middle-class ideal of physically passive womanhood and served as a model for militant labor activism. Working women reading the *Evening Journal* thus would not find the reported violence of the strikers inherently shocking, masculine, or abnormal.

Working women could also draw on their dime novel reading to interpret striking vigilantes as heroic and just. In dime novel narratives, heroines all exerted physical force when they deemed it necessary for self-defense or the defense of another. As chapter 2 argued, the dime novels redefined ladyhood to include physically aggressive behavior, including both work and some violence. Leonie Locke, for example, struggles with a villain on a pier "with almost super human strength, while he seemed nearly paralyzed at the suddenness of the attack" because he attempts to force her to marry him. Leonie pushes the villain into the sea and does not regret her actions: " 'I did not mean to do it' she gasped, 'but he drove me to it. One of our lives would have ended in a tragedy; what does it matter that it was his instead of mine.' "[37] Other heroines were equally aggressive. Working women who read dime novels could interpret the striking women protecting picketers as heroic, just, and even ladylike. Indeed, they might find the reported actions of the women inspiring and the final line of the article celebratory: "The girls are not afraid of the toughs, and they declare it will go hard with any of the ruffians who attempt to continue their recent tactics." The popular press photographs and stories thus offered working women gratifying images with which to identify.

The popular press caught the imaginations of shirtwaist workers around the city in a medium that was particularly familiar and accessible to them. As expert readers of sensational newspaper pictures and narratives, working women knew that people featured in front-page celebratory articles were "stars" of the city, at least for a day, a position usually reserved for the wealthy or powerful. Newspapers typically carried pictures of working women only if they committed a notable crime or if they were theater or film actors. In response, many working women expressed a desire for fame in "star-struck" dreams of being on the stage or screen. Their desire for fame stood in dramatic opposition to working women's systematic exclusion from public life, particularly as it was represented in the newspapers. In this case, however, the stars were garment workers like themselves, and they could *join* them in their heroism and become front-page copy in their own right. Socialist strike leader Theresa Malkiel indicated the importance of the newspaper coverage to strikers' pride in her didactic *Diary of a Shirtwaist Striker,* written for working women after the strike. Malkiel wrote about the walkout in the voice of a striker:

> Why every one of [the papers] is full of the strike and strikers; we are made so much of. It really feels good to be somebody. . . . It's strange, when you come to think of all the noise us girls have made for the last two days. Why the Vanderbilts themselves ain't in it any more—the people are too busy with us.[38]

Thus, the story that the newspapers created two weeks before the general strike call allowed both already-politicized radicals and women who had no union experience to join in with enthusiasm. The pictures did not feature individual strikers as leaders or heroes, but represented the strikers in groups. Headlines and articles predicted their inevitable success. Significantly, this story meant that no women needed to feel like followers of the more seasoned radicals, even though they might have learned from them. Rather, all could feel like stars immediately by participating.

Equally important to Jewish women's identification with the Triangle and Leiserson strikers was the coverage of the strike by the *Forverts.* This Socialist, Yiddish paper had a wide circulation in 1909 that would reach an estimated 122,500 by 1911.[39] The *Forverts'* readership concentrated in New York's Lower East Side, where family members and tenement neighbors might share a single copy of the paper. The *Forverts* did not singlehandedly solve the problem of communication among the city's tens of thousands of waistmakers, but it did provide information in Yiddish to some. Nearly daily articles in the weeks before the general strike condemned the Jewish owners of the Triangle and Leiserson shops, celebrated the cause of the strikers and, like the *New York Evening Journal,* predicted their victory. The *Forverts* carried announcements of meetings and theater benefits for the strikers, as well as regular articles and editorials condemning the violence of police and hired thugs on the picket lines. On November 17, an editorial assured readers that 50,000 waistmakers were ready to strike, and between November 17 and 22, the paper rain a daily page-two announcement of the November 22 assembly at Cooper Union to discuss a general strike.[40]

While the popular press's coverage made striking women "stars" of the city, offering them "American" validation, the *Forverts* made Jewish strikers stars of their neighborhoods as well. But the *Forverts* did not simply provide a Yiddish echo of the effect of the English-language coverage. While the English-language press presented the strikers first and foremost as "girls," engaged in a struggle for their own interests, the *Forverts* referred to them as "sisters" and "comrades," and placed their efforts in the context of a larger, Jewish and Socialist movement for freedom. The English-language dailies represented the strikers as fashionably dressed, pleasure-seeking, and regularly violent, but the *Forverts* celebrated them as "our innocent working girls," who were passive victims of violence. The *Forverts* carried only one photograph of the strikers before the general walkout: the same photograph that the *New York Evening Journal* ran on November 16 (fig. 4.3). The *Evening Journal* identified the group as a band of vigilantes committed to fighting the thugs; in contrast, the *Forverts* simply captioned the picture "A Group of Striking Ladies Waistmakers From the Triangle Company."[41] An ironic effect of the *Forverts'* focus on the larger Jewish and Socialist movement was that working women's own actions garnered scant specific attention, despite the large numbers of articles about them. To be sure, when the *Forverts* described the strikers it celebrated their "new strength and fresh energy" as they were "formulating their just struggle." But more often the *Forverts* focused on the owners, the police, the male union leadership, and editorialized in inspiring but generalized polemical language about police brutality: "Workers are enslaved through the force of the fist, the punch and the almighty buck."[42] Thus, the *Forverts* did not tell the same story that captured the city's workers after November 4, but it could provide workers some Jewish support even if their own families opposed the strike. They need not feel they betrayed their "race" by striking against Jewish owners, since other powerful Jews applauded their actions.[43] For Jewish women, becoming stars in English-language papers did not indicate an abandonment of Jewish community or identity. Indeed, shirtwaist strikers could claim "Americanization" without capitulation to oppression or loss of a Jewish identity, much as the Mexican-American female garment workers studied by George Sanchez claimed their own form of Americanization through labor union participation in the 1930s.[44]

The fact that a strong faction of Jewish community support for the Triangle and Leiserson strikers existed even before the general walkout may help account for the over-representation of Jewish participation in the strike. No such community support for the Triangle and Leiserson strikers existed among Italians, a fact due not to an inherent conservativism but most likely to a lack of information provided in Italian. The daily Italian paper, the *Bolletino della Sera*, carried only two brief announcements about strike meetings and one short article before the November 23 walkout. The article, appearing on November 2, was not particularly favorable, and portrayed strikers attacking not hired thugs but other workers. The *Bolletino della Sera* covered a number of other current strikes in considerable detail and favorable terms, but seemed to acquire its very limited information about the shirtwaist strike from the English-language papers. The other two prominent Italian papers in New York City, *Il Proletario* and the popular *Il Progresso Italo-americano*, did not cover the shirtwaist strike at Triangle and Leiserson companies at all before the general strike; even during the general strike their coverage was rare and brief.[45] The probable reason for this lack of attention, as historian Jennifer Guglielmo argues, is that Italian radicals were far more linked to the International Workers of the World (IWW) than they were to the American Federation of Labor-affiliated ILGWU. Communication links had not yet been forged between the ILGWU and Italian community groups.[46] By early December, Italian IWW members aided the strike effort by providing Italian speakers. But Italian Americans never did embrace the shirtwaist strike as an Italian issue, as they would the 1913 garment workers' strike. In that strike, Italians participated in great numbers, and *Il Progresso Italo-americano* carried nearly daily, front- and second-page coverage of the conflict.[47] In 1909, Italian workers may have thrilled to see pictures of shirtwaist strikers in English-language papers, but they would not find support among Italians comparable to that among Jews. Indeed, an Italian Catholic priest urged Italian women to stay at work, while a Jewish rabbi publicly supported the strike.[48]

Understanding the success of the mass walkout, then, requires attention to how workers who did strike came to identify with—and as—strikers and why they believed they were likely to succeed. The stories in the popular English press and the Socialist Yiddish press, part of the popular culture of working women, publicized the strike to workers and provided gratifying images of participation and assurances of victory. Organizers pushed this story further through street corner speeches and leaflets. When working women actually walked off their jobs, they dramatically enacted their first claim on a formal political identity as strikers. They reported that the walkout was an exciting and powerful experience, imbued with defiance, fun, and widespread heroism. The women arrived at their jobs as usual the morning of November 23 and at a designated time rose and left the buildings. Such defiance of the boss entailed great risk. In some shops, one or more women sprang from their seats and led the procession out. In Natalya Urosova's factory, the workers sat for two hours, all afraid to take the added risk of being first. Urosova remembered the whispering around the room: " 'Who will get up first?' 'It would be better to be the last to get up, and then the company might remember it of you afterward, and do well for you.' " Urosova recalled that finally she began to stand, and "at the same minute all—we all got up together, in one second. No one after the other; no one before. And when I saw it—that time—oh it excites me so yet. I can hardly talk about it."[49] Urosova and her co-workers joined thousands of other workers in the streets. Like many other strikes through history, the shirtwaist strike had an exhilarating "character of a revolt," as one leader called it.[50] Many had no idea what to do next, but word spread to congregate at Clinton Hall near Union Square. As workers approached, the crowds thickened and excitement mounted. Pauline Newman recalled that the power the strikers felt overcame their fear of the future:

> Thousands upon thousands left the factories from every side, all of them walking down toward Union Square. . . . I can see the young people, mostly women, walking down and not caring what might happen. The spirit, I think, the spirit of a conqueror led them on. They didn't know what was is store for them, didn't really think of the hunger, cold, loneliness, and what could happen to them. They just didn't care on that particular day. That was *their* day.[51]

The new strikers found Clinton Hall jammed, and newspapers and leaders alike reported that a feeling of festivity reigned. While leaders struggled to sign up thousands for the union, strikers recounted their shops' heroic stories and danced.

The strike, contrary to some newspaper representations, was not all play and no work. As soon as possible, strikers had to organize shop meetings to discuss and decide on grievances and picket line duties. Leaders rented or borrowed more than fifty meeting halls in lower Manhattan alone to accommodate them. Because each employer settled with the union individually, each shop needed to discuss its specific workplace grievances separately.[52] This process of developing and articulating political claims was another instance in which strikers enacted political subjectivities. The strikers had rejected existing conditions and made a utopian bid for something better. But what, ideally, would "better" look like? Unfortunately, no record exists recounting the conversations of women in their individual shop meetings. Nevertheless, we can know something about how this process occurred by reading existing evidence carefully for traces of striking women's grievances.

Histories of this strike have conflated official union demands with workers' grievances, assuming that the demands put forward by the union simply reflected the range of attitudes and interests of the workers.[53] The union officially required a fifty-two-hour week; abolition of the subcontract system; weekly payment of wages; limitation of overtime to two hours in any day, not to extend later than nine o'clock P.M.; the end of charges for materials and implements; and a union shop. Higher wages were not a standard union demand because some women worked on a piecework system and some were paid by the week, but leaders usually negotiated wages when settling with individual shops.[54] One role of strike leaders was to strategically shape strikers' diverse grievances into official union demands that would be presented to the public, based on both what workers wanted and what leaders thought they could get. While the official demands certainly represented enough of the workers' complaints to ensure their continued loyalty to the strike, the demands could not represent the workers comprehensively. Indeed, the demands had to be issued on the first day of the strike, before many workers had had a chance to express their concerns. By accepting official union demands as fully representing workers' grievances, historians have neglected to explore the ways workers articulated their complaints and developed their own demands.

Striking workers developed their first grievances largely independently of union leaders' influence. Each shop elected a "chairlady" from among their ranks to run their meetings and meet with union leaders. WTUL, SP, and ILGWU leaders traveled from one small hall to the next, meeting briefly with strikers to educate them in the basic principles of unionization, listen to them, and provide moral support. Leaders also instructed each group to discuss their specific demands and to make out a wage scale if they wished to demand an increase. Striker Natalya Urosova recalled that union leaders instructed them to "[write] out on paper what terms we wanted."[55] Helen Marot of the WTUL described the process simply as an information flow from leaders to strikers:

> When the shirtwaist strikers were gathered in separate groups, according to their factories, in almost every available hall on the East Side, the great majority of them received their first instruction in the principles of unionism and learned the necessity of organization in their own trade.[56]

However, the strike leaders were far too overtaxed to supervise workers' meetings, so most first discussions of grievances occurred in worker-only groups, led by the chairladies. These specific localized grievances often played a role in discussions with individual bosses, even when they were not expressed in the official, overarching union demands.

This process allowed the gap between workers' grievances and official union demands and policies to persist well into the strike. As one chairlady recalled, "When you're shop chairlady. . . . you have to go on the stage and take the floor and explain what's happening."[57] Jennie Matyas, who joined the ILGWU in a later strike, recalled the difference between her conception of the strike as chairlady and what was actually gained:

> I was very naive and inexperienced, naturally. The demands we made when we went out on strike were a great deal more than we subsequently got and . . . I didn't understand the theory of making a modest beginning. So I felt very disappointed, especially as I had done a good bit of speaking to the workers in the shop meetings.[58]

Workers thus maintained and developed elements of what Nancy Fraser calls a "subaltern counterpublic" during the strike, because they arbitrated information in a separate arena from the official strike negotiation.[59] At the same time, their particular grievances did have an oblique impact on the public debate.

While no direct record exists of small shop meetings in the first days of the strike, a number of grievances that are not represented in the official union demands became part of the historical record. By looking closely at them, we can trace the particular concerns that striking women brought into the public debate, including sexual harassment and issues related to clothing. The article by Clara Lemlich, entitled "Leader Tells Why 40,000 Girls Struck," published in the *Evening Journal* early in the strike is especially revealing.[60] Lemlich gained this public forum because she was already a leader, and had made the dramatic call for a general strike at the November 22 meeting. Her perspective cannot be fully representative of the range of ideas that must have existed among the working women. However, Lemlich had worked in the garment industry for five years and was very familiar with shop floor culture. In addition, she was among the leaders who spoke to numerous small shop meetings in the first days of the strike; she kept at it until her voice went hoarse. The issues she raised in the *New York Evening Journal* resonate strongly with working women's cultural practices and provide us insight into their strike experience.

Lemlich covered a range of grievances in explaining why the workers had struck. Some were official union demands; most were not. She described the piecework and weekly wage systems of payment, the numbers of hours worked, and the rationalization of labor that divided the work into small tasks. She complained about the physical conditions of the shops, calling them "unsanitary," and noted that unless workers received seats by the windows on one side of the room they experienced considerable eyestrain due to inadequate gaslighting. This complaint was common among working women but was not reflected in official union demands, perhaps because leaders did not think they could attain a change since only new factory settings would alleviate it. Lemlich also complained about the fact that bosses treated the women as machines, calling them "names that are not pretty to hear." She noted that there were no dressing rooms for women in the shops, so they had to hang their hats and coats on hooks along the walls. Women struggled to obtain decent clothing, Lemlich explained, noting the cost of clothing and the fact that women often made their own clothes from remnants. Finally, Lemlich complained about the system of fines, which was an official union demand.

Lemlich's discussion of the bosses' offensive treatment of women workers, when seen in a larger context of working women's culture, was part of an emerging critique of sexual harassment by working-class women in the 1910s. Lemlich said:

> The bosses in the shops are hardly what you would call educated men. And the girls to them are part of the machines they are running. They yell at the girls and they "call them down" even worse than I imagine the negro slaves were in the South. They don't use very nice language. They swear at us and sometimes they do worse—they call us names that are not pretty to hear.

This complaint emerges elsewhere in the records of this strike. Rose Pastor Stokes's comments to a reporter from *Collier's* implied that strikers discussed the issue of sexual harassment in their shop meetings: "[The strikers] have various grievances in various shops. It is more pay here, shorter hours there. Some of the smaller shops are unclean, filthy, in fact. There are foremen in certain factories who insult and abuse girls beyond endurance."[61] William Mailly, writing for the *New York Call*, noted that women workers endured "the tyranny, and sometimes worse, of petty bosses and foremen."[62] These complaints may seem vague. What did Lemlich mean when she said that "sometimes they do worse"? What sorts of names are "not pretty to hear"? What did Stokes mean by the words "insult and abuse"? To what did Mailly, echoing Lemlich, refer by decrying the "tyranny, and sometimes worse," of bosses?

Sexual harassment was a common occurrence in factories, but it did not yet have that label to identify it and was therefore very difficult to organize against. Nevertheless, working women succeeded in legiti-mating it as a political issue worthy of public debate. While not part of official union demands in the Uprising of the 20,000, sexual harassment was reflected in future garment strikes' demands. This was a significant accomplishment. Sexual harassment functioned as a form of worker control, creating an atmosphere of fear and intimidation. As in the 1940s factories studied by George Lipsitz, some foremen and owners demanded sexual favors from women in exchange for better posi-tions.[63] This was especially possible in piecework, where the kind of piece one was assigned to do could made a difference in pay of up to 50 percent. But as historian Mary Bularzik argues, sexual harassment was difficult to fight or even name, because women were supposed to control male sexuality through their own virtuous behavior:"To admit that sexual contact, even conversation, occurred, was to be blamed for it."[64] In political theorist Nancy Fraser's terms, the family functioned as a depoliticizing enclave for sexual issues, which were defined as private, relationship matters rooted in courtship and family. In this depoliticizing discourse, the issue was not control of the female workforce, but of attraction or of "fatherly" affection. The privatization of sexuality explains the lack of language to discuss it openly.[65]

Despite these forces denying the political import of sexual harass-ment, working women discussed this problem on the job, commiser-ating and sharing information,[66] and during the shirtwaist strike they made their complaint a matter of public debate. To understand how they could achieve this, we need to consider both the nature of the work-place subculture and the kinds of "discursive resources" available. According to Fraser, a key part of political struggle is the contest to shape interpretations of needs and rights; the contest is delineated by the discursive resources available to a given group, including the vocabulary and the narrative conventions with which people construct individual and collective stories about their grievances and their identities.[67]

The language of ladyhood, rooted in fashion and dime novel reading, provided one discursive frame in which to understand sexual harass-ment. The dime novels women read and discussed at the shop regularly narrated sexual harassment at the factories in terms that exposed and condemned it and defended the working heroine's virtue. The novels made it clear that the bosses and foremen exploited wage-earning women's need to keep jobs. In *Leonie Locke*, the foreman threatens to fire Leonie if she makes "a scene before the rest of the girls" because of his advances. At the end of the day, he uses the pretext of fining Leonie for botched work to summon her into his office, where they will be alone:

"You have spoiled the whole of the work intrusted to you today. I will point out where your mistake lies, and if you think you can remedy it, well and good; if not, it shall be charged to your account. Step this way, please." When Leonie refuses, she is fired. In *Willful Gaynell, or The Little Beauty of the Passaic Cotton Mills*, the foreman asks Gaynell for a kiss in payment for a botched piece of cloth. Indeed, shop floor sexual harassment is often the origin of dime novel villainy: the foremen in both of these books pursue the heroines throughout their adventures.[68] Dime novel heroines always resisted the harassment of foremen and bosses and eventually triumphed over their adversaries. Indeed, the ladyhood of the heroines stood in contradistinction to the ways foremen treated them.

To draw on Fraser's interpretive framework, the dime novels served as one available narrative with which women could express a grievance and ground their identities as ladies who deserved to be treated as such. The importance of working women's ladyhood to the emerging critique of sexual harassment is evident in the terms Lemlich used to explain her grievance. She began with a sentence that seems oddly classist for a great labor radical schooled in revolutionary ideologies: "The bosses in the shops are hardly what you would call educated men." Lemlich, who had fought for her own education against parents, religious authorities, and state authorities in Russia, probably drew on the rhetoric surrounding ladyhood, which came in part from dime novels.[69]

While fictional villains came from various classes, the hero who recognized the working girl to be a lady always came from a wealthy family and was well-educated and refined. Rose Schneiderman recalled that the dime novels she read gave her a "special taste in men. Among other traits, I wanted them well-read and cultured."[70] Sadie Frowne voiced this same sentiment seven years before the shirtwaist strike in her story of harassment at her shop. Explaining that the problem had been redressed, she said, "Now the men all treat me very nicely. It was just that some of them did not know better, not being educated." Frowne, a union member and avid dime novel reader, also believed that "It is good to have an education; it makes you feel higher. Ignorant people are all low. People say now that I am clever and fine in conversation."[71] Two years after the shirtwaist strike, a group of working women formed a "society" to fight sexual harassment that they called, significantly, "The Young Ladies Educational Society." One worker described it this way in *Life and Labor*:

The boss from the shop was always fresh with the girls. He liked to see us blush, so we made a society, called "The Young Ladies Educational Society," and we was not to stand the freshness of the boss. But we was afraid of him, and so we couldn't help each other. Once he touched me, very fresh like, and I cried, and he said, "Lets be good friends, Rosie, and to show you how good I means it, you take supper mit me in a swell hotel, with music and flowers, see?" And I says, "So! Supper mit you—swell hotel! Well I ask my ma," and he said, "Don't do it. You say you going to sleep at a friend's house" and I was trembling so I couldn't nearly do my work, and when my ma sees me, she says, "What's the matter Rosie?" and I says, "Nothing," because she's sad, my ma is, 'cause I have to work so hard and can't have no education.[72]

Here again, working women drew on dime novel rhetoric, combining ladyhood and "education" in the name of their organization, even though, or perhaps because, their labor meant they could not have a formal education. Their rhetoric contained both a defense of women and a poignant, utopian longing for their own schooling.

These uses of the dime novel narrative may be seen as destructive to overall class-cohesiveness. Nevertheless, the presence of the rhetoric in even seasoned radical Lemlich's description of sexual harassment speaks to the importance of the dime novel narrative for articulating such an unspeakable grievance. The other rhetorical convention that Lemlich used was to say that working women were "called down" even worse than slaves had been in the South. Here she adapted longstanding male working-class rhetoric about "free" labor versus slave labor. Some early nineteenth-century workers constructed themselves as "white" by contrasting their status with that of slaves, and demanded that as "free men" they deserved better treatment.[73] These two working-class rhetorical conventions contained contradictions and built on existing hierarchies, but they allowed Lemlich to articulate her grievance; their presence reveals the paucity of other legitimating discourses available to working women at the time.

While the issue of sexual harassment was not an official demand in the shirtwaist strike, it may have been a point of negotiation for individual shops. In addition, by making sexual harassment an issue of public debate, working women initiated a discussion that lasted beyond this strike. Later in 1910, more than 40,000 workers in Chicago's garment industry struck. The WTUL publicly demanded "all improper language in addressing the girls or in giving orders by foremen or others in authority to be strictly prohibited."[74] In addition, the WTUL interviewed strikers in the first month of the strike and created a document for wide distribution that explained women's grievances, including sexual harassment:

Abusive and insulting language is frequently used by those in authority in the shops. This is especially intolerable to the girls, who should have the right to work without surrendering their self-respect. No women should be subjected by fear of loss of her job to unwarranted insults.[75]

The WTUL further publicized striking women's claims of sexual harassment in Chicago shops by printing their stories in the WTUL journal, *Life and Labor*.[76]

Striking garment workers in Cleveland in 1911 also made an end to sexual harassment a union demand. The ILGWU widely publicized this claim in city newspapers throughout the Midwest in an effort to persuade regional merchants to cancel orders with nonunion Cleveland shops. This tactic ensured that the grievance of sexual harassment would become well known to both working- and middle-class people.[77] In 1912, the end of sexual harassment became a *primary* demand in the Kalamazoo corset strike. Workers exposed the particular injustices at the Hatfield factory, where young women received preferential treatment on the job and evening entertainment if they provided sexual favors to employers.[78] Working women continued to use language directly rooted in cultural practices of ladyhood to express their demands. In 1913, striking underwear and kimono makers in New York declared that they "wanted to be treated like ladies." As one worker said, "With the union behind us . . . [the bosses] wouldn't dare use the same language to us."[79]

Women also escaped the privatizing nature of "fatherly affection" by embracing the freedom of orphans, so celebrated in the dime novel narratives. Rose Schneiderman recalled that one boss, confronted by union representatives about pinching women workers, replied, " 'Why Miss Schneiderman, these girls are like my children.' The shop chairlady answered, 'Mr. Aptheker we'd rather be orphans.' " An entire shop took that attitude in fighting sexual harassment by a boss who claimed a "fatherly" affection. They waged the "famous 'orphan strike,' " as one union representative called it, and their single demand was: "The girls wanted to be 'orphans.' "[80]

Evidence of women's political subjectivities can be discerned in these challenges to sexual harassment. Women did not coin a term for the offensive behaviors they fought against; rather, they created terms for themselves that indicated how they demanded to be treated: as "ladies" and as "orphans." When women made dime novels part of their workplace culture, they incorporated their narratives into the range of discursive resources available to help them resist the shame and disempowerment that often accompanied daily workplace oppressions, including sexual harassment. Indeed, "ladyhood" operated as a public identity for working women which justified their presence in the workplace and city streets. When they went on strike, they drew on the identities they created in the daily life at the shop in order to form new identities as strikers. Just as the dime novel narratives centered on a validation of the working-girl heroine, women focused on validating their own worth as working women.[81]

Clara Lemlich, in her *New York Evening Journal* article, next complained that the shops had no dressing rooms in which women could hang their street clothes. This complaint was not expressed in the official union demands. Indeed, Lemlich's remarks about clothing, which comprised about 40 percent of the article, revealed an emerging language of political entitlement that leaders in the ILGWU, WTUL, and SP did not build upon. Lemlich explained that the lack of dressing rooms in the shops forced women to hang their coats and hats on hooks along the walls (see fig. 4.4). "Sometimes a girl has a new hat," she said. "It never is much to look at because it never costs more than fifty cents, but it's pretty sure to be spoiled after it's been at the shop." Lemlich then used the issue of clothing rhetorically to counter the fact that, to the bosses, the women "are part of the machines they are running":

> We're human, all of us girls, and we're young. We like new hats as
> well as any other young women. Why shouldn't we? And if one of
> gets a new one, even if it hasn't cost more than fifty cents, that

4.4 Garment workers often hung their hats on nails on the wall.

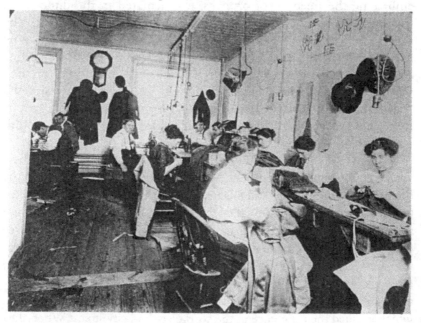

means that we have gone for weeks on two cent lunches—dry
cake and nothing else.

Lemlich was not simply arguing that women deserved to have adequate
clothing, but that they should be treated in accordance with the respect
they showed themselves, that is, as human beings, not as machines.

A demand for dressing rooms in the face of such oppressive and
dangerous conditions might seem trivial or even narcissistic. However,
Lemlich's remarks would have resonated with the concerns of working
women who dressed as ladies. She drew on their shared language to
articulate her grievance within a strike context. The wish-image
embedded in the working ladies' fashion, that is, the utopian desire to
be valued, was already tied to workplace practices and culture, as
women displayed, discussed, and even made their clothing at work.
Lemlich linked this working-class utopian imagination to the collective
action of the strike. Her demand for dressing rooms was thus both
literal and symbolic. Lemlich knew that such a demand would challenge the very ways that industrial labor devalued working women's
lives; it contained a complex defense of working women's humanity
against workplace oppression.

Lemlich continued her discussion by connecting clothing to the
prevalent strike grievance that wages were too low:

> I have known many girls who were never able to buy a hat at all.
> . . . They are the ones who earn \$3 a week. They take the clothes of
> the girls better off—those who earn \$6 or \$7 a week—after they
> have really been worn out. That's how they manage to get along.

She then contrasted the value of the goods women made with their
own value as workers, providing details on how women produced their
own clothing:

> Some girls can buy only one, perhaps two shirtwaists a year—
> while they help to make thousands of them. They make their
> own dresses after they have worked thirteen or fourteen hours a
> day, made with remnants that cost altogether \$1 or \$1.50.

Later in life, Lemlich recalled that when she joined the Socialist Party,
an older male mentor explained to her the principles of Socialist
unionism: "He started with a bottle of milk—how it was made, who
made the money from it through every stage of its production. Not only
did the boss take the profits, he said, but not a drop of that milk did you
drink unless he allowed you to." Lemlich recalled that similar ideas had
already occurred to her while working in the shops. "It was funny, you

know, because I'd been saying things like that to the girls before. But now I understood it better and I began to use it more often—only with shirtwaists."[82] Lemlich thus combined Socialist discourse with elements of women's daily practices of ladyhood in her demand for higher wages.

Lemlich was hardly typical of the striking workers. But that even Lemlich, who had the discursive resources of the radical subculture at her disposal, drew on the language of ladyhood to articulate a sense of entitlement, demands for dressing rooms, and an end to sexual harassment indicates the importance of working ladyhood to the strike culture as well as to workplace culture. Lemlich's rhetoric differed markedly from that of other leaders. Only one source, a single article in the *New York Call*, picked up on this strain of working-class culture, and claimed that women needed higher wages in order to gain "more and better clothes, larger and better lives."[83] Although the strike leaders gave attention to women's grievance about sexual harassment in the years after the shirtwaist strike, they persisted in seeing women's dress as an impediment to successful strikes, rather than a crucial part of working women's consciousness. Issues related to dress were not reflected in future strike grievances, nor did Lemlich's rhetoric about dress become union rhetoric.

In contrast to the process of articulating grievances, which happened mostly behind closed doors, women's picketing occurred daily and visibly in the public space of city streets. Both activities were crucial to the formation of women's subjectivities as strikers, but picketing publicly enacted political identity. For most strikers, picketing was far more central to the strike effort than the meetings with city officials or negotiations with owners, which they heard about secondhand. Picketing was an immediate battle: women forged subjectivities as strikers in opposition to challenges by strike breakers and the violent repression of thugs and police. As chapter 3 noted, employers, police, and magistrates contested striking women's picketing in particularly gendered terms and attempted discursively to deny their claims to political subjectivity. At the same time, they utilized longstanding strike-breaking techniques, including violence, mass arrests, and harsh sentences. Working women were familiar with middle-class perceptions of them as compromised in virtue because of their labor. On the picket lines they faced related accusations that their public actions made them "streetwalkers." Strikers did not respond to this array of challenges by becoming timid or by adopting a rational demeanor that would convince others of their respectability. Rather, they created a flamboyant strike culture that validated display, physically aggressive heroism, and even fun on the picket lines. In the process, they transformed public space and challenged its normative definition as a native-born, white, middle-class, male domain.

A sense of striking women's behavior on the picket lines can be pieced together by carefully reading a range of sources. As chapter 3 demonstrated, neither newspaper reports nor leaders' strategic representations can be accepted as "accurate." Clues to a different story can be found in admissions or contradictions in leaders' own descriptions of the strike, as well as in congruences among a wide variety of written sources. In addition, some leaders wrote about the strike in different terms after its completion, when they no longer needed to promote the strikers.

Labor leaders regularly admitted that they were not conveying all the stories about picket line activities when they defended striking women as victims. Their comments are circumspect, and probably crafted strategically to diffuse accusations of pro-union bias, but they provide important clues. Helen Marot, secretary of the WTUL, reported that "with strangely few exceptions" picketers "showed remarkable self-control":

> They had been cautioned from the first hour of the strike to insist on their legal rights as pickets, but to give no excuse for arrest.... But for many the provocations were too great and retaliation began after the fifth week. It occurred around the factories where the strikers were losing, where the peace methods were failing and where the passivity of the pickets was taunted as cowardice.

Marot thus conceded the occasional violence of the strikers, but narrativized it as a reasonable response to diminishing options. Reformers Sue Ainslie Clark and Edith Wyatt noted that the "exceptions" in which women acted violently "must, of course, be mentioned in the interests of truth." In spite of the advice of the union, picketers struck back when they were attacked "in two or three cases." Furthermore, "in a few cases they became excited and attacked strike breakers." In one, the female strikers agreed to picket "peacefully and quietly" but later "on their own admission, which was most disarming in its candor, they became careless and 'too gay.' They went picketing in too large numbers and were too noisy." Clark and Wyatt argued that if these aspects of the strike were not mentioned they would "convey a false impression that every striker arrested had as much sense and force of character as Natalya Urusova [a striker held up as an example of a virtuous victim]."[84] Clark and Wyatt narrated women's violence as part of an irrepressible adolescent spirit; they did not condone it but they also did not condemn it.

These accounts stressed that the union clearly instructed the strikers on correct behavior. This served to distance "the union" and its policies from the activities of the striking women who had been "too gay." Union leaders sought to win public approval in part by appearing to be a reasonable organization that could bargain fairly with management and, crucially, control the workers. Part of what a union agreement provides employers is an assurance that workers will not strike as long as employers hold up their end of the contract. This can place union leaders at odds with workers' own practices of resistance. Thus the union needed to control strikers' behavior on the picket line (or at least how most people perceived it) not only to prevent arrests but also to promote an image of the union as being in control of the situation. When the strikers rejected the compromise drawn up by the union and the Manufacturer's Association, they shattered this image. At this point, AFL representative Eva McDonald Valesh abandoned the leadership's line about picketers' nonviolence and actively sought to distance the union from the strikers. She painted a much more violent picture of the picketers than did any other leader:

> We do not maintain that all the girls who are arrested are dealt with unfairly. I know of two instances where the girls should not only have been arrested, but where they received what they deserved when they were sent to jail. We tell them exactly what they may not do under the law, and we are constantly urging them to remain within the law. Now and then an overzealous girl goes outside of her instructions and the law.[85]

While Valesh's comment shored up the reputation of the ILGWU, and by extension the AFL, it also hinted at a crucial fact of the shirtwaist strike: picketing was a worker-centered activity largely out of the direct control of ILGWU, WTUL, and SP leaders, particularly because women picketed at hundreds of shops across the city.

The most important source for determining the style of picketing enacted by strikers is Socialist leader Teresa Malkiel's didactic story *The Diary of a Shirtwaist Striker*, which was published serially in the *New York Call* after the strike was over. Malkiel wrote from the perspective of a fictional striker, carefully shaping her account to both appeal to working women readers and school them in the principles of unionization and Socialism. This source differs from others in two key respects: Malkiel wrote it specifically for working women rather than for the general public, and she wrote it after the strike's conclusion. Thus, there was no need to maintain the union's line that picketing women were simply nonviolent, innocent victims of aggression. Indeed, Malkiel's account indicates that even as leaders (including Malkiel herself) produced texts praising women's passivity, striking women themselves created a system of value in which picketers known for their bravery, physical aggression, and cunning gained status and notoriety. Malkiel's narrative reflects her own perspective, not that of striking workers. However, when she appealed to a working-class female audience she celebrated a physically aggressive and proud heroism that she obscured in her writings during the strike.

During the strike, Malkiel wrote an article for the *New York Call*'s special edition, which striking women sold across the city. At that time, she admitted only that picketing women occasionally called strike breakers "scabs":

> Their instructions from the union are—moral suasion all and every time, but occasionally a girl will lose her temper and call out "Scab, you took away my bread," and for this crime she is sure to face arrest, fine and very often imprisonment.[86]

In *The Diary of a Shirtwaist Striker*, Malkiel directly contradicted her earlier statements. She suggested not only that workers initiated violence on the picket lines, but that they saw it as heroic. Malkiel's diarist does not confine herself to yelling at scabs, but engages in a "fist fight" with her former best friend, Mame, who is a strike breaker—in the diarist's words, "a mean, vile, paltry scab from scabby land." The diarist recounts that she and a fellow striker, Fanny, approached Mame, who began yelling, giving a hired thug the excuse to attack Fanny. "And what could I do but lay it in to Mame, even if she had been my friend?" asks the diarist. "I'm not a bit sorry for giving her that lesson; she needed it badly." In another day's entry, the diarist reflects on strike breakers again:

> I think [scabs] deserve more pity than anything else, for they're still blind to the truth. But on the other hand, some of them scabs are so darn stupid and pig-headed that it doesn't do them any harm to get a licking once in a while.

Strikers in Malkiel's account heroically defend the picket line and the cause and do not hesitate to issue threats of physical harm and then back them up. One fictional worker, Rose, convinces her wavering co-workers to stick with the strike by arguing: "Lord help those of you who [go back to work]—we'll break every bone in your body." Malkiel narrated such stories as triumphs, moments of power in which strikers acted with bravery and heroism for their cause.[87] She probably included episodes of picket line antics and violence in order to capture readers' attention and direct it to the didactic message about Socialism contained in the diarist's reflections.

Such a value on physically aggressive heroism appears elsewhere in the historical record. Both pro-union sources and news reports described two specific picket line tactics: damaging strike breakers' clothing and throwing rotten eggs at strike breakers, employers, and the police. Early in the strike, leaders drew up and distributed an educational flyer to strikers entitled "Rules for Pickets." Most of the seven rules simply recount the legalities of picketing ("Don't walk in groups of more than two or three. Don't stand in front of the shop; walk up and down the block"). However, others provide a hint of the unwanted behavior that occurred on the line: "Don't get excited and shout when you are talking. Don't put your hand on the person you are speaking to. Don't touch his sleeve or button. This may be construed as a 'technical assault.'"[88] The specific mention of "button" is curious. Newspapers reported that police often arrested strikers for pulling the buttons off the coats of strike breakers, or even those of the police themselves. Indeed, newspapers focused extensively on how striking women attacked strike breakers' clothing, as chapter 3 discussed.[89] Although those accounts could be exaggerated or even fabricated, one arrested picketer revealed that clothing indeed posed a temptation. She insisted on her innocence by repeating the union's proscriptions: "I asked [the strike breaker] quietly and persuasively if she would not quit the job. I told her we were on the verge of winning the big battle. I was particular not to even touch her dress with my hands, for we have been warned to do peaceful picketing."[90] Buttons were an especially symbolic target. Missing buttons made coats and suit jackets less functional in the cold weather, but they also could signal a lack of self-respect. One middle-class woman who got a job as a dressmaker in order to gain material for a book found that the coat she wore specifically to pass as a "working girl" rendered her an outcast. Her coat was unacceptable not because it was shabby but because several buttons were missing, which signaled to her co-workers that she lacked pride.[91] Thus, when striking women became "too gay," they may have subjected strike breakers to an attack with significant symbolic meaning.

Striking women also threw rotten eggs at strike breakers, both to humiliate them and to harm their clothing. Bad eggs were readily available from street vendors who could not sell them. One pro-union writer, in the course of defending striking women as peaceful, admitted that they threw eggs: "There have been hundreds of arrests throughout the city. Girls still in their teens have been heavily fined or committed to the workhouse when their worst offense has been the throwing of an egg or two, which almost invariably missed the mark."[92] Likewise, newspaper reports were replete with descriptions of flying eggs and spoiled clothing. While the pro-union writer confirmed striking women's feminine gender identity by emphasizing their bad aim, newspaper reports conferred better throwing arms upon them. One article claimed that a striker, Lena, threw an egg at the foreman of her factory and missed. The foreman reportedly "turned and smiled at Lena and made scornful remarks about her throwing abilities." The article continued, "That was enough. Lena began to throw eggs. She did not miss after the first throw. In a moment Grossman looked like an animated omlet. He rushed at the line and the pair clinched, half of the omlet being tranferred to Lena." Newspapers reported that Anna Rosen was committed to Blackwell's Island for five days on the charge of assaulting a manufacturer in the face with a bad egg; five young women were fined ten dollars apiece for assaulting Police Detective Kemp with eggs; and many strikers faced fines for throwing eggs at strike breakers.[93] While it is difficult to discern if these specific reports were accurate or the accused were guilty, egg-throwing was certainly a part of women's strike tactics.

The Diary of a Shirtwaist Striker suggests that striking women enjoyed evading the police, and that picketers gained notoriety among their peers for their antics, their physical aggression, and their ability to avoid arrest. As the diarist says, "We have our fun with those cops." Malkiel's fictional account indicates that many strikers did not present the calm demeanor she described in strike publicity, but pushed the limit of what they could get away with and still evade arrest. "The wrong ones are sure to be punished," the diarist relates. "We've had twenty arrests today and, as luck would have it, the most helpless and timid were among those caught." Evasion could become a game. Some of Malkiel's stories contain a hint of dime novel adventures. The diarist specifically celebrates Rebecca, "one of our dare-devils," and the "excitement" she creates for the rest. The judge, she explains, has already placed Rebecca under bonds to prevent her from going near the factory. Rebecca is not discouraged; she "followed the forelady of her shop across the river and laid it into her so she won't be able to sit for a long time to come." Her boss subsequently goes to the striker's meeting hall with a detective and a warrant for Rebecca's arrest, but Rebecca runs into the kitchen, puts on a big apron, and sits in the corner, peeling potatoes. The diarist explains, "We girls nearly burst our sides laughing while the detective kept searching for her from roof to basement, looking into every closet, but he ain't no match for Rebecca; she knew how to evade him when he got very close to her." The diarist explains that Rebecca was later "whizzed off in an automobile" to the home of "one of them millionaires until the danger is over." Meanwhile, Rebecca dresses in fine clothes as a disguise when she attends strike events. "I wished so much that every one of us girls could dress that nice," muses the diarist.[94]

Malkiel's story is fiction, and there is no evidence that suggests such an event ever really occurred. However, Malkiel narrated Rebecca's evasion of the villainous police detective and employer in terms similar to a dime novel adventure. In addition, Rebecca is rewarded by becoming a lady, living and dressing like a millionaire, much like the dime novel heroine who gains her secret inheritance. Clearly, Malkiel appealed to workers by celebrating the strike as an adventure and strikers as heroines.

The physical aggression and antics described by Malkiel are corroborated by dozens of newspaper reports. Police arrested Annie Berman for being noisy and daring a policeman to arrest her. Ada Hoffman faced a jail term for assaulting a strike breaker who was a "former sweetheart." She reportedly told him off and slapped him in the face, at which point the other picketers broke into cheers. Two other ingenious strikers allegedly incorporated a brave prank into their tactics of preventing strike breakers from working: they snuck into the back door of the factory, took the freight elevator to the eighth floor, ran onto the shop floor and yelled, "Fire!" The strike breakers cleared the building. Papers also recounted numerous incidents of strikers rescuing arrested women from the police by charging them. While we cannot depend on the specific facts of any of these reports, the newspapers and Malkiel's story, with very different interests and agendas, both stress a physically aggressive heroism and a sense of fun on the picket lines.[95] Like the Tennessee textile workers studied by Jaqueline Dowd Hall and the Boston telephone operators studied by Stephen Norwood, women incorporated elements of a youth culture into picket line heroism.[96] Violence in the shirtwaist strike had more than one meaning. As with the Lawrence strikers studied by Ardis Cameron, violence was currency in the contest over public space, but it also functioned to sustain the strikers in their newfound identities, as dramas, antics, and bravery were applauded and approved by the group.[97] Working ladyhood and the radical subculture both could support this terrain of strikers' identities.

The gap between the terrain of strikers' subjectivities and the leaders' representations indicates that striking women created a "subaltern counterpublic," that is, a semi-autonomous public space of political debate and exchange that existed within U.S. culture but was not fully visible or comprehensible to the larger society.[98] Their subjectivities were in tension with forces in the wider culture that obscured or delegitimated them. Striking women's exclusion from full participation in the public debate enforced this division. The vast majority of striking women did not gain access to those social contexts of contact with the press, city officials, or the general public in which exhibiting the appearance of bourgeois rationality and seriousness made sense. Most white middle-class men formed subjectivities within contexts that valued and enforced a rational demeanor, but working-class immigrant women were largely excluded from those contexts.

The strike changed that for only a few. Pauline Newman, for example, conducted a fund-raising tour through the Northeast for the ILGWU during the strike, and spoke to countless middle- and upper-class women's groups. Such experiences schooled her in middle-class customs and behaviors, and Newman herself noted how dramatically she changed. (She may have drawn on working-class practices to adapt, however. Leon Stein recalled that Newman "cultivated this almost British-sounding accent" in order to win over her wealthy audiences— a practice she may have learned from working ladies in the shops.)[99] A small number of strikers served on committees that met with city officials, like one group who visited the mayor in December to complain of police brutality (fig. 4.5). The photograph of this group, published in the *New York Evening World,* reveals that the strikers dressed "tastefully," which was doubtlessly a prerequisite for being taken seriously. There are no flamboyant hats and no fur stoles, in marked contrast to other strike photographs, which reveal a range of styles from quite plain to very ornate. Indeed, it is difficult to discern in the photograph which of the six are the wealthy WTUL members Mary Dreier and Helen Marot.[100] The four strikers pictured here learned to dress tastefully, probably borrowing items to do so, and likely rendered themselves "rational girl strikers" in the meeting with the mayor as well. But these experiences were uncommon. Most of the thousands of strikers developed their own culture of heroism and their own political subjectivities from the cultural resources that *were* available to them.

This is not to suggest that women's fashion or dime novel reading made them go on strike, but that they could *use* these resources to construct political identities. Sources even indicate that some working women used the same resources to resist the pressure to strike. Teresa Malkiel noted that some middle- and upper-class women told picketers that striking was "unladylike" and reformer Lillian Wald believed that some working women themselves thought that "ladies" did not strike or belong to unions.[101] Newspapers during the shirtwaist strike reported that one scab refused to join the strike because she hoped to marry a millionaire.[102] This should not be surprising, for two reasons. First,

4.5 A strike committee en route to a meeting with the mayor.

working ladyhood inverted a notion of prestige in order to create a utopian practice of entitlement. That entitlement, however, did not lead inevitably to efforts for progressive social change. Rather, as historian Carolyn Steedman shows, such entitlement can turn to an embittered "politics of envy" that finds expression in individualism and conservativism. Steedman analyzes her mother's class envy and working-class conservativism in 1950s England, a very different situation from the one studied here. Steedman's mother did not forge or share her consumer practices within an active community of workers; indeed, she was quite isolated. Nevertheless, Steedman's analysis provides an example of one conservative use of a working-class rhetoric of entitlement.[103]

Second, we should expect that if women used shared cultural practices to *support* identities as strikers—"we want to be treated as ladies"—then strike breakers would be all the more likely to choose the same powerful metaphors to *resist* a strike call, claiming that striking was not ladylike. When workers constructed themselves as strikers and ladies, they also defined scabs—the numerical minority—as traitors and outsiders. As Judith Butler argues, interpellation both fixes one's identity with a label, and opens up a space of agency as one's social existence is recognized, albeit often in unfavorable terms.[104] When strikers interpellated strike breakers as "scabs," they endowed them with a political identity, albeit a negative one. Strike breakers resisted the terms of their definition by drawing on available discursive resources, including the same tropes of ladyhood. It cannot be overemphasized that the cultural practices of ladyhood did not make women take up a particular political position; rather they provided resources that could be marshalled for a number of ends. Thus, we must acknowledge that even though this dramatic story of more than 20,000 women creating pro-union political subjectivities involves the vast majority of New York's shirtwaist workers, there is another story about a minority of workers who concurrently created anti-union political subjectivities.

The strike breaker who reportedly planned to marry a millionaire drew on a particularly powerful resource: the dime novel ending. Recall that the working-girl heroines of dime novels did *not* pursue collective action to remedy their workplace oppression. Rather, they engaged in a series of adventures rewarded ultimately by marriage to a millionaire and transcendence of the workplace altogether. Of course, as chapter 2 argued, the endings did not constitute the whole of the reading experience. Through the bulk of the novels the heroines successfully met demanding adventures, potentially providing support for working women's physical aggression while picketing. Nevertheless, the endings are significant: marriage to a millionaire *could* be read as incompatible with a strike. The woman who did not want to strike because she planned to marry a millionaire staked her defense on this trope of reward and transcendence.[105]

Even the apparently conservative dime novel ending could have another meaning for strikers, however, because of the participation of Rose Pastor Stokes in the strike. Rose Harriet Pastor was a working girl who fulfilled the dime novel fantasy and married millionaire Graham Phelps Stokes in 1905, just four years before the shirtwaist strike. Lower East Side women instantly made her a popular hero. Pastor caused a sensation whenever she appeared in working-class neighborhoods; the *New York Herald* reported that "the young Hebrew girls on the east side regard her as an oracle and a friend." Journalist Ella Wheeler Wilcox bemoaned the fact that many working women saw the marriage as a fulfillment of the "Laura Jean Libbey" novels, "which turn the heads of hundreds of poor girls."[106] Rose Pastor Stokes, who became an active Socialist, returned to New York City to serve as a leader in the shirtwaist strike. She spoke at large rallies and dozens of small shop meetings, and newspapers noted that she was immensely popular (fig. 4.6). A reporter described one speech in which "a score of girls surrounded her, listening rapt. 'Nothing can be gained unless you hold together,' she told them—just what any number of other people had told them, but somehow it hadn't made the same impression."[107] Stokes's support suggested that there was no contradiction between the dime novel ending and a strike. Indeed, in the dime novels, the married heroines regularly returned to the factories in the last pages of the book to greet their old co-workers and to assert their working-class loyalty. The ending of *Willful Gaynell* features Gaynell visiting the factory, where her former co-workers receive her with cheers. "Little Gaynell would be a great lady now, they well knew; but they knew, too, she could never be proud and cold—would be in the future what she had been in the past, the staunch true friend of the noble working girls."[108] Rose Pastor Stokes's return could be read by strikers as the ultimate fulfillment of the dime novel ending. Indeed, her popularity as strike leader hinged on her status as popular hero, a status rooted in women's cultural practices of ladyhood.

Striking women enacted a diversity of political subjectivities in the shirtwaist strike, drawing on a cultural repertoire that included the meanings women made with fashion and dime novel fiction. Certainly, these were not the only resources available to working women. Women

4.6 Rose Pastor Stokes, the working girl who married a millionaire, speaking at a shop meeting during the strike.

like Clara Lemlich and Pauline Newman drew on Socialist principles when constructing themselves as strikers, and passed those principles along in strike meetings. However, for many working women, lady-hood already functioned as a public identity that resisted class, gender, and ethnic hierarchies. Ladyhood played upon working women's exclusion from full admittance to the cultural categories of "worker," "lady," or "American," despite their labor, their gender, and their country of residence. Working women likewise found themselves, as a group, excluded from a recognized political identity: they did not have full access to the resources of public exchange, nor did they gain admittance to contexts in which a rational and serious demeanor carried cultural capital. Working women had to "invent themselves" what it would mean to be strikers, and how to do it. Through the walkout, the process of forming grievances, and the daily task of picketing, striking women built on what was available to them to enact formal political identities. The specific ways they accomplished this were doubtlessly multiple and shifting; nevertheless, an understanding of women's cultural repertoire allows us to see that the terrain on which women built political identities included popular culture.

Consumer culture did not operate in opposition to political actions in the shirtwaist strike; nor did it cause radicalism. The analytical binary opposition between consumer culture and politics has caused us to lose some of our sense of political possibility. When we assume that consumer culture deflects people from political concerns, we foreclose an understanding of how people exercised limited agency, using the resources available. Furthermore, by assigning all historical subjects who acted in formal politics an Enlightenment subjectivity, we erase the struggle with cultural contradictions and hierarchies that many people faced when acting in the public arena. In addition, we perpetuate a dominant cultural myth that a stable Enlightenment-based subjectivity is necessary for political participation. By looking at the multiplicity of ways working women wrested political subjectivities from a society that meant to exclude them, we recover a glimpse of the diversity of political identities and the interrelationship of forms of social resistance.

Shirtwaist strikers effectively challenged who and what could be considered political. It is little wonder that their example sparked similar strikes across the country as women workers heard and read about their dramatic heroism. Leaders regularly credited the shirtwaist strike for initiating this trend in the nation's garment industry, among workers of many ethnicities and languages.[109] This strike wave not only organized the most women workers to that point in United States history, it also established strong garment industry unions that would represent immigrant workers throughout the twentieth century.

But in February 1910, such victories were not yet known. They can best be seen when taking a long view, across various strikes and over decades. Indeed, the shirtwaist strike failed to win union agreements with several of the large shops, including the Triangle Shirtwaist Company, and about 1,000 workers went back to their jobs with conditions unchanged. Gains in the other shops quickly eroded as manufacturers, knowing the limits of the union's strength, competed with the nonunionized shops. By late 1911, only a year and a half later, shirtwaist local 25 requested permission from the ILGWU for another general strike, and in 1913 shirtwaist workers did strike again, this time in concert with kimono and lingerie workers. For 145 shirtwaist workers, even this was too late: they died in a fire at the Triangle factory in 1911. Management kept doors locked to prevent workers from taking breaks—a safety issue that striking had attempted to reform—and workers could not escape the blaze. More than anything else, the Triangle fire pointed out the limitations of the 1909 strike.

For the former shirtwaist strikers, the 1909 strike brought sacrifice, hard work, excitement, and some moments of heroism—but it did not immediately change their oppressive working conditions. As important as the strike was to women's sense of dignity and their long-term interests in improved conditions and democratic participation, it did not allow them to transcend their daily struggles. Shirtwaist strikers went back to their everyday experiences, including long hours, dangerous conditions, a few fine articles of clothing, and discussions of dime novels and romance. Our story thus should not conclude with this strike, but return to women's everyday experiences. For to conclude here would be to place the strike in the same narrative position in this history as the marriage to the rich hero holds in dime novel romances: that of reward and magical transformation. Instead, chapter 5 returns to women's popular culture, and in particular that burgeoning industry that boomed at the same time that thousands of working women became strikers: the movies.

CHAPTER FIVE

MOVIE-STRUCK GIRLS

Motion Pictures and Consumer Subjectivities

[Working women walking on Eighth Avenue see] the flashing, gaudy, poster-lined entrances of Hickman's and of the Galaxy. These supply the girls with a "craze," the same that sends those with a more liberal allowance to the [stage] matinees. Their pictures spread out adventure and melodrama which are soul-satisfying.

—Ruth True, *The Neglected Girl* (1914)[1]

Mary's eyes were smoldering that day with the fire of strange yearnings. She moved about her work as one walking in a dream— burning with a life that was not the life around her.   —opening lines, print version of *What Happened to Mary* (1912)[2]

During the same years that working women went on strike in unprecedented numbers, they were creating a motion picture "craze." Working women attended movies by 1905, but only formed a distinctive "fan" relationship with them after 1908. As reformer Ruth True noted, women's fascination with the movies exceeded the experience of the films themselves. Young working women gazed at the "flashing, gaudy" posters that lined the entrances to nickelodeon theaters, daydreamed about stars and about becoming stars themselves, and attended motion pictures regularly to socialize and to imaginatively step into the visual fantasies of the silver screen. When these women consumed motion pictures, they created new urban experiences and occupied the public spaces of streets and theaters in new ways. They built particular and distinctive social practices around motion picture consumption and incorporated the movies into their established consumer practices around dime novels and fashion, weaving motion pictures into their identities as ladies. Like the strikes of the 1910s, the movies signaled a new relationship of working women to public life. Of course, the motion picture industry did not promote the democratic participation in economic decisions that unions had sought. But for working women, the movies became a parallel site of social change in the public realm.

Neighborhood theaters, called nickelodeons, boomed after 1905. In the scramble for more narratives to satisfy eager audiences, producers translated a plethora of print fiction genres into film form, including dime novel romances. Working women saw elements of the dime novel romance formula in a variety of short melodramas after 1908, as producers presented working heroines who encountered adventures, gained inheritances, or married millionaires. In July 1912, the Edison Company and *The Ladies' World*, a popular magazine, collaborated to produce the sensationally popular serial story *What Happened to Mary*. Edison released the story about a New York working woman in twelve twenty-minute film episodes to coincide with publication of the segments in print form in *The Ladies' World*. This successful collaboration would be the first in a long line of motion picture serials featuring female heroines. Mary and her successors excelled in their work, triumphed over personal danger, heroically saved others, and gained promotion and respect. Romance took a back seat to adventure in these narratives; the working heroines captured robbers, raced through burning buildings, and leapt from moving freight trains. They did not, however, go on strike.

The motion picture theaters constituted a new public space in the early twentieth century, uniquely open to working-class women of all ethnicities.[3] As historian Kathy Peiss notes, when movies moved from the arcade kinetoscopes to nickelodeons after 1905, women's attendance soared.[4] There were at least six hundred nickelodeons in greater New York City by 1910, showing movies to 1.5 million people, or a quarter of the city's population, each week. Most of this early audience was working class. Historian Steven Ross notes that 72 percent of those attending were blue collar workers, 25 percent were clerical workers, and only 3 percent belonged to the "leisure" class. Women's attendance was greater for this amusement than for any other in the city: they comprised 40 percent of the working-class audience in 1910.[5] Whereas many working-class parents believed that other places of public amusement, such as dance halls or amusement parks, were not appropriate for unchaperoned daughters, they thought the nickelodeons were safe and respectable. The motion picture theaters thus constituted a new public sphere. Film historian Miriam Hansen argues that while the movies certainly did not operate like Habermas's ideal of democratic exchange, they did serve as a new "public space, part of a social horizon of experience" for a new kind of collective, the audience.[6] Motion pictures, then, offered both new urban experiences and new kinds of commodities to working women.

Working women's public mobility allowed them to enact public subjectivities within consumer culture. As part of these new subjectivities, working women claimed an active gaze in the streets and in the local theaters. This gaze was a consumer gaze—that is, it was tied to and justified by a consumer activity—but it was not merely acquisitive. Rather, it was interwoven with complex narratives and fantasies. When working women gazed at posters, dreamed of stars, and attended shows, they enacted subjectivities in a new public arena and engaged contradictions that they experienced as immigrant women workers, just as they did in their consumption of fashion and dime novel products. The motion picture serials directly catered to working women with visual fantasies related to their established practices of ladyhood. The serials solicited an identification with heroines who desired—and achieved—lavish social recognition both as workers and as women, in jobs that delivered adventure. This is not to say that motion pictures were an arena of freedom for working women; theaters and the range and content of films themselves regularly replicated hierarchies working women found elsewhere in society. Nevertheless, women's social practices of motion picture consumption generated new resources for the creation of public identities.

This chapter explores working women's relationship to the movies with the methods used to examine their experiences with fiction and fashion in chapters 1 and 2. First, I analyze motion picture production, particularly how the industry shaped and limited the range and content of the products available for women's consumption. I will trace the emergence of the serials compared to other types of film narratives, and the film industry's production of early "fan" products. I turn next to working women's consumption of motion pictures, focusing on the social practices they made in relation to the movies. As in chapter 2, I will distinguish between the acts of consumption—buying tickets, looking at posters, attending theaters—and the imaginative experiences of the films themselves. All of these aspects of consumption worked together as women imbued "the movies" with significance.

Studying working women's experiences with motion pictures presents a unique problem: identifying which specific films to study. While working women's consumption of all types of popular culture was varied, many read an identifiable set of dime novels and dressed in particular and distinctive styles. However, they saw *all* types of motion pictures. Nickelodeons typically showed four or five short films on the same bill, interspersed with singers or vaudeville acts. Exhibitors demanded that distributors provide a mixed bill of different types of narratives. Working women saw them all: social problem films, Westerns, melodramas, comedies, labor-capital films, travel films, railroad dramas, adventure serials, and military films. The problem of assessing women's relationship to the movies is thus complex. Historian Kathy Peiss has focused on comedies produced before 1910, citing a 1907 source indicating that comedies were the most popular with early movie audiences. Peiss's results are important and pathbreaking, but largely predate 1908, the era when more complex dramatic narratives developed and working women formed more specific fan practices. Historian Elizabeth Ewen has looked at popular stars and the types of stories that they played in. This too stands as an important beginning, but is focused primarily on the feature film era, 1915 and after.[7]

Here I focus on the adventure serials, in particular *What Happened to Mary* and the long-lived *Hazards of Helen* (Kalem, 1914), because they had roots in dime novel formulas and were aimed at working women as well as a broader audience. The market for motion pictures was relatively undifferentiated; that is, everyone attended all the time rather than dividing into particular market segments according to different interests. However, by 1909, producers standardized and differentiated fictional film products into types of narratives that they knew would be more appealing to some segments of the audience than others. Like the early story papers of the 1840s, the mixed bill of nickelodeon theaters operated on the principal of "something for everyone." Working-class women constituted a significant portion of the motion picture audience; it was in producers' interests to maintain their loyalty while ensuring that films would entice the widest possible audience approval. The adventure serials, beginning with *What Happened to Mary*, grew directly out of dime novel romance conventions and tapped a female reading public through their connection with *The Ladies' World*, a "low-brow" women's magazine. More than any other type of narrative, they emerged from, and intended to reproduce, established fiction consumption practices of working women. Thus, the serials are the best place to start examining specific film texts in relationship to working women's social practices of film consumption during the formative years of 1909 to 1916.

The motion picture industry struggled to become big business in the early 1900s, and that struggle profoundly shaped the films that working women could see by 1909. Leading producers pursued three related goals in their efforts to organize the early film industry and maximize their profits. First, they attempted to control the production, distribution, and exhibition of films. Second, they increased the pace and volume of production, and third, they standardized the film product to make it as predictable and interchangeable as possible, while maintaining audience enthusiasm. These forces shaped and limited the narratives, but they did not eliminate creativity. Rather, scenario writers, directors, actors, and producers applied their creative energies at once to economic and aesthetic challenges in this rapidly developing form of visual storytelling. As with dime novels and fashion products, the relations of production conferred both limits and possibilities on the products. When those commodities entered social circulation, working women wound them into their own social practices and imbued them with their own meanings.

Some film and social historians have celebrated the relative lack of organization of the young film industry before Hollywood, seeing it as providing a particular possibility for working-class expression. They note the predominantly working-class immigrant audience for movies before World War I, the preponderance of narratives representing working-class life, and the large number of immigrants among the independent film producers, particularly after 1912. The silent movies, according to these historians, were largely produced by, represented, and were viewed by the working class. These historians celebrate the silent era as a time of relative freedom of expression for film makers.[8] In contrast, they see the Hollywood era as the time when movies became a big business and drove out working-class interests.

The relationship between working-class audiences and the developing popular culture industry of film is more complex than this view suggests. As a number of other film historians have pointed out, the industry wooed a middle-class audience as early as 1908. This is not, however, to claim that the movies were "middle class" rather than "working class." Indeed, to ascribe a class designation to a set of products deflects attention from how the capitalist marketplace shapes cultural products for all classes. The view that Hollywood signaled the decline of free expression because of the rise of rationalized production misconstrues the early industry and seems to assume that meaningful film can only be produced outside of the capitalist marketplace. Ironically, critics of the later, Hollywood era unwittingly maintain the bourgeois myth that some cultural artifacts under capitalism are free of market interests. However, as chapter 1 argued, this myth operated principally to maintain class distinction through commodities while

denying that it was doing so. When some film and social historians celebrate the early movies as free or working-class expression, they under-
estimate the ways that the young industry's strenuous attempts to rationalize and organize production profoundly shaped its products by 1909,
including those that overtly represented class conflict.

The emergence of the adventure serials was itself a result of economic
interests and requires a more nuanced analysis. The serials engaged
central issues of gender and class, but were standardized products of the
most rationalized arm of the film industry. They offered powerful representations of women as heroic workers but, like the dime novel
romances, did not represent working-class women's strikes or overt
political action. Indeed, with very few exceptions, the motion picture
industry did not make films that represented groups of women on strike.
While this omission was consistent with the dime novel formula, it
seems odd in the context of the dramatic strikes of the 1910s, especially
considering the fact that movies about male strikers were rather
common. As Steven Ross has pointed out, motion picture producers
created a genre they called the "labor-capital film," which represented
strike scenes from a variety of perspectives and served as a medium for
social debate about the role of labor unionism in U.S. society.[9] But
labor-capital films only very rarely represented groups of women strikers.
As a public realm of debate, the motion pictures replicated and even
accentuated exclusions that existed elsewhere in public life. These exclusions did not occur naturally; they were effects of producers' efforts to
standardize film production between 1908 and 1912.

Before 1908, many producers perceived the young U.S. film
industry to be in a crisis. The simultaneous emergence of the fictional
story film and the growth of nickelodeons around 1905 drew an ever-
expanding audience with a voracious appetite for new motion pictures.
As film historian Eileen Bowser notes, the French company Pathé-
Frères filled most of the spectacular demand for films in the United
States. Companies based in the United States felt hampered by the
depression of 1907 and by the distribution and exhibition system, and
were reluctant or unable to increase the capital investment necessary to
expand production. The system of distribution and exhibition in the
U.S. was entirely unregulated; films could be rented out repeatedly,
providing increased profits to distributors and exhibitors but limiting
producers' sales.[10]

The Edison Company led the move to gain control over production,
distribution, and exhibition by founding the Motion Picture Patents
Company (MPPC) in December of 1908 with a group of eight other

large producers, a distributor, and Eastman Kodak, the principal manufacturer of film stock. The MPPC consisted of many companies, such as Edison, that held patents for technology used in production and projection of motion pictures. By limiting rights to use of such technology to its members and licensees, the MPPC gained control of the industry, including the distribution system. Independent companies could and did exist, but they faced shortages of good materials and equipment, limited access to distributors, and regular lawsuits for patent infringement. Once the MPPC ensured that licensed producers would make tidy profits on their capital investments, the rate and scale of film production increased rapidly. The MPPC held the reins of the industry until 1912, when independent producers, and eventually the U.S. government, successfully challenged its monopolistic practices in court. During those four years, however, the film industry stabilized and underwent dramatic and irreversible changes.[11]

The crisis in the film industry was not only economic but also aesthetic. As producers created more, and more complex, narratives to please clamoring audiences, they found viewers could not follow the silent stories. After the formation of the MPPC, producers responded by changing the mode of narration to utilize visual cues that could be widely understood across differences in class or national origin, including an increased number of camera cuts, closer shots, and new styles of acting.[12] Bowser argues that the changes in American film production originating in 1908 and 1909 were as radical as those at any other time in film history, and profoundly altered the relationship between spectator and film narrative. Before 1905, motion picture producers supplied a variety of narratives to the new theaters, including "actuality" films, comedies or jokes rooted in vaudeville traditions, lantern-slide shows, and comic strips. Directors shot these early narratives in presentational style; that is, the camera viewed the action as though it were on a stage, mimicking the live theater experience. Such techniques did not work well with more complex fictional narratives. In response to this problem, producers layered an increased number of camera shots to create depth and point of view, effectively bringing the spectator's view into the frame of action. Spectators now viewed scenes as invisible participants rather than as a removed audience. Closer shots accentuated this sense of intimacy, as spectators could see subtle shifts in emotion in actors' faces and postures. As a result, acting styles moved away from the large gestures and pantomime that worked to convey emotion on the stage. All of these techniques made possible a more distinctive and elaborate imaginative relationship between film viewers and motion pictures, particularly viewers' closer identification with film stars, and led to the birth of the star system.

Once producers reformed the system of distribution so that it granted them more control and profit, they rationalized production in order to increase their rate and volume of film output. A principal change involved modifying the role of the director. Previously, directors typically came up with stories, conveyed their intentions to actors, and worked the photoplays out in short rehearsals before shooting. As producers sought to increase the number and complexity of fictional narratives this system became impractical. First, it was too slow. Second, it worked better with shorter, less complicated narratives than it did with the longer films in which directors layered shots in more complex ways. Increasingly, companies hired scenario writers to craft visual stories according to the emerging types or genres of film narratives. Producers incorporated editorial practices from the cheap fiction industry, or "the fiction factory," as writer William Wallace Cook called it, and hired many writers who also wrote for that industry. The *New York Times* in 1913 noted that scenario writers were valued most for their ability to write according to specific instructions: "Many of [the scenario writers] work on order. A company suddenly requires a play about a certain actor, a certain locality, or possibly an animal it has purchased. Immediately, the company communicates with one of its writers, tells its needs and asks for a script, 'within a day or so.' . . . Companies are always desirous of finding new authors in this by-order method." The *Times* asserted that story ideas themselves were a dime a dozen. Companies paid scenario writers to explain "in short, jerky clauses, the direction for every movement on the part of each actor." Bannister Merwin and James Oppenheim, both of whom wrote scenarios for *What Happened to Mary*, were two of the six successful writers that the *Times* named as making scenario writing a "lucrative profession" because they were willing and able to provide what producers wanted.[13]

In some cases, scenario writing was even more rationalized. While writers like Merwin, Oppenheim, and Cook supplied fully developed visual narratives in scenario form, others simply sent plot ideas to editors who then assigned them to staff writers to develop into movie scenarios. For the freelance writers or amateurs supplying ideas, scenario writing was not particularly lucrative. As in dime novel fiction writing, much of the financial risk and unpredictability of the business was borne by the writers rather than by the producers. In 1909, Cook answered a Vitagraph advertisement he saw in the newspaper that claimed "We pay $10 to

$100 for Picture Plays." Cook sent in an idea, and was shocked to receive a $10 check in return. Upon querying Vitagraph, Cook received a letter from the editor explaining that "The manuscript has to be revised in almost every instance in order to put it in practical shape for the directors. . . . The members of our staff, who are obliged to write practical working scenarios, appreciate the above facts because they know what it means to perfect a scenario with the synopsis of the story, the properties, settings, etc., etc." But mastering the art of "short, jerky clauses" would not raise Cook's rate appreciably: "The editor merely surmises, or so we think, that a thoroughly original manuscript in practical shape would be worth at least $25, but we seldom get one of that kind." Cook eventually did master the art of scenario writing, and in 1910 wrote a "good many" scenarios for an unnamed company that paid him $35 each. Cook complained that scenario writers were paid poorly, endured slow responses on scripts from movie companies, and were not listed as authors in the film credits. From his experiences in both dime novel and scenario writing, Cook considered, "Possibly the film manufacturers borrow their ideas of equitable treatment for the writer from some of the publishing houses."[14]

Such editorial control over scenario writing went hand-in-hand with creating a standardized product, which would make the industry more predictable and profit margins more stable. Films before 1909 ranged from 200 feet to 1000 feet in length; setting a standard length made it possible to set a single price for films, making them more interchangeable from a marketing perspective. In addition, producers sought to create customer loyalty by promoting films through company brand names as well as by genre. A distributor could put a Biograph drama in a package with an Kalem adventure serial episode and a Vitagraph comedy, for example, and exhibitors and audiences would have an approximate idea of what they would receive. Bowser notes that Biograph films were the most popular with U.S. audiences by 1910. As early as 1909, then, standardization meant that the creative energy of motion picture makers would be channeled into particular "lines" of roughly predictable products. Finally, the shift in film techniques was also part of the effort to standardize film products. Producers needed the widely understood visual cues to ensure audience involvement with the films. The new use of camera cuts and close shots invited strong emotional responses to the film.[15]

Ultimately, the purpose of a standardized product was to standardize audience attendance and emotional response to the films as much as possible. Producers wished not only to make *movies* but also to create a pleasurable movie-going *experience* that could be replicated on a weekly or even nightly basis. This involved shaping both industry structures and audiences' desires into a workable system of motion picture production and reception. Perhaps the most challenging element of this was capturing audience members' imaginations and desires in predictable and reproducible ways. Thus, it was at this point in film history (1908–1915) that producers began speaking of "spectators" conceived as individuals responding emotionally to a screen fantasy, as often as they used the older term "audience," which positioned viewers as a group.[16] It would prove very difficult to control the various meanings that viewers took from films, but quite possible to create enough of a satisfying emotional response to ensure increasing popularity and success for the newly structured industry.

The final ingredient necessary to make motion pictures big business was a wider audience at the theaters. Because the industry had developed with a predominantly working-class audience, this meant reaching out to the middle class. Some exhibitors did so by building new, large theaters in theater districts to remove motion pictures from their association with the immigrant, working-class neighborhood nickelodeons.[17] In addition, producers like Edison adopted a Progressive tone, arguing that films could be a tool of uplift for working and middle class alike. Like vaudeville producers two decades earlier, producers tailored films to please the desired middle class and even agreed to self-censorship to convince the public of their respectability.[18] But producers could not ignore their working-class customers altogether. Bowser notes that they tried to create "educational" films, but working-class audiences rejected them so exhibitors refused to rent them.[19] Nevertheless, the middle class had an effect on motion pictures long before its members attended movies in great numbers. Indeed, the need to please a middle-class audience, real or only wished-for, played a large role in determining which representations of working women would become standard in the movies.

According to Steven Ross, "social problem" films regularly featured groups of women workers, while labor-capital films almost never did. Social problem films emerged as part of the Progressive mission of some producers and focused on current social issues, including the exploitation of so-called "dependent" workers—women, children, and the elderly. While they regularly exposed the dark side of industrial capitalism, they represented women workers as victims, not as politically empowered strikers. Indeed, Ross notes that in social problem films, "working women were portrayed less as workers than as women in need of constant protection by well-intentioned males." Labor-capital films, however, represented male—not female—workers on strike. According to Ross, who counts 274 labor-capital films produced between 1905 and 1917, this genre conveyed a variety of political perspectives on strikes. But I have found only one film that definitely represented a group of women on strike. Young working-class female characters did appear in labor-capital films, sometimes in heroic roles, but usually as daughters of strikers, not workers or strikers themselves: their loyalty and heroism were defined by their family relationships. In addition, labor-capital films typically represented a single working-class heroine rather than groups of women.[20]

As chapter 3 noted, many middle-class people were accustomed to and comfortable with representations of working women as victims rather than as strikers. This may explain why film producers largely avoided the women's strikes as starting points for labor-capital films. A narrative that positioned working women as strikers would challenge both unregulated industrial capitalism and the prevalent masculine definition of political actors. Ross, however, praises the labor-capital film for "concentrat[ing] on a more controversial sector of the working class. Instead of focusing on unorganized women, children, and elderly wage earners, their plots dealt with adult male workers who labored in the nation's most contentious and highly organized industries." Such male workers, he notes, could not be construed as victims.[21] Ross fails to consider that the controversial element of a film sprang not from the sector of the working class it pictured, but from the modes of representation and narration it utilized. As vulnerable victims, immigrant women workers on the screen could solicit pity from audiences. But as political actors, young immigrant women were far more controversial than skilled white men who worked in the highly organized industries of the early twentieth century. Indeed, as chapter 3 showed, some middle-class commentators who *supported* the shirtwaist strike persisted in representing striking women as victims asking for charity even in the context of overt, dramatic, and often militant political action. Labor-capital films usually focused on the workers most favored by the AFL and those closest to attaining political legitimacy in the eyes of the middle class, particularly Progressives. Both social problem and labor-capital films bore the imprint of producers' goal to please—or minimally offend—a middle-class audience.

The one film that I have found that represented a group of women on strike, *The Girl Strike Leader* (Thanhouser, 1910), relied as much on the dime novel formula as on labor-capital film conventions to tell its story. Thanhouser released *The Girl Strike Leader* only five months after the

New York shirtwaist strike. In this film, producers did not represent working women merely as victims. Rather, the heroines take action by striking successfully to better their working conditions. At the end, the girl strike leader marries the factory owner, which validated her adventures as a striker and extricated her from labor altogether.[22] This film placed the strike in the position of adventures in the dime novel formula, treating women viewers to a familiar ending, but one quite different from the actual conclusion of the shirtwaist strike. Film historians have interpreted the marriage to the factory owner as undercutting the representation of class conflict, but for working women well-versed in dime novel romance conventions, the story could profoundly validate their actions as strikers by rewarding the heroine for brave adventures.[23]

The Girl Strike Leader fit into a developing genre of female adventure films, popular between 1908 and 1912, as much as into the labor-capital genre. Female adventure films drew on a variety of cheap fiction formulas and formed the basis for later adventure serials. A film "series" was a set of shorts featuring the same characters, such as the Keystone Cops, but unconnected by plot and released on no particular schedule. A "serial," however, tied episodes together by some element of an ongoing plot and was released regularly, usually weekly. Eileen Bowser notes that in 1909 the Kalem Company produced a series about a female spy working for the South in the Civil War that was an important precursor to the serials. The independent Yankee Film Company started a female detective series in 1910 in which a male detective's daughter takes over his job after he is killed.[24] Railroad dramas also regularly featured heroic women workers. *The Lonedale Operator* (Biograph, 1911, d. D. W. Griffith) shows a girl telegraph operator capturing robbers in a scene that at once anticipates both *Hazards of Helen* and an episode of *What Happened to Mary*. Indeed, Kalem's popular *Hazards of Helen* serial reused a railroad drama produced years earlier in order to avoid lags in the production schedule. *The Grit of the Girl Telegrapher* first appeared in the theaters as a regular short in 1912, and appeared again under the title *The Girl Telegrapher's Nerve* in March 1916 as episode number 69 of *Hazards of Helen*. Thus, the serials emerged from a group of films that were already popular with motion picture audiences and drew on popular fiction conventions for female adventures.[25] These films largely avoided representing women as victims or as overtly political actors.

The Edison Company joined forces with the magazine *The Ladies' World* to create the first female adventure serial, *What Happened to Mary*, in 1912. Edison was the leader in rationalizing film production, and

What Happened to Mary was largely a product of producers' attempts to standardize production and reception even further. Edison and *The Ladies' World* released the twelve-episode story monthly in both film and print formats. The two producers sought a story with elements proven popular with fiction and film audiences. They hired seasoned scenario writer Bannister Merwin to write the first scenarios and texts for both the film and print versions of the story. Later, James Oppenheim took over the scenarios while Frank Blighton continued the print episodes. The Edison Company used both Merwin and Oppenheim on a regular basis and could be confident that they would supply stories "on order."[26] The film company and the magazine publisher overtly aimed to share audiences: the magazine printed photographs from the movie set as illustrations, urged readers to see the film version at the close of each segment, and supplemented the story with articles on how films were made. Film episodes closed with a title urging viewers to read about Mary in *The Ladies' World*. The continuity of the story helped the Edison Company create a sustained interest in a set of related film products and linked film directly to women's established reading practices.

With *What Happened to Mary*, *The Ladies' World* gained motion picture fans as readers and associated itself with the glamour and modernity of the movies. *The Ladies' World* already had an established audience of working-class and lower middle class female readers. It had begun as a "mail order journal," that is, it made money from mail-order advertisements printed throughout the magazine rather than from subscriptions. Hundreds of such journals existed at the turn of the century. They were highly accessible: producers mass-mailed the journals to homes free of charge. They typically printed "low-brow" fiction to draw consumers to look at the advertisements. Though considered a step down from the "legitimate" women's journals, such as *Ladies' Home Journal* or *Woman's Home Companion*, mail-order journals distributed a great deal of fiction to working people. In 1907, the post office withdrew mail-order journals' second-class mailing privileges unless they produced legitimate subscription lists, paid in advance. This drove many journals out of business immediately, and by 1912 the future of *The Ladies' World*, whose subscription rate was fifty cents per year, was in question. But within less than a year, after five episodes of *What Happened to Mary*, the editor credited the serial for the bulk of 100,000 new subscriptions.[27]

The Edison Company and *The Ladies' World* heavily promoted the film and print story through the new star system and together shaped a fan culture. Before 1909, producers did not divulge the names of film actors. Rather, they operated with a stock system in which they steadily employed a group of actors whom they assigned to play parts as needed. By 1909, audiences were clamoring to know the names of the actors with whom they emotionally identified. Producers soon realized that this avid interest among the new fans, many of whom were working women, could be very lucrative, and began advertising motion pictures with the stars' names and photographs.[28] The Edison Company hired the popular Mary Fuller to play the leading role and launched an aggressive promotional campaign (fig. 5.1). Fuller had starred in female adventure shorts already and was a proven hit with audiences. One reviewer remarked on the Edison Company's "striking advertising campaign," which made him confident that all of his readers knew Fuller was the film's star even before the motion picture opened. In addition, *The Ladies' World* included photographs of and articles about Mary Fuller.[29] As part of the promotion of Mary, *The Ladies' World* and the Edison Company offered some of the film industry's first fan products. *The Ladies' World* encouraged admirers to buy "the Mary hat," modeled in the advertisement by Mary Fuller, a "What Happened to Mary Board Game," and a "What Happened to Mary Jigsaw Puzzle." The producers invited additional suggestions from readers: "It would seem only logical that we should have 'Mary' hats and gowns—perhaps a 'Mary' color for the women who are her admirers. . . . Perhaps there are other entertaining or utilitarian purposes to which the character of 'Mary' may be applied; and perhaps there are readers . . . who can originate ideas that have not occurred to the originators of 'Mary.' If so, let us have them."[30] Serial producers navigated uncharted territory in the consumer culture industry by requesting the guidance of working-class and lower-middle-class women.

Producers also relied on consumers to guide them in creating the plot of *What Happened to Mary*. Through promotional contests, producers encouraged fans' imaginative engagement with Mary and gained audience response from women readers. Each month *The Ladies' World* staged a contest that awarded $100 for the essay that best answered the question "What Happened to Mary Next?" The magazine reported that it received 2,000 entries in the first month of the contest and that by the fifth month the numbers approached 10,000. Three or four contest winners were published each month. On two occasions the winning essays for the contest did indeed outline the plot for the story that month.[31] The ongoing contest informed the producers of audience desires that they could then utilize in shaping the unfolding narrative. In addition, the contest encouraged readers to create an imaginative fantasy world around *What Happened to Mary*. Such participation in the narra-

5.1 Publicity photograph of Mary Fuller.

tive could promote loyal purchases of movie tickets and magazines.

Other film producers soon tried to replicate *What Happened to Mary*'s great success with serials of their own. The Selig Company joined with the *Chicago Tribune* to produce *The Adventures of Kathlyn* in 1913, and dozens of others followed. While *What Happened to Mary* was released on a monthly basis, later serials appeared weekly. The adventure serials quickly became a new and noted genre in silent film. By April 1914 *Variety* magazine declared that, "The serial thing in movies has come to stay. There's hardly a big concern now that isn't getting out a melodramatic series in which a young woman is the heroine and the camera has her having hair breadth escapes by the score."[32] Many of the serials featured wage-earning women and some were detective stories, but all centered on adventure. As a group, the serials were products of producers' well-planned efforts to capture and sustain audience interest. For working women, though they contained no depictions of collective action, they constituted an exciting type of film product with roots in familiar fiction formulas.

Despite producers' self-conscious efforts to rationalize production and shape consumption, the movies took on new meaning once in social circulation. Producers could not fully control how working women wove motion pictures into the social fabric of their daily lives. Indeed, the cultural impact of the movies was far greater than the visual experience of the films themselves. Like dime novels and fashion, the meanings of motion pictures emerged in part from the social practices of the working women who consumed them. When working women bought tickets, viewed posters, dreamed of stars, and attended theaters, they made motion pictures part of their collective culture, including their workplace culture.

The ways working women acquired their movie tickets greatly influenced the kind of experience they had at neighborhood theaters. As working-class communities incorporated motion pictures into their daily routines, they blended family and ethnically based leisure customs with women's new patterns of consumption. Working women attended motion pictures with family groups, dates, and alone. Motion pictures became a new ethnic community event that everyone could attend, like picnics in the park, religious holiday celebrations, and weddings. One observer noted that motion picture theaters were practically the only place, along with public parks, where "whole families can together enjoy any kind of recreation." Another remarked in 1907, "Father and mother, the baby, the older children, the grandparents—all were there."[33] Depending on how family economies were managed, the price of a working daughter's ticket might come from the family purse or from her own wages after the bulk had been turned over to the mother. Either way, women's wages contributed to ticket purchases, but their position as dependent daughters would be reinforced if their tickets were paid out of family funds. Many girls and young women probably had their first experiences at the movies with their families, reinforcing their family-based identities in the new public arena.

Even as motion picture theaters fit into established neighborhood leisure practices, they fostered new forms of dating that were free of direct supervision and also considered respectable. Working women often attended motion pictures with young men who paid for their tickets. Reformer Ruth True noted that many workers did not hurry home after work but would "linger with a boy companion making 'dates' for a 'movie.'" This way of getting through the nickelodeon door set in motion a quite different set of social relations than when women attended with families. At motion picture theaters, working women had unprecedented opportunities for social intimacy with men. Jane Addams noted that the "very darkness of the room, necessary for an exhibition of the films, is an added attraction to many young people, for whom the space is filled with the glamour of love making." Such glamour must have been intensified by the occasional larger-than-life representations of romance on the silver screen. Many middle-class reformers found this attraction alarming and warned regularly against the "danger of undue familiarity made possible by dim lights."[34] Nevertheless, working-class parents continued to see the space as safe and respectable, perhaps because there were so many families there. Young working women and men thus made the movies a site of romantic and sexual experimentation and change.

When women gained access to motion picture theaters through dates with men, they participated in a developing sexual economy in which their appearance carried high value. The purchase of the movie ticket was only one item in a series of exchanges. According to middle-class reformers, men regularly expected "payment" for their movie tickets in the form of sexual relations: "They do not treat for nothing," warned one. Reformer Mary Simkhovitch noted that when a young woman went weekly with a man to the movies, he expected in return that she would "go with no one else and . . . [would] give him the privileges of engagement." Simkhovitch noted that this could lead to trouble: "Sometimes a passion for the theater will lead a girl to go with a man with whom she is unwilling to keep company and yet who expects his payment." The movies thus fit into the sexual economy of "treating" described by Kathy Peiss, in which payment for dates carried a tacit expectation for reciprocal payment of engagement or sexual favors.[35]

From many working women's perspectives, however, they had already paid up front. In this sexual economy, the first step often was women's cultivation of an attractive appearance, which solicited the men's purchase. Fashion was necessary to achieve visibility. Jane Addams recorded that one young woman stole a "mass of artificial flowers with which to trim a hat," because she believed that "a girl has to be dressy if she expects to be seen." The woman was reportedly afraid of losing the attention of a man who had taken her to the nickelodeon. "If he failed her," Addams explained, "she was sure that she would never go again, and she sobbed out incoherently that she 'couldn't live at all without it.'" As chapter 2 noted, in a context in which women were systematically paid less than men, clothing could be seen as an investment in the future if it helped women make a good match. Dates to the movies were smaller prizes, but functioned as part of the same system. Reformer Clara Laughlin observed two women who "limited their indulgence in nickel shows" for several weeks in order to save money to buy very dressy clothes on the installment plan. Their clothes, in turn, won them dates that led to weeks' worth of regular movie tickets.[36] Though successful, the two women found themselves doubly in debt: to the store that sold them the clothes, and to the men whom they "owed" for the movie tickets, and who did not recognize their initial payment. Thus, women's love of the movies could socialize them simultaneously in the new practices of heterosexuality and in U.S. values of capitalist investment, and potentially also teach them the pitfalls of both for those in economically disadvantaged positions. Even when women attended the movies with dates for the "glamour of love making," they could find themselves enmeshed in new gendered hierarchies.

The newest pattern of leisure at the motion picture theaters was working women attending alone or with female friends. They bought their own tickets with their wages and often met groups of other young people once at the theater. While some working women also went to dance halls and amusement parks with female friends, the cheapness and respectability of the movies made them especially accessible. Louise Odencrantz notes that though young Italian women rarely socialized without a chaperon, many "were allowed to go out without their parents [to] moving-picture shows." Filomena Ognibene, an Italian woman garment maker, recalled that "the one place I was allowed to go by myself was the movies. I went to the movies for fun. My parents wouldn't let me go out anywhere else, even when I was twenty-four." Reformers noted that many working women attended the movies at least once a week, some with even greater frequency. Ognibene went to the movies two or three times each week.[37] When women used their wages for their own evening amusements, they laid claim to the practices and privileges of male wage-earners, just as they did when they bought clothing and dime novels. In addition, in these cases they occupied the public space of motion picture theaters outside of family or dating relationships.

Women's social practices of attending theaters and engaging in related fan activities also inflected the motion picture experience with specific meanings. For working women, the films themselves were not the only, and sometimes not the principal, draw. The nickelodeon served as a "general social center and club house," in Jane Addams' words, for people of all ages. For one woman worker who lived in a New York boarding house, having a place to talk in mixed-gender groups was the primary reason to go to the movies. She and a group of friends talked one night in her hallway "as it was too wet and cold to walk around the streets. After shifting from one foot to the other several times and being very tired of standing, some one suggested that we either go to a moving picture theater or to a cafe to have a drink." Likewise, a study of Progressive-run organized "homes" for working women showed that "in houses where there was only one reception room, the girls usually preferred to go to the movies or places giving an opportunity for intimate conversation."[38] Women who lived in tenements also lacked space for socializing. Movie audiences often talked through the films, interacting with the characters or ignoring the screen to continue a conversation.[39] The film itself was certainly important, but such testimony demonstrates how women used motion picture theaters to create a new public site for themselves. They imbued the movies with a sense of unprecedented freedom of mobility—a new and exciting public identity—quite apart from the content of specific films.

Working women's emerging fan practices claimed access to public space through the assertion of an active consumer gaze. Women's consumption of new fan products—particularly the posters at theater entrances and the photographs of stars that exhibitors often handed out free of charge—shaped a distinctive "fan culture" that far exceeded the event of motion picture attendance. Their fan practices also became part of workplace culture as women discussed motion picture stars and plots, much as they talked about dime novels, at the shops. In this way, women imbued both their night life and their daytime life with the glamour of the movies. Fan paraphernalia certainly was not working women's own cultural creation, but the product of producers' promotional efforts. Nevertheless, when fans wove the posters and photos into their own lives, they created what historian Kathryn Fuller called "a truly popular culture of film."[40]

Specifically, posters functioned like shop windows to legitimate women's presence in the urban landscape and their active gaze at products and images that filled the modern city. Walter Benjamin notes that the rationalization of industry and the reverence for "reason" that characterized modern life did not drain the urban landscape of myth and magic.

On the contrary, capitalist industry caused a re-enchantment of modern life within the urban consumer spaces of arcades and amusement parks, in the city streets plastered with theater and movie posters, and in the cinema itself.[41] Stores created window displays to beckon and entice; department stores used glass and mirrors to focus shoppers' gazes upon products newly packaged to capture attention and promise delight. While shop windows and nickelodeon exteriors covered with posters existed primarily to sell products, they also became women's spaces. Historian William Leach notes that department stores became important spaces for middle-class women,[42] but the degree to which working-class women participated in a similar space of visual spectacle and consumer desire on the streets is less acknowledged. Many had an established practice of window shopping on their way home from the factory, laundry, or sweatshop. One reformer noted that for working women "the shop windows . . . were one of the chief sources of entertainment and delight."[43] Gazing at the posters that lined nickelodeon entrances connected closely to this practice. When working women made the nickelodeon exteriors a site for their public subjectivities they made the enchantment of the city part of their own subcultural landscape, and made an active and desiring gaze a part of their public identities. Like the use of fashion, the social practice of motion picture consumption negotiated a modern culture that privileged looking in the construction of meaning.

Young working women created somewhat different patterns of consumption of movie posters in the evening than during the day. At evening, poster-lined nickelodeon entrances became sites where both men and women could meet and socialize. Jane Addams recorded that one group of women refused her efforts to interest them in a sponsored day in the country, "because the return on a late train would compel them to miss one evening's performance. They found it impossible to tear themselves away not only from the excitements of the theater itself but from the gaiety of the crowd of young men and girls invariably gathered outside discussing the sensational posters." Social workers Robert Wood and Albert Kennedy found this phenomenon threatening to young women, noting that "the crowds outside the door [of the motion picture theater], the lurid and sensational advertisements, and the absence of all chaperonage, are sources of danger."[44] Posters allowed working women to linger on the street in mixed-gender groups that were not composed primarily of dating couples.

During the day, working women looked at motion picture posters on their way to and from work, much as they gazed in shop windows at the latest fashions. Louise de Koven Bowen noted that two workers at a candy factory combined window shopping and gazing at posters: "On their way to and from the factory Hilda and Freda would often stop and gaze longingly in the shop windows ... or they would read the fascinating posters which described the delights of the theatre they had no money to enter."[45] Some working women also looked at posters while on their lunch breaks. The brief time allowed—usually only thirty to forty minutes—and inclement weather often kept women inside the factories. But on occasion they took the opportunity to leave and linger on the streets. Reformer Harriet McDonal Daniels worried that the short lunch periods could lead the working woman astray. "On every side the picture shows flaunt their lurid posters before her eyes and on every corner and before every entrance groups of young men congregate to 'treat.' " The lunch break was usually too short for women to actually attend the movies, but like reading a dime novel, gazing at a poster could interrupt the tedium of the workday with a splash of color and a romantic image. Workers gazed at stars whose fame represented a counterpoint to their own devalued labor. Daniels believed Italian women to be particularly susceptible to such pleasures, precisely because their parents otherwise limited their freedom of movement in public. Some Italian women did not even walk to work without escort, but were accompanied to the factory door by brothers. Daniels wrote, "During working hours she is under the watchful eye of the boss, out of working hours she is under the strict surveillance of her parents; during this one little hour she is free and it would be strange indeed if in many cases she were not led astray."[46] Thus, although Italian women generally had less mobility in public than Jewish women, their social practices of moviegoing, including viewing posters, did allow them to occupy new public settings.

When working women looked at shop windows and movie posters they legitimated their public presence through a consumer gaze. But this gaze was not simply acquisitive. Rather, it connected to a complex realm of fantasy, imagination, and desire. In particular, posters prompted the imagination by presenting single images from larger narratives. Commentators noted the power of these large, colorful, and dramatic displays to capture attention. Reformer Michael Davis called the motion picture poster "a psychological blow in the face." He explained that "the poster is to catch the eye of the street passenger; it must hold him up," and described how a poster could suggest a sensational story with a single image:

> The poster takes some feature or even suggestion of the performance having an elemental appeal, and exaggerates this to a point sometimes passing all resemblance to the actual show. Thus, a black-whiskered villain stands flourishing a revolver; Slouch-hat

Charlie smites the swell with a bludgeon, while pals make off with the lady; by the side of the bleeding father, the pale hero utters a fully printed oath of revenge; a short-skirted female dances upon a globe of the world, supported by three gilded youths gazing upward! These are but four recollections of reality.[47]

Working women's social practice of gazing at posters connected to a larger imaginative world, just as looking at shop windows connected to working ladyhood. Crucially, working women had great latitude to make their own meanings from the posters, both individually and in conversation with each other.

The significance of this active and imaginative gaze in public spaces has often been dismissed as acquisitive consumerism. But in important ways, this gaze created a possibility for women's desires, and not only desires for *stuff*.[48] The consumer gaze legitimated women's presence in public spaces on a daily, informal basis, altering entrenched gendered patterns of mobility. In addition, in U.S. society, conventions of looking have long operated as a way to signal dominance or deference. Custom allowed propertied white men to look directly at everyone, while women in public had to avert their eyes if they wished to avoid appearing "brazen" or sexually available. While white men became autonomous subjects in part through looking, people of color and all women were properly the objects of that look. When working women gazed at posters in public, they did not overturn established practices, but they did open up a new site of desire that could exceed the expectations of producers. I am not making a liberal pluralist argument that women gained freedom because they now could do what men had done; women's consumer gaze was certainly imbued with new hierarchies. Indeed, the capitalist marketplace repeatedly promised women a "modern" freedom from patriarchal constraints, even as it promoted subjectivities oriented to consumption and reconfigured gendered power relations. Just as the clothing that working women wore was not in itself "democratic," the new gaze was not inherently liberating. However, in both cases producers could not fully control the desires women would develop in relation to consumer culture.

In a context of unrelenting labor and inadequate compensation, the pleasure and power of participating in the new, modern public could be a way to maintain dignity and even a sense of hope, as one striking woman's story about the death of a co-worker indicates. During the Chicago garment strike of 1910, one young woman died after becoming ill while selling union newspapers. A striker described her grief to a reporter for *American Magazine*: "When I hear for sure thing a girl striker is dead, I lay on the bed crying' like everything. And then

Anna, my chum, she lays on the bed cryin', and we both cry together so, on the bed. I don't know the girl, but I was feel so sorry that I must to cry. Oh, she was a poor girl, poorer'n we . . . and when I think on how it is with poor girls, I can't help from cryin.' "This young woman cried for herself and her poverty as well as for her co-worker. Strike leaders feared the despondency that could overcome workers who saw little in their futures but toil and poverty. The Chicago striker explained how she resisted giving in to her fear and despair:

> Then suddenly I stop cryin' and I say to Anna: 'For why do we cry? Ain't she better off'n we! She ain't cold; she don't have to buy no winter underwears; she don't have to worry for the eats; she won't never go scabbin.' She's lucky, lucky more as we.' And Anna says 'Sure she is.' And then we both say ain't it a foolishness for to cry for someone as is luckier'n we. So we get dressed and we goes out on Halsted Street and we looks on nickel picture shows and mill'n'ry windows. Honest, I ain't been to a nickel show in nine weeks and I'm forgettin' how they looks![49]

These young strikers' trip to look at shop windows and films could be termed an "escape" from their troubles, but this would simplify a complex survival mechanism. The two women certainly did not deny their connection to the dead striker and her oppression—indeed, they declared themselves in a *worse* condition. Still, they sought out public activities that granted them a modicum of mobility, an active gaze, and a sense of possibility. The next day, they were back at their strike duties.

The quality of some women's desires in relation to motion pictures can be discerned in what contemporaries termed the "movie-struck" fantasy, that is, the dream of a job in motion pictures. As Jane Addams noted, the motion pictures and the evenings at the nickelodeon became "the sole topic of conversation" for working women through the week, "forming the ground pattern of their social life."[50] A central part of this was discussion of stars and the potential pathways to stardom. Indeed, many working women even applied at the motion picture studios in hopes of gaining more lucrative and rewarding jobs. This reflected close identification with female film heroines, and deep-seated desires for jobs that paid well and valued workers rather than exploiting and discarding them. The movie-struck fantasy was a dream of lavish recognition much like that showered on the working-girl heroines in dime novel romances. It imaginatively combined women's workplace struggles with their rewarding consumer culture experiences and pleasures. Through this collective fantasy, working women wove the movies into the established fantasies of romance, adventure, and sudden changes in fortune that characterized working ladyhood.

Working women became movie-struck after 1908, when the shift in film techniques to closer shots and more cuts fostered a closer identification with players. Audiences clamored for information about and names of particular stars, and in response producers slowly shifted from a stock to a star system. Some neighborhoods, impatient for information from producers, named the stars themselves. *The Survey* noted in 1909 that "One little girl who plays a prominent part in the pictures of a certain New York manufacturer has been named Annette by her admirers on the East Side. Her appearance on the screen [always] brings a round of applause."[51] Posters aided the imaginative process of identifying with or following particular stars, and producers supplied exhibitors with free photographs of stars to hand out as promotional tools. Working women could fuel their fascination with motion pictures and stars through the penny papers, which regularly carried articles about the movies; trade and fan magazines; and gossip. One observer noted that whatever their means of information, "the children of New York are sophisticated and . . . know quite as much about motion picture stars and the latest productions."[52]

Many young people still fantasize about being in the movies, but such dreams were considerably less abstract during the nickelodeon era in New York City. Movies were literally being made on the streets all around working women. Most of the studios still were based in New York, including Biograph and Kalem, and journalists remarked that "a crowd always gathers" to see movies being shot at popular locations like Grand Central Station, a street lined with pushcarts on the Lower East Side, Midtown, or Brooklyn. It was well known that most of the studios hired "extras" or "supers" at the rate of three to five dollars per day, though extras seldom got work on a daily basis.[53] This was an enormous sum of money for a factory worker used to making six dollars per week, and the work seemed exciting and easy. In addition, working as an extra was known to be one route to a position as a stock player for a company. Applying for a motion picture position was little different than applying for a factory position, until assigned to a role, as one journalist described: "[The applicant] will have to report every day at eight o'clock, stand in line before the directors as their assistants pick out the 'types,' and then, if she is picked, she will have to make up as a Spanish girl, a factory girl, a 'society lady' wearing a borrowed evening gown, or anything else the director may suggest." The Biograph Company studio at 11 East Fourteenth Street was especially accessible to workers on the Lower East Side, many of whom worked in factories within easy walking distance. Kathryn Fuller noted that the Biograph studio was daily besieged by movie-struck young women hoping to win jobs, and some stars like Lillian and Dorothy Gish actually got their start in this manner.[54]

The ways that producers promoted the earliest stars may have encouraged working women to dream of motion pictures as a possible employment option. Before 1908, commentary on the films focused on technology and explained how the films were made and projected. By 1907 to 1908, the shift in filming techniques and acting styles directed more attention to the actors themselves. Articles about stars in popular and trade papers and magazines from 1909 to 1914 focused on the *work* of acting in motion pictures, rather than on stars' private lives, as they would by 1915. As film historian Richard de Cordova notes, promotional material created a discourse on acting that participated in the larger effort to assert the respectability and "art" of the cinema, and thus draw a middle-class audience. Nevertheless, the early articles clearly represented the stars as workers whose main task was to express emotions with facial expressions, "gesture," and "motion." Articles regularly explained the action of a picture from the point of view of an actor who endeavored to communicate a particular emotion or perform a stunt. De Cordova rightly argues that this should not be viewed as a demystification of the means of production, but as a creation of a certain kind of knowledge about film.[55] Indeed, trade papers, newspapers, and magazines portrayed acting both as paid labor and as involving real adventures: "at times the moving picture woman is subjected to dangers. Her horse may throw her when she is doing fast riding, or the wolf dogs may become unmanageable and bite." Articles about Mary Fuller described her work routine of real-life dangers, including sliding down a rope from a seventh-floor window, driving a motor boat, and riding a bucking bronco.[56] For working women reading the penny press or cheap magazines, this knowledge encouraged fantasies of new, exciting jobs and provided tips on how to act. A *Ladies' World* article entitled "The Photoplay: An Entertainment and an Occupation" reported that a successful motion picture actress must "be so inspired with her theme, and really feel the part so thoroughly, that she can go through it at a moment's notice. Her facial expressions and movements carry the whole idea to the audience. Then, too, she must learn to move very slowly and deliberately or the actions on the screen will be blurred."[57] Such press coverage could fan the flames of fantasy by collapsing the distance between paid labor and familiar narratives of adventure. Whereas in the dime novel romances, heroines encountered adventures after losing their jobs, in the movie-struck fantasy stars got paid for adventures in the course of their work.

The movie-struck fantasy is significant not because working women really got jobs in motion pictures—certainly few did. The encouragement women received through promotional material intended to capitalize on movie-struck women's intense loyalty as consumers. Nevertheless, the fantasy provides clues to the imaginative element of movie consumption. In many ways, the movie craze dovetailed with the practices of ladyhood. The latter was a signifying practice, a shifting identity that built upon the exclusions working women faced and the possibilities that consumer culture provided for appropriation of cultural codes. The imaginative self-construction of ladyhood could prepare women to embrace the movie-struck fantasy. Many working ladies would be confident of their ability to fulfill the requirements Mary Pickford claimed qualified one for motion pictures: "A girl cannot take the part of a lady unless she is one—she can not fake poise, grace, repose, the courteous gesture and air of good breeding unless she has the instincts of a lady and the necessary training in manners."[58] Like the dime novels, the movie-struck fantasy figured a magical transformation that served to confirm one's true inner qualities. Film historian Charles Musser has argued that immigrant audiences constructed fantasies around early stars of silent films, and also enjoyed the ways that the same star could take on dramatically new identities week after week, including diverse ethnic roles. Musser has suggested that immigrants' daily practices of constructing themselves as Americans, with new dress, mannerisms, and patterns of speech, could make them identify with, and enjoy watching, stars do the same thing in the movies. The way that such rapid change was accepted in the movies made them appealing as a counterpoint to the oppressions that immigrants faced. As Musser said, "the movies provided [immigrants] with an alternative to the alienation and struggle experienced while constructing a new world during the course of their everyday lives."[59] For working women who enacted identities as ladies, the movies provided fantasies and models of magical transformation.

Women's social practices of film consumption thus created a collective culture connected to their consumption of other commodities, such as dime novels and fashion. Film became more than an object or a narrative in women's lives; it became part of their imaginative landscape—or collective dreamworld—and as such was integral to their enacted identities. This collective culture framed women's viewing of specific films, though as with dime novels and fashion, individual idiosyncrasies and multiple possibilities for interpretation ensured that working women made a variety of meanings from those films. We cannot know how different women responded to the content of the posters or the serials. Nevertheless, a close look at how the serials *What Happened to Mary* and *Hazards of Helen* solicited audiences' identification and offered them visual fantasies can reveal more about the contours of working women's collective culture of film.[60]

The specific process and mechanism of identification with a fictional character and scenario in print or film has been the subject of great debate in film and literary theory. It is generally accepted that the identifications people make with fictional characters can be very important in how people develop their own identities. Film critics argue that identity emerges not as the sum of the content of images with which people are presented, but from a *process* of identification rooted in the affective experience of the film. When a spectator comes to identify with a character, she or he takes up residence in a fictional world. The story that the spectator participates in is not real, but his or her responses to it certainly are, and can be formative in the construction of the self. Individuals bring different identities, perspectives, and histories of interpellation to the viewing experience and inevitably make a variety of meanings as they interpret the films for themselves. It is crucial, then, to work with a sophisticated notion of identification that can accommodate the complexity and variability of individual responses.

Film critic Elizabeth Cowie argues that identification occurs not when we see or read about someone who is "like" us, but when we see a character who has a similar "structural relation of desire" to our own. That is, when we can come to *desire with* a character, we can identify with them, even if the character is of a different gender, class, or race, or is in a story about a different time or culture. According to Cowie, "The pleasure in identification lies not only in what is signified—a meaning—in that traditional realist sense, that is, a coming to know; it also lies in a coming to desire made possible by the scenario of desire which I come to participate in as I watch a film, view an image, or read a text."[61] The protagonist's "characteristics" are less important to the process of identification than her desires and how spectators are invited to participate in them. Following Cowie, I will examine *What Happened to Mary* and *Hazards of Helen* for the structural relations of desire of the working-girl heroine, and the ways an identification with her is solicited through print and visual narrative devices. The serials offered working women an identification with a heroine who desired and received dramatic social recognition as a worker and a woman.

What Happened to Mary, like the majority of silent films, no longer exists in film format. However, the print version of the story from *The Ladies' World* has survived. Comparison of scenario plot descriptions and the print episodes reveals that the film and fiction versions of *What Happened to Mary* followed the same plot line, although they necessarily used different devices to solicit the identification of viewers and readers. While the film relied on visual cues and conventions, the print version could narrate characters' thoughts and emotions. This created inevitable differences in storytelling. For example, the first film episode began with Mary as an abandoned baby found in a basket on Moseses Island by Billy Peart. A *Bioscope* review reported that "Mary rapidly grows up, as is the way in films" and the film story continues when she is eighteen. By centering on Mary and her rapid growth, the film signaled to viewers that she, not Billy Peart, would be the protagonist of the story. Through the new techniques of film cuts, the viewer would be a silent observer of the basket being left, and of Mary quickly growing to young woman-hood. The print version, in contrast, begins with a description of Mary's appearance as a young woman. Readers learn that she was left on Moseses Island in a basket in a later scene, told as Billy Peart's memory.[62]

Despite these differences, the print version of *What Happened to Mary* was remarkable for print fiction in that it solicited readers' iden-tification in large part by portraying looking relations. Bannister Merwin, who wrote both the print and film versions of the early episodes, appears to have structured the magazine story to describe the scenes in the film. *The Ladies' World* encouraged readers to approach the story as a narration of the motion picture, and provided articles describing how particular central film scenes were made.[63] Indeed, the print narrative is almost completely devoid of dialogue; it consists predominantly of visual description. Along with the photographs from the movie set as illustrations, the print version sought to parallel the film experience and allow fans to "read" the movie. Of course, the print version is not the same as the film version and cannot stand in for it. However, a close look at the print version reveals something of the overall experience of the serials. In addition, it reveals a solicitation of identification, through looking and a particular set of desires in the working-class heroine, that would be common to other serials.

The print version of *What Happened to Mary* designates Mary as the protagonist and solicits identification with her not by consistently narrating from Mary's point of view, but by setting up a suspenseful series of looking relations that encourages an emotional response on her behalf. The opening lines of the story describe an open-ended desire in Mary, a longing for something she cannot name: "Mary's eyes were smoldering that day with the fire of strange yearnings. She moved about at her work as one walking in a dream—burning with a life that was not the life around her." While the story gives an intimate if vague portrayal of Mary's emotional state, like the film it also invites the reader to position herself as part of the scene, observing Mary as one of the villagers: "If you who had known her long had asked her suddenly, 'What is different with you, Mary?' she would have looked at you with startled query . . . for she did not know that anything was different. Her new yearnings had not yet burst into flames." Readers knew that Mary was the protagonist because it was her desire that they follow and watch. But what did Mary desire? Suddenly, readers discover that Mary is at the harbor, looking at a yacht that has just landed. Four wealthy people get off a launch from the yacht: two older people who are rudely "aloof to her," and a young man and woman. "And the girl's eyes had met Mary's, and something subtle had passed between them—the secret unspoken password of maidenhood."[64] This scene figures class distinction and the alienation and longing that can go with it for the working class.

Scenes 2 and 3 invite an emotional identification by prompting anxiety and indignation on Mary's behalf. Readers see Mary enter the store owned by her adoptive stepfather, Billy Peart. She does not look at him as she heads to the ice cream parlor in the rear, but readers see him watching her: "Billy glanced at her in his quick, hard, speculative way, and clamped his lips together in a fashion even more frog-like than usual . . . and shifted his weight from foot to foot." Thus readers are cued that Billy is not a person to be trusted: he's speculative, shifty, and nervous. The fact that readers see Peart but Mary is not watching inaugurates a device common to the *What Happened to Mary* story and later serials: readers know something the protagonist does not. The scene might mildly prompt readers to be wary of Billy for Mary's sake. In scene 3, readers witness Mrs. Peart yelling at and physically threatening Mary for being away from the shop for too long. Mary, however, does not answer, but "smiled faintly at the two children, who were tasting [ice cream]." This scene demonstrates that Mary is oppressed in her household, and that she is good and kind to children in spite of it. These two scenes solicit an identification imbued with feelings of indignation or anxiety for Mary, so good yet treated so badly. Readers may have wanted to defend her.

Scene 4 of the first episode sets up the soon-to-be-familiar pattern of suspense, in which the audience knows more about the heroine's danger than she initially does. Readers and film viewers learn that when Peart found Mary in the basket, he also found a note promising him $1,000 if he marries her to a local man before she turns twenty-one years old. Mary, however, is unaware of her adoptive status or Peart's financial interest in her marrying. Readers see Mary in town, approached by a young local man. They then learn that this whole scene has been witnessed by Billy Peart. The print version has to narrate Billy's gaze sequentially, but the film version could have placed Peart in the background through much of the encounter, letting the viewer know that this scene was of interest to him. The print version notes, "Billy stopped in his tracks, his bulging eyes fixed on the young couple with an astonishment that quickly gave place to satisfaction."[65] While Mary casts an active, desiring gaze toward the yacht and the rich girl, she is often unwitting of, and therefore vulnerable to, the gaze of others. This scene solicits anxiety for Mary, distrust of Billy, and perhaps a desire for her liberation. Through a set of accidents and incidental kindnesses of strangers, by the end of the first episode Mary learns of Billy Peart's plot and that her parentage is a mystery, and acquires a bit of money to escape the island. Readers identifying with Mary would feel relief and exhilaration at the denouement of the first episode. The whole audience is invited to identify with the freedom of a young woman alone, newly released from patriarchal authority and her established social identity.

The narrative strategy of letting the audience know more than the protagonist is common in suspense thrillers. Suspense arises not simply because we do not know what will happen, but because readers or viewers know *something* will happen, but not exactly what. Knowing more about the situation than the characters prompts anxiety on their behalf. Cowie cites Alfred Hitchcock's distinction between surprise and suspense: a bomb going off is a surprise; the audience seeing a bomb planted under a table where people are sitting is suspense. Hitchcock notes that in suspense "the public is participating in the scene. The audience is longing to warn the characters on the screen."[66] In *What Happened to Mary*, the suspenseful scene is not as dramatic as a bomb under a table (though subsequent episodes and later serials did utilize such extreme devices), but readers do know about a plot of which she is entirely unaware and are invited to desire her escape and liberation, that is, to come to desire *with* Mary.

The process of an intensely pleasurable identification hinges on readers participating in Mary's predicament. The story's mechanisms invite readers to take up her cause and align their desires with hers. They will then become implicated in a dramatic moment, full of an intensity of feeling, even though some of it, like anxiety, might seem unpleasant. In the suspense plot of *What Happened to Mary*, readers could come to desire *more* than Mary did. While Mary's desires and her sense of danger are vague, readers know the details of her predicament and can wish for her liberation all the more. By Cowie's model, when readers identify, they align their own loss, lack, or desire to the character's, so that they are feeling on behalf of the character, and indirectly on their own behalf as well. Thus, the apparently unpleasant aspect of the identification process may be imperative for an emotionally intense and satisfying experience. Of course, such identification is not inevitable. Readers can resist narrative cues or impose other emotional tones upon them. But if readers long with Mary in some way during the episode, they can feel an intense thrill when she escapes the island and achieves liberation.

At the close of the first episode, Mary arrives at a status familiar to dime novel enthusiasts: she is an orphan. As chapter 4 demonstrated, the metaphor of the orphan as free from patriarchal control was one that some working women had already incorporated into their own imaginative resources from the dime novels, and they used it to express a desire for freedom from sexual harassment. Like the dime novels, *What Happened to Mary* follows a melodramatic structure in which a heroine loses her established social identity, encounters a number of challenges and adventures, gains new social recognition for her adventures, and finally receives a reward. The first episode of the Mary serial merely initiates this larger plot formula. A good part of Mary's enigma has not been resolved. What more does she really want? Who were her parents? And how will Mary make it alone in the world? Indeed, even as readers might find the ending to the first episode satisfying, they may feel a curiosity and perhaps an anxiety about Mary's future.

Homeless and penniless, Mary is freed from her established social identity; the next several episodes portray her adventures in finding and performing work and confer new social recognition on her as both a worker and a woman. Mary's job is full of challenge and danger, but she ultimately receives fabulous rewards and recognition from co-workers, bosses, clients, and audiences. Later episodes maintain a similar emphasis on visual description and methods of soliciting identification with Mary by first prompting anxiety or indignance on her behalf.[67] Mary inevitably faces some adventure or challenge in which others oppose her unjustly or secretly plot against her. In episode 3, Mary gets a job as a chorus girl in a play. When the lead falls ill on opening night, Mary performs in her place, and like one dime novel heroine, is a smash hit. Readers might cheer her success particularly because she has been unjustly ridiculed by the other chorus girls. Unlike the dime novel heroine, Mary is a paid stage worker when she performs, which links work and adventure more closely.

Mary's adventures, like those of the dime novel heroine, revolve around her status as a woman worker. The constructed categories of honorable "worker" and honorable "woman" both largely excluded working women. Dime novel and serial narratives centered on the contradictions at the juncture of those exclusions. For example, *What Happened to Mary* raises the question of whether Mary can succeed in her workplace *despite* being female. Though Mary excells at her job, a competitive co-worker, a covert embezzler, regularly spoils it purposely to make her look bad. Mary proves her status as a worker, and gains revenge, by lying in wait in the office for him one evening, catching him stealing from the safe, and holding him with at gunpoint for several tense moments. Finally, the co-worker lunges at Mary, knocks the gun from her hand, and wrestles with her until the boss arrives with the police. When they ask Mary how she held a male rival with "superior masculine strength" for so long, Mary shows them the gun. Then the boss reveals that the gun, which Mary found in his desk, is not loaded. Lacking maleness—or a loaded gun—Mary achieves social recognition as a worker even as the episode reaffirms her femininity by marking her "natural" weakness—she is more vulnerable than a male hero would be. In recognition of Mary's proficiency, her boss gives her a promotion.

The plot of *What Happened to Mary* significantly revised the dime novel formula of social recognition and reward for adventure: Mary's reward hinged on recognition for her work rather than marriage to a rich hero. Her final reward in the last episode of the story was to gain her inheritance, while the dime novel heroine received her inheritance about half way through the narrative, in what Peter Brooks calls the "recognition" in the melodrama. Readers and viewers of *What Happened to Mary* learned that Mary was a "missing heiress" by episode 5, but dastardly villains and adventures kept her from collecting the cash for seven more episodes. Literary critic Rachel Brownstein argues that the traditional novel ending of marriage, for example in Samuel Richardson's *Pamela*, offered the female protagonist not just a husband but a realized feminine identity. Others' recognition of the protagonist's new status was as important, she argues, as the marriage itself.[68] In dime novel romances, marriage essentially affirmed the working heroine's adventures and her feminine worth, so that she could visit her former co-workers as an honorable working woman. *What Happened to Mary* omitted this narrative tradition of signaling female social recognition, reconfiguring the affirmation of femininity within the praise she won from coworkers and bosses for her adventures.

The Ladies' World and the Edison Company drastically broke from formula by *not* ending the serial with the heroine's wedding. While Mary had occasional romantic episodes, romance did not structure the plot. This innovation was probably a fluke. Producers fully expected their female and male audience to be anxiously awaiting Mary's romantic fate, and encouraged that expectation with the regular appearance of admirers. A male reviewer for the *Bioscope* complained about this aspect of the serial, revealing the importance to him of a recontainment of Mary's power—and her cash. "One regrets the absence of any real 'love interest.' At one moment in her career, Mary seems about to succumb to the tender passion, but a new adventure crops up, and the eligible young man is forgotten. We must confess that we should have liked to see him brought in again at the end, to share Mary's dollars, which we feel sure are far too many to be safe in the keeping of a lonely spinster, even though she is so capable a manageress as our heroine." Producers' prime motivation in subverting audience expectations was additional profit: they had already planned a sequel, *Who Will Marry Mary*, based entirely on romance. However, the sequel never approached the popularity of *What Happened to Mary* and was terminated after six months. *Who Will Marry Mary* lacked the adventure and the struggle in work that readers and viewers found exciting. Serials that followed kept romance marginal. Despite the popular culture industry's initial assumption that women always cared most about romance, it recognized that this profit-motivated accident revealed audience desires.

Later serials learned from the mistake of *Who Will Marry Mary*: they emphasized adventure over romance and accentuated suspense and sensationalism. One reviewer even criticized *What Happened to Mary* for being too mild: "One fancies that the author, or the producer, might have 'taken his gloves off' more effectually to one or two of the more sensational passages. One doesn't desire horrors, but it is possible to be realistic without incurring the censor's displeasure."[69] Perhaps Edison held back in order to please a cross-class audience. But later serials chocked their episodes full of hair-raising feats of daring, car chases, fires, and the capture or death of numerous villains.

Hazards of Helen, which began in 1914, combined the workplace-based adventures of *What Happened to Mary* and popular fascination with the powers and dangers of technology. *Hazards of Helen* featured a female telegraph operator who weekly encountered life-imperiling mishap or villainy in the course of her job (fig. 5.2). Helen was constantly running atop trains to prevent them from crashing. Viewers were invited to identify with the working woman in a setting that typically connoted masculinity, modernity, and the paradoxes of industrialization for working-class audiences. "Railroading," as historian Walter Licht says, "held out the lure of adventure, travel and escape." The world of railroading was the world of men: the homosocial space of railroad work and the regular absences from family and community created a camaraderie around labor that became the source of many popular stories.[70] Women were just beginning to work in the railroad industry in 1914. Their numbers would climb during World War I, but when *Hazards of Helen* ran, Helen was particularly modern—she worked at a kind of job long celebrated as epitomizing the honorable *male* worker.[71]

5.2 Advertisement for *The Hazards of Helen* in the *Motion Picture World*.

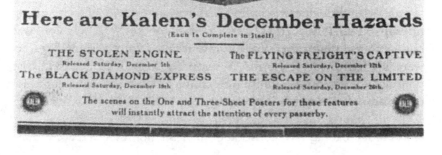

Railroads themselves were distinctly modern and epitomized the power and danger of the machine. Although railroads had transformed the U.S. economy and social life, the industry had a particularly high accident rate. Trains signaled workers' heroic achievements in production as well as their significant vulnerabilities.[72] *Hazards of Helen* played on people's fascination with this potential danger. While Helen usually prevented a crash, occasionally the audience got to see trains collide. Such catastrophes had cross-class appeal, but had become particularly common in "low-brow" cultural forms and in working-class spectator events. Some cheap stage melodramas at the turn of the century featured train wrecks. Additionally, in 1907, nearly 250,000 New Yorkers turned out at Brighton Beach to see two locomotives in a staged head-on collision at sixty miles per hour, an event repeated at the 1909 Chicago Labor Day celebration. The *Union Labor Advocate* noted that "thousands of railroad operating employees will be on the ground to study the 'disaster.' " Labor-capital films often included such sensationalism as well. For example, an advertisement for *The Wage Earners* (Atlas, 1912) read, "Everyone will want to see this great picture of Labor and Capital. Many thrilling and exciting scenes, such as the big train wreck, auto wreck, the wild ride on the handcar, the flying leap onto a moving train, the big walkout, the mob scene and many others."[73] A female heroine, traditionally seen as particularly physically vulnerable, could epitomize the dichotomy between the power of machinery and the vulnerability of humans for both male and female audiences (see fig. 5.3). Through cunning and bravery, as well as strength, Helen always prevailed. Thus, the railroad serial maintained *What Happened to Mary*'s focus on the female character's desire for social recognition as a worker and a woman, while linking this theme to a working-class cultural motif that had an established history with a male audience.

Close analysis of episode 58, "The Wrong Order," demonstrates that the serial solicited an identification with Helen through suspense and offered a fantasy of recognition and admiration. This episode opens with an intertitle that reads: "Helen, a telegraph operator, returns from her vacation." Audiences then see Helen walking into the telegraph office and greeting her male co-workers. The camera positions viewers as an invisible part of the staff, visually following Helen as she greets each man heartily. The men are clearly delighted to see her, and shake her hand in a demonstration of camaraderie. Part of the group goes out to the yard, where an express train awaits. An intertitle signals the action to come: "The observation car is a better place for you to ride than this dirty engine." The camera views the group from the back as Helen starts

5.3 Helen makes a flying leap from the telegraph station onto a moving train to capture escaping crooks in episode 45, "A Girl's Grit."

to climb onto the engine car. One of the men stops her and mouths the line of the intertitle, and Helen shrugs and agrees. This sets up one question of the short: Should Helen be treated differently because she's a woman? Does she need to keep her clothes clean? The audience then sees Helen and her boyfriend on the observation car, the last car on the express. Medium-close shots allow an intimate view of Helen and her easy manner with her boyfriend. Camera cuts to the engine car show that there is a mechanical problem, while Helen and her boyfriend grow impatient. The boyfriend goes to investigate, leaving Helen alone on the back of the car reading an issue of *Collier's*. Cross-cutting between the engine and observation cars serves to accentuate Helen's isolation from the work of the men. The train leaves twenty minutes late.

The episode next sets up a suspenseful situation and an identification with Helen as the only person who can save the day. The camera shows the engineer abandoning the train to tend his injured wife, leaving the express, now late and running out of control, on a collision course with a freight train. The audience learns about the problem, but Helen is unaware. The camera, in medium shots, shows the last station before the collision point receive a wire with instructions to stop the express, but it is too late—the express has just sped by. But the audience, viewing the action via a long shot from Helen's point of view on the back of the train, sees a man running out of the station waving his arms. Helen is thus notified of the problem. This point-of-view shot reinforces audience identification with Helen partly because only she, from her "feminine" position on the observation car, realizes the danger. The audience sees a medium-close shot of Helen's face as she registers the horror of the situation and then springs to action. The doors from the observation balcony to the train itself, however, are locked. Always resourceful, Helen immediately climbs up onto the top of the speeding train and runs along it to the engine car. An intertitle explains the action to come: "Unable to enter the steam filled cab, Helen makes a desperate attempt to stop the train." In medium-close shots the audience watches Helen climb on top of the engine and then slide down on one side to reach the handbrake at the front (fig. 5.4). Pulling hard on the brake, Helen slows the express enough that, as the camera cuts to a long shot, the freight has time to change tracks at the switch before the express train speeds past it. A medium shot shows Helen leaping from her precarious perch into the ditch when the express is almost stopped. Immediately, Helen is surrounded by railroad men, who help her up and congratulate her. The final scene parallels the opening scene: Helen is back in the office at a new desk, signaling a promotion. A medium-close

5.4 Helen in front of the engine in episode 58, "The Runaway Freight."

shot shows her proudly admiring the desk. The final shot shows Helen standing while the men help her brush the dirt off her skirt.[74]

Hazards of Helen thus solicited an emotional identification from viewers. If they became indignant for Helen when she was excluded from the male workers' activities, or anxious when she was unaware of her danger, they would also feel a vicarious thrill at her physical bravery and heroism. Helen faces a limit because of her femininity, placed on the observation car in order to keep her clothes clean, and she literally goes over the top to demonstrate her ability to be a good worker. In the process, she gets her clothes dirty, indicating that the imposed limits on her were, in fact, rather silly. Helen is affirmed in her job with a new desk and a promotion, but she is also affirmed as a woman when the men help her brush off her skirt. The male camaraderie of the workplace is extended to Helen, and is charged with a special intimacy or mild eroticism. Like the dime novel heroines who proved their ladyhood in part through physically aggressive adventures, Helen proved her worth through physically demanding work that did not abrogate her femininity.

Helen could represent the disadvantaged overcoming social restraint in spectacles similar to those staged by the Jewish immigrant Houdini. Helen was often placed in a position of vulnerability and peril to the nearly ubiquitous train robbers. Trapped, tied, gagged, locked away, Helen routinely performed Houdini-like tricks of evasion and escape. Though the villains were always armed, Helen, like Mary, rarely had access to a loaded gun. When she did require one, she used her creativity to procure it. In the thirty-first episode, villains lock Helen into a cattle car on a freight train that, unbeknownst to the conductor, is on a collision course with a passenger train. As the bad guys fight the good guys on the platform outside Helen's cell, one drops his gun. Helen makes a fishing line out of a hairpin and a strip of her dress, drags the gun to her in the cattle car, and shoots and severs the wire holding the semaphore arm so it swings to DANGER, prompting the conductor to stop the train (fig. 5.5). Here Helen uses her feminine accoutrements to make up for her initial lack of a gun and emerges, again, the hero.[75]

Hazards of Helen played on the space of contradiction inhabited by women workers and provided fantasies of power and belonging. Her reward was neither an inheritance nor marriage but simply warm recognition at the end of every episode. (Indeed, the *refusal* of a marriage proposal appears to have become a common narrative device.) Helen was fired from her position and had to prove herself to her bosses in at least two episodes. In episode 42, Helen is discharged because management believes she failed to turn a copy of an order over to a conductor,

5.5 Helen cleverly obtains a gun and saves the day, despite her imprisonment in a cattle car, in episode 31, "The Pay Train."

resulting in a near train collision. In fact, she did so, but cannot prove it because a spiteful coworker has destroyed the order. Through an array of spectacular adventures, Helen captures both the conductor, who has gone insane, and the spiteful employee, who plotted to dynamite the train. Helen is exonerated and restored to her duty with special recognition. In episode 13, Helen loses her job after being robbed by two crooks. Later, she sees the culprits flee on a freight. Hot in pursuit, Helen drops off a bridge onto the moving train, fighting until she falls off the train with one of the robbers and lands in the water. The thieves are thus captured and Helen is given her job back, with honor.[76]

The serials were products of the most rationalized arm of the film industry, and bore the limiting effects of industry priorities. Most notably, they did not represent strikes as a kind of female adventure like the labor-capital films did with male strikers, nor did they represent heroines as overtly political. But the serials' sensationalism and melodrama were not meaningless or trite. Like the dime novels, adventure serials engaged contradictions that working women faced on a daily basis and offered them gratifying fantasies of social recognition as women and workers. Of course, the movies invariably ended and working women went back to their daily lives of devalued labor and social contradiction. But while the serials did not directly change women's material conditions, they did, in Cowie's words, make possible "the scene of the wish." That is, like labor unions, motion pictures provided a legitimate place for women to imagine recognition and value as workers.

The meanings of the movies emerged from an array of social practices that working women created around their motion picture consumption. Motion picture theaters were new kinds of social spaces in which women could enact public identities. Looking at posters, dreaming of stars, and viewing the films all privileged looking and appearance in the construction of meaning and the self. Women's participation in this certainly implicated them in new gendered hierarchies. But working women's consumer gaze was more than simply superficial or acquisitive. It entailed complex fantasies of worth connected to their workday; to their status as workers, women, and immigrants; and to their established practices of ladyhood. The films themselves were far from simply emancipatory for working women. However, working women made them into resources for the ongoing tasks of maintaining dignity and creating identities. Just as they embraced the shirtwaist strike and its utopian promises, working women could make motion pictures a site for new public identities and new dreams of being valued.

CONCLUSION

A Place to Dream

She [left school at fourteen and] went to work. She entered one of the New York factories and began her new life. While at the machines Regina was dreaming of her past days, days which were dear to her. At times the foreman of the factory would stop near her machine and tell her that she must learn to do her work quicker and that the factory was not a place to dream.

—Bertha Levy, garment worker, "Regina's Disappointment" (1913)[1]

In 1913, the ILGWU's *Ladies Garment Worker* published a poignant story of Regina, a girl of fourteen forced to leave school "with an aching heart" and go to work in a factory to help support her family. Bertha Levy's story expresses a powerful longing for education, and the disappointment Regina feels as she resigns herself to a life of poorly compensated and repetitive labor. While the story details Regina's family circumstances and leaving school, the majority of it narrates Regina's struggle to live on a daily basis with longing and a sense of loss. Her mother does not understand her new irritability, since her experience is not exceptional: "How could [her family] understand her? Was she then the only one who was being deprived of the opportunity to learn? Was she the only one who, though so young, yet was already disappointed in life?" At work, Regina's dreams precipitate the censorship of the boss. Garment workers' tedious tasks did not require creativity, but they did necessitate close mental attention. It was in owners' interests to keep workers entirely engrossed by the labor in order to produce at the greatest speed. Levy's prose reveals the connections between management's attempts to control workers and the suppression of imagination: "the foreman of the factory would . . . tell her that she must learn to do her work quicker and that the factory was not a place to dream."

Of course, despite the goals of capitalist rationalized production, working women did dream at the factory. They dreamed about education and a brighter future. They dreamed about the dime novels they read, the fashionable clothing they wished to buy, the motion pictures they saw. They dreamed of marrying millionaires, inheriting millions themselves, becoming motion picture stars—of being valued rather than devalued, recognized instead of oppressed. They dreamed of being part of a larger world than the factories that they inhabited for ten, twelve, or even fourteen hours per day. Many of working women's dreams had roots in the daily, material practices of their shared work, consumption, and common disappointments. Indeed, Levy's story casts Regina as misunderstood by all, except for her co-workers—"we who work with her together." Working women's dreams and their subjectivities were inextricably entwined with the products of consumer capitalism, but the women were not simply duped customers. Though producers wished to control the terms and meanings of consumption, they could not anticipate or dictate the social practices through which working women incorporated fashion, fiction, and film products into their daily lives. The meanings of the particular products emerged not simply from the objects themselves, but from those social practices that gave them currency and shared value among working women.

This book has explored the pains and the pleasures of consumer capitalism in working women's lives at the turn of the twentieth century. Women's work drained their energy and health, but required little of their intelligence or creative capacity. Their jobs—in garment factories and sweatshops, laundries, box factories, department stores, artificial flower factories, etc.—emerged directly from the booming consumer industries that supplied a diverse population with new products. The rationalization and mechanization of these jobs meant that employers gave little, if any, attention to human needs for health, comfort, interest, or pride in labor. The women were pioneer workers in an economic system that has persistently been willing to put profits ahead of people, and dollars ahead of dreams.

Despite this dehumanizing system, working women embraced dime novels, fashion, and film products and used them to create distinctive and pleasurable social practices and to enact identities as ladies. Consumer culture producers thus profited from the women's capacity to imagine and create, even as factory bosses sought to remove those abilities from women's daily part in the production process. Capitalist owners could not fully rationalize human existence; rather, consumer capitalism generated new urban landscapes and social relations that fostered new ways of dreaming and forming subjectivities. This was not a free realm and women could not construct subjectivities in any way that they chose. Rather, they had a limited cultural repetoire imbued with the marks of existing gender, class, and race hierarchies. Specifically, capitalist economic and social relations shaped the products available to working women, rendered some subjects off limits, and categorized the goods as "cheap" and without moral value. However, when these products entered social circulation, working women endowed them with another set of meanings that became resources for resisting the daily oppressions of the workplace and the insidious oppression of the spirit. Working women experienced the pains and the pleasures of consumer capitalism simultaneously.

Consumer culture thus became central to working women's subjectivities. The practices of ladyhood built upon dime novel and fashion consumption, and directly engaged the exclusions women experienced in a society where the honorable worker was male, the honorable American was a native-born, Anglo-Saxon Protestant, and the honorable woman was middle class. Occupying a site of dramatic cultural contradiction, working ladies claimed all three valued statuses and not only occupied public streets and factories, but did so with proud display. When tens of thousands of working women went on strike in New York City in 1909, their shared culture provided identities and language with which to construct political subjectivities. Indeed, since consumer culture had become central to who they were, they could not help but bring those identities into the strike context. Participation in ladyhood did not necessarily mean that working women would support the strike; indeed, at least a few women used the same powerful tropes to resist unionization. However, the practices of ladyhood became resources for women constructing formal political subjectivities in a society that did not readily recognize them as political actors.

We have inherited a political language that declares consumer culture to be a fantasy and holds up a model of the citizen as Enlightenment subject, refracted through nineteenth-century middle-class ideals of "character." Indeed, labor leaders obscured the role of working ladies in the strike in an effort to represent strikers as political actors to the white middle class. The idea that a subject formed in relationship to certain commodities cannot engage in political exchange has had profound effects on the writing of history, including the history of popular culture. Following Warren Susman's influential article, " 'Personality' and the Making of a Twentieth Century Culture," many critics implicitly or explicitly juxtaposed a nineteenth-century culture of "character," rooted in values of work, duty, and citizenship, with a twentieth-century culture of "personality." For Susman, the "personality model" of the self is rooted in consumer culture, which places a high value on appearance and image.[2] As Janice Radway has noted, many anticapitalist critiques have elevated the "character model" of the self as intrinsically more capable of political action, especially oppositional political action.[3]

The juxtaposition of nineteenth-century character and twentieth-century personality itself comes from nineteenth-century middle-class ideology. As chapter 1 argued, the culture of character was also a culture of commodities. Indeed, the notion of character shaped the meanings that the middle class attached to their own commodity consumption. They used this notion to distinguish commodities with values, supposedly shaped by morals, from commodities clearly shaped by market interests and therefore lacking in values. This obscured the working of the market in the production and dissemination of all consumer products: middle-class fashions as much as the flamboyant dresses of workers, advice manuals and "literature" as much as dime novels and story papers. Thus, the middle class could obscure but also perpetuate its use of commodities to produce class distinction. Ironically, when scholars harken back to a nineteenth-century culture of character as part of an anticapitalist critique, they replicate middle-class ideologies.

Likewise, the corollary assumption that a self formed in relation to commodities is superficial—exhibiting mere personality rather than depth of character—echoes a nineteenth-century middle-class attack on working-class consumption. The notion of "personality" vaguely describes an overt value placed on appearance and image created through commodity purchase that became widespread in the twentieth century, but it says next to nothing about how people's social relations shaped the meanings of commodities in their lives and, simultaneously, shaped their subjectivities. Because commodities became meaningful only in social relations, their use also engaged issues of power that profoundly affected historical actors' daily lives. It should not be surprising, then, that working-class women utilized commodities to construct and to negotiate gender, class, and ethnic identities quite as much as did the middle class, albeit in starkly different ways. Similarly, while we might expect working-class women's political subjectivities to differ from the middle-class definition of rational participation, there is no reason to assume that their consumption would prevent political action.

The belief that consumerism is diametrically opposed to politics is so widespread that it pervades not only works that dismiss or attack popular culture, but also some excellent contributions to the study of popular culture. Historian Susan Glenn's pathbreaking *Daughters of the Shtetl* includes an entire chapter on women's workplace culture and the fantasies that surrounded fashion and other popular culture activities. However, she believes that the workplace culture could foster *either* fantasy *or* politics: "work groups could either function as an outlet for romantic fantasy or become a vital mechanism for focused and purposeful labor protest." Glenn does not ask how fantasy was *related* to politics and to the process of becoming a political subject; in her view, once workers chose labor protest they presumably left fantasy behind. Steven Ross's excellent analysis of class issues and the early film industry, *Working-Class Hollywood*, celebrates the early movies for giving workers substantial stories of class struggle in a new public culture. However, he contrasts this golden age when audiences dealt with the "reality" of class relations with later Hollywood cinema, which he terms a "fantasy industry." For Ross, fantasies are dangerous distractions from real politics.[4] Both of these historians have advanced the field of labor and social history in important ways, but each also shores up a notion of a resistant political subject that juxtaposes politics with fantasy and consumerism.

The analytical binary between consumerism and politics creates a myth of a rational political actor who does not obtain an identity within commodity culture, and precludes understanding the diverse paths to political identities. This myth then leads to a heroic history of political actors who have exhibited remarkable, if inexplicable, autonomy, rationality, and agency despite the myriad of forces arrayed against them. While most historians agree that identity is socially constructed, that people cannot freely create themselves, in historical studies agency often seems to inhere in the political individual. Such histories can be inspiring in their clarion calls for justice and collective action, but ultimately they can be defeating as well: people today can seem to fall far short of those earlier heroes who possessed such marvelous character and will.

Pauline Newman certainly thought so. Former shirtwaist worker and labor leader, Newman in the 1970s found workers lacking the seriousness of purpose that she recalled in the garment workers of the early 1900s. Her memory of the women she organized in the 1910s came to match the ideal that labor leaders constructed: "I'm a little discouraged sometimes when I see the workers [today] spending their free hours watching television—trash. We fought so hard for those hours and they waste them. We used to read Tolstoy, Dickens, Shelley, by candlelight, and they watch the 'Hollywood Squares.' "[5] Newman and some other women probably *did* read Tolstoy, Dickens, and Shelley. However, many women read dime novel romances instead. Indeed, in articles published in the ILGWU's *Ladies Garment Worker* in the 1910s, Newman regularly urged women to stop reading dime novels and take up "serious" reading, even if they found it dull.[6] But in the 1970s, Newman relied on a historical narrative that denied the earlier generation's relationship to mass-produced entertainment and positioned the women of the 1910s as serious and rational political subjects. However, Newman's description of the heroic working women *also* depended on a particular set of commodities: she asserted the character of early women workers through high literature. Newman did not see these literary products as commodities, nor did she see their fictional narratives as fantasies.

This is not to suggest that we celebrate consumerism and the fantasies related to it as somehow free of the influence of capitalism or social hierarchies. The arena of popular culture is not an arena of freedom, but is at every point interwoven with larger social discourses and relations. The commodities available to particular groups are shaped and categorized by a combination of economic and cultural interests that opens up certain possibilities but also imposes limits. It is little wonder that for Newman, access to high literature could feel like a transcendence of the types of goods marketed to working women. But Newman did not consider the ways in which high literature was also limited. Rather than searching for an arena of freedom, we might more fruitfully look at the ways people make dreams and identities—including political identities—within their limited arenas and with the resources available.

It is my hope that this book will contribute to an ongoing process of creating new political visions and narratives. The notion that political subjectivity requires a demonstration of rationality or an appearance of seriousness or character tacitly privileges people who have access to cultural institutions teaching such values and behaviors, and thus tends to replicate gender, class, and race exclusions. We need to understand how political ideals have at times foreclosed options and rendered some possibilities unintelligible. Popular culture allowed working women to claim a place to dream in their daily lives. Of course, their dreams, no less than their material conditions, were inevitably rooted in and limited by the hierarchical structures of U.S. society. But precisely because working ladies found themselves excluded from the honorable categories of "worker," "American" and "woman," the resources of popular culture were of particular importance in their efforts to claim identities out of contradictions, and gain a sense of dignity and worth. As Walter Benjamin argued, the wish images embedded in many popular culture products are important not because they are radicalizing in themselves, but because they engage a utopian impulse within the imagination. If we want to know where agency comes from and how people manage to challenge oppressive hierarchies that shape their world, then we have to know who they have become and what resources are available to them. In the context of nearly debilitating oppressions, having a place to create shared dreams is crucial for the formation of a self that is resilient, capable of survival, creativity, and the production of new social forms. These new forms, in turn, may help us to envision new political identities or to recover old ones that had been lost to history. Indeed, the challenges of promoting political change in the context of a global capitalist system may require close attention to the particular pleasures, dreams, and subjectivities that become our imperfect resources. When dreams based in consumer culture are revealed to be collective, integral to the formation of the self and to political identities, it is time for the historian to take up the interpretation of dreams.[7]

NOTES

Introduction: Mud in Our French Heels

1. For excellent discussions of this iconography see Barbara Melosh, *Engendering Culture: Manhood and Womanhood in New Deal Public Art and Theater* (Washington, D.C.: Smithsonian Institution Press, 1991), 83–109; Elizabeth Faue, *Community of Suffering and Struggle: Women, Men and the Labor Movement in Minneapolis, 1915–1945* (Chapel Hill: University of North Carolina Press, 1991), 69–99.

2. Judith Butler, *Gender Trouble: Feminism and the Subversion of Identity* (New York: Routledge, 1990), especially 142–48; Butler, *Bodies That Matter: On the Discursive Limits of "Sex"* (New York: Routledge, 1993), 189–91, 206. See also Denise Riley, *Am I That Name?: Feminism and the Category of "Women" in History* (New York: Macmillan, 1988).

3. Elizabeth Spelman, *Inessential Woman: The Problems of Exclusion in Feminist Thought* (Boston: Beacon, 1988), 158–59. Sandra Harding similarly argues that many feminists have replicated the theories of liberation that have been used to oppress women and to keep them situated as "other." Feminists have placed themselves in the position of subject, unwittingly positing a new "other"

outside themselves. See Harding, "The Instability of the Analytical Categories of Feminist Theory" in Sandra Harding and Jean O'Barr, eds., *Sex and Scientific Inquiry* (Chicago: University of Chicago Press, 1987), 294.

4. David R. Roediger, *The Wages of Whiteness: Race and the Making of the American Working Class* (New York: Verso, 1991). See also David Montgomery, *Citizen Worker: The Experience of Workers in the United States with Democracy and the Free Market During the Nineteenth Century* (Cambridge: Cambridge University Press, 1993).

5. In addition, Ava Baron has argued that women and people of color were systematically excluded from categories of work considered "skilled," which was often a designation having more to do with who did the work than the amount of learning required to perform it. See Baron, "Questions of Gender: Deskilling and Demasculinization in the U.S. Printing Industry, 1830–1915," *Gender and History* I:178–99.

6. For a discussion of Samuel Gompers and the American Federation of Labor's attitude toward women workers see Alice Kessler-Harris, *Out to Work: A History of Wage-Earning Women in the United States* (New York: Oxford University Press, 1982), 153–58.

7. Tania Modleski, "Femininity as Mas(s)querade" in *Feminism Without Women: Culture and Criticism in a "Postfeminist" Age* (New York: Routledge, 1991), 23. For related discussions see Andreas Huyssen, "Mass Culture as Woman: Modernism's Other" in Tania Modleski, ed., *Studies in Entertainment: Critical Approaches to Mass Culture* (Bloomington: Indiana University Press, 1986), 188–207; Patrice Petro, "Mass Culture and the Feminine: The 'Place' of Television in Film Studies," *Cinema Journal* 25 (3): 5–21; Mary Louise Roberts, "Gender, Consumption, and Commodity Culture," *American Historical Review* 103 (3): 817–44; Victoria de Grazia with Ellen Furlough, eds., *The Sex of Things: Gender and Consumption in Historical Perspective* (Berkeley: University of California Press, 1996), introduction.

8. Modleski, "Femininity as Mas(s)querade," 24–26. Modleski pairs her excellent critique of Ann Douglas with a critique of Jean Baudrillard, who in this respect is similar to de Certeau in affirming what he sees as the "effeminate" nature of consumer culture. Michel de Certeau, *The Practice of Everyday Life*, trans. Steven F. Rendall (Berkeley: University of California Press, 1984), 21.

9. The notion of "mass deception" comes from the Frankfurt school of cultural critics, who argued persuasively in the 1940s that consumer culture bears the imprint of the production process that created it, which results in an impoverishment of variety and content. Theodor Adorno and Max Horkheimer argue that consumer culture products, such as films, leave no room for contemplative response, so their function is to degrade culture and transmit dominant ideologies. Whereas art could be a mechanism of critique and community building, resisting totalitarianism, consumer culture negates the contemplation crucial to it. Consumer culture thus must be resisted in order to resist totalitarian

domination. This aspect of their thought has been taken up by more recent scholars such as Stuart and Elizabeth Ewen and Neil Postman, who assume that a leftist political consciousness is by definition opposed to a participation in consumer culture. Theodor Adorno and Max Horkheimer, "The Culture Industry: Enlightenment as Mass Deception" in their *Dialectic of Enlightenment* (1944; reprint, New York: Herder and Herder, 1972), 139. Stuart and Elizabeth Ewen, "Consumption as a Way of Life," in *Channels of Desire: Mass Images and the Shaping of American Consciousness* (Minneapolis: University of Minnesota Press, 1982), 51. Neil Postman, *Amusing Ourselves to Death* (New York: Penguin, 1985). Leslie Tentler applied this notion to working-class women at the turn of the century, claiming that women's participation in consumer culture reinforced dominant notions of femininity and was, by its nature, conservative. Leslie Woodcock Tentler, *Wage-Earning Women: Industrial Work and Family Life in the United States, 1900–1930* (New York: Oxford University Press, 1979).

10. See George Lipsitz, *Time Passages: Collective Memory and American Popular Culture* (Minneapolis: University of Minnesota Press, 1990), 16–17.

11. Meredith Tax, *The Rising of the Women: Feminist Solidarity and Class Conflict, 1880–1917* (New York: Monthly Review Press, 1980); Nancy Schrom Dye, *As Equals and as Sisters: Feminism, the Labor Movement, and the Women's Trade Union League of New York* (Columbia: University of Missouri Press, 1980); and Annelise Orleck, *Common Sense and a Little Fire: Women and Working-Class Politics in the United States, 1900–1965* (Chapel Hill: University of North Carolina, 1995) all give scant if any attention to consumer culture practices among women strikers. Historians who focus their studies on immigrant groups rather than on labor history tend to include more discussion of consumer culture. See Susan Glenn, *Daughters of the Shtetl: Life and Labor in the Immigrant Generation* (Ithaca: Cornell University Press, 1990).

12. Kathy Peiss, *Cheap Amusements: Working Women and Leisure in Turn-of-the-Century New York* (Philadelphia: Temple University Press, 1986). A few historians do note that women engaged in popular culture and participated in strikes, but analyze the two phenomena separately. See Joanne Meyerowitz, *Women Adrift: Independent Wage Earners in Chicago, 1880–1930* (Chicago: University of Chicago Press, 1988), Elizabeth Ewen, *Immigrant Women in the Land of Dollars: Life and Culture on the Lower East Side, 1890–1925* (New York: Monthly Review Press, 1985), and Glenn, *Daughters of the Shtetl.* Tentler, *Wage-Earning Women*, explores the work culture of working women, and argues that it had a conservative effect, reinforcing the view that "female culture" is contrasted with serious politics.

13. Jacqueline Dowd Hall, "Disorderly Women: Gender and Labor Militancy in the Appalachian South," *Journal of American History* 73:354–82; Stephen H. Norwood, *Labor's Flaming Youth: Telephone Operators and Worker Militancy, 1878–1923* (Urbana: University of Illinois Press, 1990), 12; Robin D. G. Kelley, "The Riddle of the Zoot: Malcolm Little and Black Cultural Politics During World War II" in *Race Rebels: Culture, Politics, and the Black Working Class* (New York: Free Press, 1994), 162–63; Tricia Rose, *Black Noise: Rap Music and Black*

Culture in Contemporary America (Hanover, N.H.: Wesleyan University Press, 1994), 4. Historians George Sanchez, Vicki Ruiz, and Lizabeth Cohen similarly argue that participation in consumer culture does not necessarily undermine ethnic or working-class identity but can even be a means of maintaining it. George Sanchez, *Becoming Mexican American: Ethnicity, Culture and Identity in Chicano Los Angeles, 1900–1945* (New York: Oxford, 1993), 171–206; Vicki Ruiz, " 'Star Struck': Acculturation, Adolescence, and Mexican American Women, 1920–1950" in Elliott West and Paula Petrik, eds., *Small Worlds: Children and Adolescents in America, 1850–1950* (Lawrence: University Press of Kansas, 1992), 61–80; Lizabeth Cohen, *Making a New Deal: Industrial Workers in Chicago, 1919–1939* (New York: Cambridge University Press, 1990), 99–158.

14. Lipsitz, *Time Passages*, 253.

15. For critiques of this phenomenon see Ellen Willis, "Consumerism and Women" in Vivian Gornick and Barbara K. Moran, eds., *Woman in Sexist Society* (New York: Basic Books, 1971), 480–84; Carolyn Steedman, *Landscape for a Good Woman: A Story of Two Lives* (London: Virago, 1986); Cynthia Wright, " 'Feminine Trifles of Vast Importance': Writing Gender into the History of Consumption" in Franca Iacovetta and Marianna Valverde, eds., *Gender Conflicts: New Essays in Women's History* (Toronto: University of Toronto Press, 1992), 229–60.

16. Angela McRobbie, *Feminism and Youth Culture: From "Jackie" to "Just Seventeen"* (Boston: Unwin Hyman, 1991), 13. In her chapter "Settling Accounts with Subculture: A Feminist Critique," McRobbie argues that the early group of male scholars of subcultures defended the popular culture activities of the boys they were studying against the frivolous and consumerist use of popular culture among girls. This attempt to legitimate the seriousness of their subject matter, argued McRobbie, unwittingly prompted them to write "homages to masculinity."

17. Lisa Lewis, *Gender Politics and MTV: Voicing the Difference* (Philadelphia: Temple University Press, 1990); Janice Radway, *Reading the Romance: Women, Patriarchy and Popular Literature* (Chapel Hill: University of North Carolina Press, 1984).

18. *New York Evening Journal*, November 26, 1909.

19. Dye, *As Equals and as Sisters*, 21.

20. For a discussion of workplace conditions in the garment industry, see Orleck, *Common Sense and a Little Fire*, 32–33, and Glenn, *Daughters of the Shtetl*, 103–6. For discussions of the Triangle Shirtwaist Factory fire see Orleck 130–31.

21. Mary Brown Sumner, "The Spirit of the Strikers," *The Survey* 13:554.

22. Jewish women usually handed their pay envelopes to their mothers, because mothers managed household finances. However, fathers remained the heads of households. For discussions of working women's use of fashion within the family see Ewen, *Immigrant Women in the Land of Dollars*, 186–205; Peiss, *Cheap Amusements*, 56–87; Glenn, *Daughters of the Shtetl*, 161–65; Barbara A.

Schreier, *Becoming American Women: Clothing and the Jewish Immigrant Experience, 1880–1920* (Chicago: Chicago Historical Society, 1994), 121–46. These issues will be explored in more depth in chapter 2.

23. For discussions of clothing and Americanization see Schreier's excellent museum exhibit catalogue (ibid.), 56–62, 126–29; Ewen, *Immigrant Women in the Land of Dollars*, 202–3; Glenn, *Daughters of the Shtetl*, 160–61.

24. Miriam Cohen, *Workshop to Office: Two Generations of Italian Women in New York City, 1900–1950* (Ithaca: Cornell University Press, 1993), 69–72; Schreier, *Becoming American Women*, 121–48; Peiss, *Cheap Amusements*, 56–87. See also Judith E. Smith, *Family Connections: A History of Italian and Jewish Immigrant Lives in Providence, Rhode Island, 1900–1940* (Albany: SUNY Press, 1985); Donna Gabaccia, *From Sicily to Elizabeth Street: Housing and Social Change Among Italian Immigrants 1880–1930* (Albany: SUNY Press, 1984).

25. John D'Emilio and Estelle B. Freedman, *Intimate Matters: A History of Sexuality in America* (New York: Harper and Row, 1988), 278.

26. This idea will be developed in further depth in chapter 2. Other critics who discuss the capacity of popular culture to undermine family-based patriarchy because of its appeal to different members of the family in different market segments include Joel Kovel, "Rationalization and the Family," *TELOS* 14 (1978); Fred Pfeil, "Makin' Flippy Floppy" in his book *Another Tale to Tell: Politics and Narrative in Postmodern Culture* (New York: Verso, 1990).

27. It is not my argument that this movie was directly influential on Lemlich; its release over two years after the Uprising of the 20,000 ensures that this was not the case. Rather, I am arguing that this short movie exemplified new ideologies about consumption pervasive in the early twentieth century. Such strategies outlived the pre–World War I era. Perhaps the most famous of these is the Virginia Slims cigarette advertisement that reads "You've come a long way, baby." The success of R. J. Reynolds in associating the consumption of cigarettes with women's liberation can perhaps be measured by the plethora of feminist newspaper and journal articles that have repeated or altered this slogan.

28. Judith Walkowitz, *City of Dreadful Delight: Narratives of Sexual Danger in Late-Victorian London* (Chicago: University of Chicago Press, 1992), 9.

29. Angela McRobbie, "New Times in Cultural Studies," *New Formations* 13:13.

30. My study focuses accordingly on the construction of gender, class, and ethnic identities and ideologies. Race is also important to this story in several ways. The racial status of Jewish and Italian women at the turn of the century was a matter of debate. In addition, there are many parallels between how the women we now think of as "white ethnics" and African American women inverted dominant power structures through their use of fashion and tropes of "ladyhood."

31. For example, see Joan W. Scott, "Experience," in Joan W. Scott and Judith Butler, eds., *Feminists Theorize the Political* (New York: Routledge, 1992), 22–40.

32. My thinking about this issue is indebted to Elsa Barkley Brown's lecture, "Telling Democratic Stories: the Politics of African American Women's Lives," Mellon Foundation Lecture Series, Duke University, September 19, 1995; and Robin D. G. Kelley, "Introduction: Writing Black Working-Class History From Way, Way Below" in *Race Rebels*, 1–16.

1. Cheap Dresses and Dime Novels

1. Quoted in Glenn, *Daughters of the Shtetl*, 163.

2. James Oppenheim, "Peg O' the Movies," *The Ladies' World* (Nov. 1913): 5.

3. Louis Althusser, "Ideology and Ideological State Apparatuses," in *Lenin and Philosophy*, trans. Ben Brewster (New York: Monthly Review Press, 1971), 170–86; see also Teresa de Lauretis, *Technologies of Gender: Essays on Theory, Film and Fiction* (Bloomington: Indiana University Press, 1987).

4. Martyn J. Lee, *Consumer Culture Reborn: The Cultural Politics of Consumption* (New York: Routledge, 1993), 39, 49.

5. Warren Susman, " 'Personality' and the Making of Twentieth-Century Culture," in *Culture as History: The Transformation of American Society in the Twentieth Century* (New York: Pantheon, 1984), 271–85.

6. This myth has been repeated in numerous scholarly treatments of the Lawrence strike. Recently, Gerald M. Sider has revealed the mythic nature of the connection between "Bread and Roses" and the Lawrence Strike. He suggests that the poem, published in the I.W.W.'s *Industrial Worker* in 1946, reflects a Fordist sentiment for company paternalism. Neither is correct. It is impossible for Oppenheim to have been inspired by the Lawrence strikers or Fordist policies when he wrote "Bread and Roses," because he first published the poem in December 1911, a month before the 1912 strike began. Despite the fact that Sider did not check to see when the poem was written, I agree with his statement that "close textual analysis can be done as a way of getting your hands on (rather than washing your hands of any responsibility for) the social relations from which 'texts' come." See Joyce L. Kornbluh, ed., *Rebel Voices: An I.W.W. Anthology* (Ann Arbor: University of Michigan Press, 1964); Gerald M. Sider, "Cleansing History: Lawrence, Massachusetts, the Strike for Four Loaves of Bread and No Roses, and the Anthropology of Working-class Consciousness," *Radical History Review* 65:77, 82; James Oppenheim, "Bread and Roses," *American Magazine* 73 (2): 214.

7. Claudia B. Kidwell and Margaret C. Christman, *Suiting Everyone: The Democratization of Clothing in America* (Washington, D.C.: Smithsonian Institution Press, 1974), 19–23, 27–31, 65–69.

8. Ibid., 39, 43–49; Joan L. Severa, *Dressed for the Photographer: Ordinary Americans and Fashion, 1840–1900* (Kent, Ohio: Kent State University Press, 1995), 25.

9. Christine Stansell, *City of Women: Sex and Class in New York, 1789–1860* (New York: Knopf, 1986), 90.

10. Kidwell and Christman, *Suiting Everyone*, 135–37; Severa, *Dressed for the Photographer*, 9, 297; Stansell, *City of Women*, 107–8, 164.

11. Stuart Blumin argues that the middle class emerged by the mid-nineteenth century as a class with a "distinctive way of life," rooted in specific patterns of work and consumption, as well as particular family strategies, changing spatial structures of urban neighborhoods, and participation in voluntary associations. Consumption became not only a line of conflict between classes, but even in the absence of overt conflict was a means of distinction and definition of class boundaries. Stuart Blumin, *The Emergence of the Middle Class: Social Experience in the American City, 1760–1900* (New York: Cambridge University Press, 1989), 11–12. For his discussion of the role of consumption in class formation see 138–91.

12. The nineteenth-century middle class built upon colonial consumer practices. "Gentility" was an upper-class ideal that middling colonists sought to appropriate. They could not afford full-fledged gentility per se: their expendable income simply was not great enough. Nor should their consumption be interpreted simply as an imitation of the consumer activity of the upper crust. Rather, middling people wove consumer products into their own culture, creating what Bushman called "vernacular gentility." Indeed, Donald Hall argues that print products allowed colonists, particularly New Englanders, to challenge the authority of the church and practice a syncretic religion more openly than in the seventeenth century. T. H. Breen extends this argument to suggest that the spirit of consumerism very much affected the middle class: infused with liberalism, many believed it was now their right to consume regardless of rank. Richard L. Bushman, "American High-Style and Vernacular Cultures" in Jack Greene and J. R. Pole, eds., *Colonial British America: Essays in the New History of the Early Modern Era* (Baltimore: Johns Hopkins University Press, 1984), 345–83; T. H. Breen, "The Meanings of Things: Interpreting the Consumer Economy in the Eighteenth Century" in John Brewer and Roy Porter, eds., *Consumption and the World of Goods* (New York: Routledge, 1993), 249–60; David D. Hall, *Worlds of Wonder, Days of Judgment: Popular Religious Belief in Early New England* (New York: Knopf, 1989), 49–52; Carole Shammas, "Changes in English and Anglo-American Consumption from 1550 to 1800" in John Brewer and Roy Porter, eds., *Consumption and the World of Goods*, 185–91.

13. John Kasson, *Rudeness and Civility: Manners in Nineteenth-Century Urban America* (New York: Hill and Wang, 1990), 38–43.

14. See in particular Kidwell and Christman, *Suiting Everyone*. This book draws heavily on Daniel Boorstin's *The Americans: The Democratic Experience* (New York: Random House, 1973), which celebrates industrialization as a democratizing force in history, dismissing workers' experiences. For a recent extensions of the "democratization" thesis, see Severa, *Dressed for the Photographer*, and Nancy L. Green, *Ready-to-Wear and Ready-to-Work: A Century of Industry and Immigrants in Paris and New York* (Durham: Duke University Press, 1997), 21–25.

15. Blumin, *The Emergence of the Middle Class*, 138–91; Mary Ryan, *Cradle of the Middle Class: The Family in Oneida County, New York, 1790–1865* (New York: Cambridge University Press, 1981). My understanding of cultural capital draws from Pierre Bourdieu's notion of "habitus," the matrix of culturally determined beliefs and ways of seeing that enable a person's cultural classification of the world around them. The habitus is internalized, rather than necessarily conscious, and manifests partly in terms of "class taste," with "class" considered broadly to mean a classification of society, including race, ethnicity, social class, etc. See *Distinction: A Social Critique of the Judgement of Taste* (Cambridge: Harvard University Press, 1984), 169–72.

16. Quoted in Karen Halttunen, *Confidence Men and Painted Women: a Study of Middle-Class Culture in America, 1830–1870* (New Haven: Yale University Press, 1982), 80.

17. Ibid., 90.

18. See Lee's excellent discussion of Marx's notion of the fetishization of the commodity, *Consumer Culture Reborn*, 17.

19. Fashion and other commodities, however removed from the production process, were not empty of meaning or "blank slates" waiting to be inscribed by an all-powerful advertising industry, as some cultural critics have argued. Rather, products always already have associations with related commodities and take up circulation within established consumer practices. Thus, a historical perspective of consumers' ideologies and practices is crucial.

20. Halttunen, *Confidence Men and Painted Women*, 79; see discussion 72–80. See also Kathy Peiss's related discussion of the changing class and race meanings of makeup in the eighteenth and nineteenth centuries in *Hope in a Jar: The Making of America's Beauty Culture* (New York: Holt, 1998), 22–35.

21. Quoted in Halttunen, *Confidence Men and Painted Women*, 67.

22. Severa, *Dressed for the Photographer*, 3.

23. Quoted in Halttunen, *Confidence Men and Painted Women*, 70.

24. Quoted in Severa, *Dressed for the Photographer*, 89.

25. Ibid., 95.

26. Quoted in ibid., 4, emphasis in the original.

27. While middle-class styles developed in large part to express class and race distinctions, these styles certainly held other meanings as well. Middle-class women undoubtedly took pleasure in dress, just as did women of the working class, and the constricting styles could have powerful aesthetic and sexual connotations. In addition, middle-class women could have devised a number of strategies to turn their resources of dress to their greatest advantage. Indeed, the very confluence of power and constriction in Victorian era women's clothing provided fodder for eroticism that continues to fascinate many over one hundred years later. In this chapter, however, I am focusing on the role of dress in constructing and maintaining class hierarchies, rather than pursuing a

comprehensive analysis of the meanings of middle-class women's dress in their own homes and social gatherings.

28. Stuart Blumin, "The Hypothesis of Middle-Class Formation in Nineteenth-Century America: A Critique and Some Proposals," *American Historical Review* 90 (Apr. 1985), 307–9.

29. Both quoted in Stansell, *City of Women*, 94 and 164. The first quote is from *Godey's Lady's Book*; the second is from the *New York Tribune*.

30. Ibid., 100.

31. Kidwell and Christman, *Suiting Everyone*, 135–45; Severa, *Dressed for the Photographer*, 297, 372–73.

32. Bertha June Richardson, *The Woman Who Spends: A Study of Her Economic Functions* (Boston: Witcomb and Barrows, 1904), 75–76.

33. Quoted in Kidwell and Christman, *Suiting Everyone*, 142. These kinds of ball dresses cost as little as $7.50.

34. Rose Pastor, "Just Between Us Girls," *Yiddishes Tageblatt* (December 27, 1903).

35. Lillian D. Wald, *The House on Henry Street* (New York: Henry Holt and Company, 1915), 191.

36. Sue Ainslie Clark and Edith Wyatt, *Making Both Ends Meet: The Income and Outlay of New York Working Girls* (New York: Macmillan, 1911), 7.

37. Cornelia Stratton Parker, *Working With the Working Woman* (New York: Harper & Brothers, 1922), 88; Elizabeth Hasanovitz, *One of Them: Chapters From a Passionate Autobiography* (Boston: Houghton Mifflin, 1918), 193; Clark and Wyatt, *Making Both Ends Meet*, 106. Dorothy Richardson describes laundry workers who labored in stockings or barefoot because their shoes were so uncomfortable. However, without protection their feet were burned by the floors, hot from the steaming equipment. *The Long Day: The Story of a New York Working Girl* (New York: The Century Company, 1905), 243, 248. Shoes also signified American "affluence," as some immigrants had gone barefoot, except on holidays, in the old country. See Schreier, *Becoming American Women*, 62–63.

38. Richardson, *The Long Day*, 70, 108–9, 232; Hasanovitz, *One of Them*, 93; Clark and Wyatt, *Making Both Ends Meet*, 88–89.

39. Severa, *Dressed for the Photographer*, 205, 380.

40. Richardson, *The Woman Who Spends*, 76.

41. Michael Schudson, *Discovering the News: A Social History of American Newspapers* (New York: Basic Books, 1978), 35.

42. Alexander Saxton, *The Rise and Fall of the White Republic: Class Politics and Mass Culture in Nineteenth Century America* (New York: Verso, 1990), 96.

43. Daniel Czitrom, *Media and the American Mind: From Morse to McLuhan* (Chapel Hill: University of North Carolina Press, 1982), 14–15.

44. Conde B. Pallen, quoted in ibid., 20.

45. See Peter Stallybrass and Allon White, *The Politics and Poetics of Transgression* (Ithaca: Cornell University Press, 1986). As they write, "Disgust always bears the imprint of desire," 191.

46. See Saxton, *The Rise and Fall of the White Republic*, 95–105.

47. My understanding of the history of dime novels is greatly indebted to Michael Denning's pathbreaking study, *Mechanic Accents: Dime Novels and Working-Class Culture in America* (New York: Verso, 1987). For a discussion of the early story papers, see 10–12.

48. Street and Smith boasted sales of 80,000 for the *New York Weekly* by 1859, nearly a 400 percent increase in the four years of its existence. Average sales grew to 150,000 by 1863, and 350,000 in 1877. Dime novels showed similar success. See ibid., 10–11; Mary Noel, *Villains Galore: The Heyday of the Popular Story Weekly* (New York: The McMillan Company, 1954), 110–12; and Lydia Cushman Schurman, "The Publishing Firm of Street and Smith: Its First Fifty Years, 1855–1905," *Dime Novel Roundup* (Apr. 1988):20–24.

49. Following Michael Denning's terminology, I will refer to the body of popular fiction that included the related forms of story papers, dime novels, cheap libraries, and inexpensive books as "dime novels." See Denning, *Mechanic Accents*, 10–12; advertisement for George Munro's Sons, Publishers found in Laura Jean Libbey, *Leonie Locke: The Story of a New York Working Girl* (New York: George Munro's Sons, Publishers, 1884).

50. For another discussion of this topic, see Denning, *Mechanic Accents*, 17–26.

51. Cathy Davidson, "The Life and Times of *Charlotte Temple*: The Biography of a Book," in Davidson, ed., *Reading in America: Literature and Social History* (Baltimore: Johns Hopkins University Press, 1989), 157, 165, 174, 178.

52. William Wallace Cook, *The Fiction Factory* (Ridgewood, N.J.: The Editor Company, 1912), 33–42; Denning, *Mechanic Accents*, 23–26.

53. Cook, *The Fiction Factory*, 43–44, 58.

54. Fredric Jameson, "Reification and Utopia in Mass Culture," *Social Text* 1 (1) (1979): 130–48.

55. Denning, *Mechanic Accents*, 85, 94–96.

56. Ibid., 96–97; 104–5.

57. Ibid., 73, 94–95, 104–5; Saxton, *The Rise and Fall of the White Republic*, 97–98; Peter Brooks, *The Melodramatic Imagination: Balzac, Henry James, Melodrama, and the Mode of Excess* (New Haven: Yale University Press, 1976), 1–23.

58. I base this synopsis on my close reading of the following working-girl dime novels by Laura Jean Libbey: *Leonie Locke, or, the Romance of a New York Working Girl* (New York: Monro, 1884); *Only a Mechanic's Daughter: A Charming Story of Love and Passion* (New York: Monro, 1892); *Willful Gaynell or the Little Beauty of the Passaic Cotton Mills* (New York: Monro 1890); *The Heiress of*

Cameron Hall (New York: Monro, 1897); *Ione: A Broken Love Dream* (New York: Street and Smith, 1887); *Little Leafy the Cloakmaker's Beautiful Daughter* (New York: J.S. Ogilvie, 1891); *A Master Workman's Oath or Coralie the Unfortunate* (New York: Monro, 1892); and two other "Laura Jean Libby type" dime novels: Mrs. Georgie Sheldon, *A True Aristocrat* (New York: Street and Smith, 1882); Geraldine Fleming, *Only a Working Girl* (New York: Monro, 1895). Most of these dime novels were published first as story papers and continued to be reprinted well into the twentieth century. I also randomly selected thirty-seven additional dime novel romances (not necessarily with working-girl heroines) held at the Kerlan Collection at the University of Minnesota to obtain a picture of the range of dime novels available.

59. Stansell, *City of Women*, 112–13.

60. Denning, *Mechanic Accents*, 186; Noel, *Villains Galore*, 277–78.

61. Dorothy Pam, "Exploitation, Independence and Solidarity: The Changing Role of Working Women as Reflected in the Working Girl Melodrama, 1870–1910," (Ph.D. dissertation, New York University, 1980). See also Denning, *Mechanic Accents*, 186.

62. Charles Foster, "Bertha, the Sewing Machine Girl; or Death at the Wheel," script, New York Public Library, Billie Rose Theater Collection.

63. Denning, *Mechanic Accents*, 168–73.

64. "Bertha M. Clay" originated as a pen name for a British author of sensational romances, Charlotte Mary Braeme. It became a house name for Street and Smith Publishing Company. See Noel, *Villains Galore*, 186–90; Denning, *Mechanic Accents*, 23–24; Arlene Moore, "Searching for Bertha M. Clay: Problems in Researching the Topic and Areas for Further Study," *Dime Novel Roundup* (Feb. 1991):10–14.

65. Mrs. Georgie Sheldon, *A True Aristocrat* (New York: Street and Smith, 1882), 287. *A True Aristocrat* was reprinted at least three times, in 1891, 1910, and in the 1920s.

66. See Denning, *Mechanic Accents*, 188–89.

67. Jane Tompkins, *Sensational Designs: The Cultural Work of American Fiction, 1790–1860* (New York: Oxford University Press, 1985), 143–44. See also Nina Baym, *Woman's Fiction: A Guide to Novels by and About Women in America, 1820–1870* (Ithaca: Cornell University Press, 1978); and Mary Kelley, *Private Woman, Public Stage: Literary Domesticity in Nineteenth-Century America* (Oxford: Oxford University Press, 1984).

68. Brooks, *The Melodramatic Imagination*, 14–17.

69. Middle-class women's assertion that domestic fiction had value was not accepted by literary critics who constructed an American literary canon in the late nineteenth and twentieth centuries. Critics dismissed this writing as "sentimental" and feminine and considered its popularity evidence of its lack of literary value. See Tompkins, *Sensational Designs*.

70. Libbey, *Leonie Locke*; Libbey, *Ione: A Broken Love Dream* (New York: Street and Smith, 1887).

71. "Laura Jean Libbey Hoped to Achieve Immortality," *New York Times*, November 2, 1924,VII:11.

72. Cook, *The Fiction Factory*, 173.

73. Denning, *Mechanic Accents*, 50–52.The new pressure to "clean up" dime novels was felt in vaudeville as well. See Robert W. Snyder, *The Voice of the City: Vaudeville and Popular Culture in New York* (New York: Oxford, 1989).

74. Joyce Shaw Peterson, "Working Girls and Millionaires: The Melodramatic Romances of Laura Jean Libbey," *American Studies* 24 (1) (Spring 1983): 19–35.

75. Meyerowitz, *Women Adrift*, 56–60.

76. Lawrence Levine argues that the upper class "rescued" the arts, particularly the symphony, theater, and museums, from the market in order to "win freedom from the pressures of the marketplace." However, this analysis is problematic for two reasons. First, as Paul DiMaggio contends, it is only when elites and a sizable middle class joined forces that high culture institutions were economically viable.The upper class did not eliminate economic influence on the arts, but simply shifted the nature of that influence. Second, Levine's analysis supposes that this "freedom" from the marketplace would lead to "free expression."This is simply the ideology that elites and the middle class promoted. Such elite institutions were not really free from the marketplace, and while their expression certainly was meaningful, as was expression in vaudeville, it was not "free." Styles, canon formation, and the need to profitably express middle-class values shaped the expression of elite cultural forms as much as the need to sell tickets, please the many, and displease the fewest shaped popular forms. Paul DiMaggio, "Cultural Entrepreneurship in Nineteenth-Century Boston: The Creation of an Organizational Base for High Culture in America" in Chandra Mukerji and Michael Schudson, eds., *Rethinking Popular Culture: Contemporary Perspectives in Cultural Studies* (Berkeley: University of California Press, 1991), 374–77, 383; Lawrence W. Levine, *Highbrow/Lowbrow:The Emergence of Cultural Hierarchy in America* (Cambridge: Harvard University Press, 1988), 132, 230.

77. See James Oppenheim,"The Story of the Seven Arts," *American Mercury* 20 (78) (June 1930): 156–57 for a discussion of his desire to write without the need to make a living shaping what or how he wrote.

78. Lincoln Steffens, *The Autobiography of Lincoln Steffens*, vol. 2 (New York: Harcourt, Brace and Co., 1931), 536, 541, 575–76.

79. Oppenheim,"The Story of the Seven Arts," 156–58.

2. Ladies of Labor

1. Richardson, *The Woman Who Spends*, 77–78.

2. Butler, *Gender Trouble*, 148.

3. Wald, *The House on Henry Street*, 172. Priscilla Murolo notes that even women who took part in the working-girl clubs, organized by middle-class reformers, often resisted the advice of club leaders to dress "tastefully." *The Common Ground of Womanhood: Class, Gender and Working Girls' Clubs, 1884–1928* (Urbana: University of Illinois Press, 1997), 42–44.

4. Rose Pastor, "Talks With Girls," *Yiddishes Tageblatt,* July 12, 1903. Pastor wrote regularly on this Yiddish paper's English page, which attempted to appeal to younger people. See also Pauline Newman, "Our Women Workers: When You Have Time to Read," *Ladies Garment Worker* 4 (7) (June 1913): 34.

5. Pauline Newman, "Working Girl's Homes," *Ladies Garment Worker* 1 (6): 3. See also Gertrude Barnum, "At the Shirt Waist Factory," *Ladies Garment Worker* 1 (2): 3.

6. Rose Pastor, "Just Between Ourselves, Girls," *Yiddishes Tageblatt,* June 7, 1903; Jane Addams, "The Subtle Problem of Charity," *Atlantic Monthly* 83 (Feb. 1899): 168–69.

7. Butler, *Gender Trouble,* 144.

8. Jane Gaines, "Introduction," in Jane Gaines and Charlotte Herzog, eds., *Fabrication: Costume and the Female Body* (New York: Routledge, 1990), 15.

9. Janice Radway, "Interpretive Communities and Variable Literacies: The Functions of Romance Reading," *Daedalus* 113 (3): 66–67.

10. Kelley, *Race Rebels,* 17.

11. Colin Campbell, "The Sociology of Consumption" in Daniel Miller, ed., *Acknowledging Consumption: A Review of New Studies* (New York: Routledge, 1995), 111–19; Fred Davis, *Fashion, Culture and Identity* (Chicago: University of Chicago Press, 1992), 5–12. See also Dick Hebdige, *Subculture: The Meaning of Style* (London: Methuen, 1979).

12. Film critics developed theories of active reception largely in response to Laura Mulvey's "Visual Pleasure and Narrative Cinema," *Screen* 16 (3): 6–18. See Deidre Pribram, *Female Spectators: Looking at Film and Television* (New York: Verso, 1988); Radway, "Interpretive Communities," 51–53.

13. See Radway, ibid. and *Reading the Romance*; Susan Porter Benson, *Counter Cultures: Saleswomen, Managers, and Customers in American Department Stores, 1890–1940* (Urbana: University of Illinois Press, 1986).

14. For a discussion of Benjamin's notion of the "dream world," see Susan Buck-Morss, *The Dialectics of Seeing: Walter Benjamin and the Arcades Project* (Cambridge: MIT Press, 1989), 253–54, 125–26.

15. Cohen, *Workshop to Office,* 69–72; Peiss, *Cheap Amusements.*

16. Andrew R. Heinze, *Adapting to Abundance: Jewish Immigrants, Mass Consumption, and the Search for American Identity* (New York: Columbia University Press, 1990), 193–98.

17. Archibald A. Hill, "The Pushcart Peddlers of New York," *Independent* 61

(October 18, 1906): 917; quote is from "Thursday in Hester Street," *New York Tribune*, September 15, 1898, 7.

18. Hill, "Pushcart Peddlers of New York," 920, 916.

19. See Glenn, *Daughters of the Shtetl*, 86–88, 154–55; Cohen, *Workshop to Office*, 114–24.

20. Peiss, *Cheap Amusements*, 52–53.

21. Rose Schneiderman with Lucy Goldthwaite, *All for One* (New York: Paul S. Eriksson, 1967), 40.

22. See Abraham Cahan, "Rabbi Eliezer's Christmas" in Moses Rischin, ed., *Grandma Never Lived in America: The New Journalism of Abraham Cahan* (Bloomington: Indiana University Press, 1985), 63–70. This story was originally published in *Scribner's Magazine* in 1899. It's possible that the novels, which the proprietor described as "trash," were in Yiddish only. However, it would make good business sense for the proprietor to carry both Yiddish and English novels. See also Rose Cohen, *Out of the Shadow* (New York: George H. Doran Company, 1918), 187.

23. Schneiderman with Goldthwaite, *All for One*, 40.

24. Cohen, *Out of the Shadow*, 249.

25. Sadie Frowne, "The Story of a Sweatshop Girl" in David M. Katzman and William Tuttle, Jr., eds., *Plain Folk: The Life Stories of Undistinguished Americans* (Urbana: University of Illinois Press, 1982), 56. Originally published in the *Independent* in 1902.

26. "Laura Jean Libbey Hoped to Achieve Immortality," *New York Times*, November 2, 1924, VII:11.

27. Denning, *Mechanic Accents*, 36–37.

28. Cohen, *Out of the Shadow*, 187–91.

29. Orleck, *Common Sense and a Little Fire*, 39. Orleck uses this fact to back up her claim that Jewish women were serious readers of literature and Socialist theory. While this was undoubtedly true for some, it seems more likely that the large numbers of women that checked reading were thinking of romances, particularly because they knew this was a study surveying their amusements.

30. Natalie Zemon Davis, "Printing and the People," in Mukerji and Schudson, *Rethinking Popular Culture*, 65–66, 70–71. Reprinted from Davis's 1975 book, *Society and Culture in Early Modern France*.

31. Richardson, *The Long Day*, 73–74.

32. Ibid., 75–85.

33. Radway, "Interpretive Communities," 62.

34. Gertrude Barnum, "Talks With the Girl Who Works: The Perfect Lady," *New York Call*, March 20, 1909, 8; Barnum also discusses shirtwaist workers reading dime novel romances on their lunch hour in "At the Shirtwaist

Factory," *Ladies Garment Worker* 1 (2) (May 1910): 3.

35. Richardson, *The Long Day*, 72–73.

36. "Zelda on Books," *Yiddishes Tageblatt*, August 4, 1903. Rose Pastor was drawing on her own reading experiences as part of "The Friendly Club," a club organized by middle-class women for the uplift of working-class women. Herbert Shapiro and David L. Sterling, eds., *"I Belong to the Working Class": The Unfinished Autobiography of Rose Pastor Stokes* (Athens: University of Georgia Press, 1992), chapter 2. See Anne Ruggles Gere, *Intimate Practices: Literary and Cultural Work in U.S. Women's Clubs, 1880–1920* (Urbana: University of Illinois Press, 1997), 182–86, 67–68 for a discussion of working women's reading practices in these clubs.

37. "The Mail Bag," *Life and Labor* (May 1911): 160.

38. "Zelda on Books," *Yiddishes Tageblatt*, August 4, 1903. The preceding quotes are also from this article.

39. Richardson, *The Long Day*, 96–97.

40. Hasanovitz, *One of Them*, 204; Frowne, "The Story of a Sweatshop Girl," 52. Dorothy Richardson also records being assigned a number that she would be "known as," *The Long Day*, 51. Cornelia Stratton Parker, a lady in disguise, labeled five of her six chapters by the numbers assigned to her at her six jobs: "No. 1075 Packs Chocolates" "286 on Brass" "195 Irons 'Family'," etc. *Working With the Working Woman*, 1, 42, 75.

41. See Joe Austin, "Taking the Train: Youth Culture, Urban Crisis and the Graffiti Problem in New York City, 1970–1990" (Ph.D. dissertation, University of Minnesota, 1996) for a related discussion of graffiti writers' use of consumer culture codes.

42. See especially Ewen, *Immigrant Women in the Land of Dollars*; Schreier, *Becoming American Women*, 60.

43. Louise C. Odencrantz, *Italian Women in Industry: A Study of Conditions in New York City* (New York: Russell Sage Foundation, 1919), 64.

44. Wald, *The House on Henry Street*, 192.

45. Hasanovitz, *One of Them*, 212.

46. Frowne, "The Story of a Sweatshop Girl," 57.

47. Clara E. Laughlin, *The Work-a-day Girl: A Study of Some Present-Day Conditions* (1913; reprint, New York: Arno, 1974), 147. Laughlin recorded working-class speech more than most middle-class advocates of working women. However, she weaves her own analysis with narration of the women's conversations, creating doubt that they are directly transcripted. Nevertheless, her narration in this case is combined with a wealth of other material on the economic motives of women's dress.

48. Peiss, *Cheap Amusements*, 108–14.

49. Hasanovitz, *One of Them*, 247.

50. Odencrantz, *Italian Women in Industry*, 202, 228; "East Side Fashions," *New York Tribune Illustrated Supplement*, August 26, 1900, 13; "Thursday in Hester Street," 7.

51. Odencrantz, *Italian Women in Industry*, 228.

52. For New York, see Laughlin, *The Work-a-day Girl*, 144–47. In Chicago, the installment system may have been even more important because there were fewer pushcarts. See S. Breckinridge, *New Homes For Old* (New York: Harper and Brothers, 1921), 137; Viola Paradise, "The Jewish Immigrant Girl in Chicago," *The Survey* 30 (Sept. 6, 1913): 702.

53. Ewen, *Immigrant Women in the Land of Dollars*, 101–2, 106.

54. Quoted in Schreier, *Becoming American Women*, 137.

55. Quoted in Ewen, *Immigrant Women in the Land of Dollars*, 107; see also 106–8, 200; Mary Odem explores young working-class women's generational rebellions in *Delinquent Daughters: Protecting and Policing Adolescent Female Sexuality in the United States, 1885–1920* (Chapel Hill: University of North Carolina Press, 1995), 157–84.

56. Clark and Wyatt's *Making Both Ends Meet* is full of specific budgets of working women, and reveals that a great number of them stretched their budget for clothes by making simple accessories and shirtwaists. See especially 49–61.

57. "East Side Fashions," 13.

58. Odencrantz, *Italian Women in Industry*, 228; "Thursday in Hester Street," 7; Hill, "Pushcart Peddlers of New York," 921.

59. Angela McRobbie, *Postmodernism and Popular Culture* (New York: Routledge, 1994), 135.

60. "Thursday in Hester Street," 7.

61. Hasanovitz, *One of Them*, 227. Shops that made higher quality clothing paid significantly higher wages, and jobs there were sought after. In addition, the season for good-quality clothing ended slightly earlier than the season for lower-quality clothes. Women who worked in those shops tried to shorten their "slack season" by moving to shops that made cheaper goods. Some shop owners also switched to contracts for cheaper goods when the first season ended. Thus, women gained a variety of experiences. See Hasanovitz 61–62; 187.

62. "East Side Fashions," 13.

63. Ibid.

64. The term "moral economy" originated with E. Thompson, "The Moral Economy of the English Crowd in the Eighteenth Century," *Past and Present* 50 (February 1971): 76–135; see also Robin D. G. Kelley, "Shiftless of the World Unite," in *Race Rebels*, 17–34.

65. Hasanovitz, *One of Them*, 227.

66. De Certeau, *The Practice of Everyday Life*, 25–26.

67. Richardson, *The Long Day*, 106–7; see also 70–71, 95.

68. Laughlin, *The Work-a-day Girl*, 145; Hasanovitz, *One of Them*, 93; Richardson, *The Long Day*, 67.

69. Ibid., 68, emphasis mine.

70. McRobbie, *Postmodernism and Popular Culture*, 151.

71. Kelley, *Race Rebels*, 169. There are also many parallels between these practices and those of domestic workers, both immigrant and African American, who resisted wearing uniforms. See Elizabeth Clark-Lewis," 'This Work Had an End': African American Domestic Workers in Washington D.C., 1910–1940" in Carol Groneman and Mary Beth Norton, eds., *To Toil the Livelong Day: America's Women at Work, 1780–1980* (Ithaca: Cornell University Press, 1987), 196–212; Tera W. Hunter, *To 'Joy My Freedom: Southern Black Women's Lives and Labors After the Civil War* (Cambridge: Harvard University Press, 1997), 152–53, 182–83.

72. Richardson, *The Long Day*, 70.

73. Hasanovitz, *One of Them*, 46.

74. See Buck-Morss's elucidation of Benjamin's *Passagenwerk* in *The Dialectics of Seeing*, 114–20; Angela McRobbie, "The *Passagenwerk* and the Place of Walter Benjamin in Cultural Studies" in *Postmodernism and Popular Culture*, 96–120. See also Fredric Jameson, *The Political Unconscious: Narrative as a Socially Symbolic Act* (Ithaca: Cornell University Press, 1981), 285.

75. Jacob A. Riis, *How the Other Half Lives: Studies Among the Tenements of New York* (1890; reprint, New York: Dover, 1971), 118.

76. Richardson, *The Long Day*, 120. Jane Addams noted that working women exhibited a "self-conscious walk" along with "giggling speech" and "preposterous clothing." See Addams, "Some Reflections on the Failure of the Modern City to Provide Recreation for Young Girls," *Charities and the Commons* 21 (Dec. 5, 1908): 366.

77. Pastor, "Just Between Ourselves, Girls," *Yiddishes Tageblatt,* June 7, 1903.

78. Rose Pastor, "Heart-to-Heart Talk," *Yiddishes Tageblatt*, October 18, 1901.

79. Barnum, "Talks With the Girl Who Works: The American Girl's Language," *New York Call*, April 24, 1909, 8. The term "vulgar vanity" belongs to Richardson, *The Long Day*, 198.

80. Radway, *Reading the Romance*, 10.

81. Brooks, *The Melodramatic Imagination*; Denning, *Mechanic Accents*, 170–71.

82. Elizabeth Cowie, *Representing the Woman: Cinema and Psychoanalysis* (Minneapolis: University of Minnesota, 1997), 72–121.

83. Geraldine Fleming, *Only a Working Girl*, 79; Libbey, *The Heiress of Cameron Hall*, 34.

84. See Cowie's discussion of *Coma* in *Representing the Woman*, 36–71.

85. This argument is similar to one made by Radway in her study of women romance readers of the 1970s. Radway notes that the Smithton women saw the romance heroines, greatly maligned by scholars as weak and vapid, as intelligent and independent. Radway argues that the readers did not apply a "rule of unity" that required all character information be consolidated into an assessment of the character. Rather, they employed a different "philosophy" of language, reflecting a different kind of literacy or method of reading altogether. See "Interpretive Communities," 58–59.

86. Laura Jean Libbey, *Willful Gaynell, or The Little Beauty of the Passaic Cotton Mills* (New York: Munro, 1890), 3.

87. Libbey, *The Heiress of Cameron Hall*, 15.

88. Alice Kessler-Harris, *A Woman's Wage: Historical Meanings and Social Consequences* (Lexington: University of Kentucky Press, 1990), chapter 1.

89. "The Mail Bag," *Life and Labor* (Nov. 1913): 352.

90. Josephine Casey, "Why Women Organize," *Union Leader Advocate* 10 (October 1909): 20.

91. Fleming, *Only a Working Girl*, 214.

92. Libbey, *Willful Gaynell*.

93. Ibid., 125–26. See also 227, for a description of Gaynell breaking the glass of a carriage with her bound wrists. The heroine overcomes a drugged state to break a window and escape in *The Heiress of Cameron Hall*, 152.

94. Libbey, *Willful Gaynell*, 64.

95. Ibid.

96. Libbey, *The Heiress of Cameron Hall*, 116–17.

97. Brooks, *The Melodramatic Imagination*, 27.

98. Jane Gaines, "Introduction: Fabricating the Female Body," in Gaines and Herzog, eds., *Fabrication*, 12.

99. Libbey, *Willful Gaynell*, 151.

100. For example, consider the 1930s melodramas, such as *Stella Dallas* or *All About Eve*, the gothic romances such as *Rebecca* or *Gaslight*, and the comedies such as *Adam's Rib* or *His Girl Friday*. See Christine Gledhill, ed., *Home Is Where the Heart Is: Studies in Melodrama and the Woman's Film* (London: BFI, 1987).

101. Peiss, *Cheap Amusements*, 88–114. See also Pastor, "Heart to Heart Talk."

102. "East Side Fashions," 13.

103. See Daniel Harris, "The Aesthetics of Drag: Homosexuality, Cross-dressing and Sexual Politics," *Salmagundi* 108 (Fall 1995): 16. I am not suggesting that working ladies had a "postmodern" subjectivity. Rather, evidence suggests that they insisted that ladyhood revealed who they "really" were inside. Postmodern theories of subjectivity, however, can help us understand their actions.

104. Fred Davis, *Fashion, Culture and Identity*, 14.

105. "The Observer," *Yiddishes Tageblatt*, January 13, 1902.

106. "East Side Fashions," 13; Addams, "Some Reflections of the Failure of the Modern City to Provide Recreation for Young Girls," 366.

107. O. Henry, *The Trimmed Lamp* (New York: Doubleday, Page and Company, 1917), 4; "East Side Fashions," 13.

108. Ibid.

109. Anzia Yezierska, *The Bread Givers* (1925; reprint, New York: Persea Books, 1975), 2.

110. Pastor, "Just Between Ourselves, Girls," *Yiddishes Tageblatt*, December 12, 1902.

111. Parker, *Working With the Working Woman*.

112. Wald, *The House on Henry Street*, 190–91.

113. Pastor, "Just Between Ourselves, Girls," *Yiddishes Tageblatt*, December 14, 1902.

114. See George Lipsitz's *Time Passages*, 18, for a similar point in relation to music.

3. Fashioning Political Subjectivities

1. Sarah Comstock, "The Uprising of the Girls," *Collier's* (December 25, 1909): 14–16, 20–21.

2. Enlightenment thinkers based an ideal of political exchange on man's capacity to be rational. From its inception this ideal built upon exclusions, as they believed only some men, and no women, to be capable of rationality. In the United States, the founding fathers believed that only white, propertied men had a capacity for rationality, and they codified these assumptions in the requirements for the franchise. All people of color and all women were seen as by nature dependent and therefore incapable of autonomous thought. The nineteenth-century middle class used these ideals to construct a notion of a public sphere in which rational exchange could occur, and a corresponding notion of a private sphere characterized by emotion, nurturing, dependency, and desire. The middle class assigned females to the private realm, and thus declared them unfit for public life. This ideal of public exchange and the division between public and private was never fully realized. Indeed, working-class white men and black men successfully overturned federal legal restrictions on the franchise, and men and women of various races and ethnicities regularly imposed themselves on the United States' political landscape. Strikes were one way in which this occurred, and male strikers in particular held a controversial but recognized place in public life. Nevertheless, ideals of rational political exchange based in a division between public and private became *normative*, serving as a basis for regulating access to public space and political participation well into the twentieth century. See Steven Seidman, ed., *Jürgen Habermas on Society and Politics: A Reader* (Boston: Beacon Press, 1989); Nancy Fraser, "What's Critical About Critical Theory? The

Case of Habermas and Gender" and Iris Marion Young, "Impartiality and the Civic Public: Some Implications of Feminist Critiques of Moral and Political Theory," both in Seyla Benhabib and Drucilla Cornell, *Feminism as Critique: On the Politics of Gender* (Minneapolis: University of Minnesota Press, 1987), 31–55, 56–76; Mary Ryan, *Civic Wars: Democracy and Public Life in the American City during the Nineteenth Century* (Berkeley: University of California Press, 1997); Miriam Hansen, *Babel and Babylon: Spectatorship in American Silent Film* (Cambridge: Harvard University Press, 1991), 9.

3. A common narrative structure in labor histories delineates the oppressions that workers faced on the job and in their lives, and positions the strike as the culminating action or narrative climax that changes their lives. Strikes are thus positioned in narrative opposition to oppression and limitation, indicating that they are arenas of willed action and freedom. While strikes are indeed often exhilarating refusals of workplace hierarchies, they do not extricate workers entirely from the social forces that limit their agency and inscribe them into social hierarchies. Recent labor histories explore how workers replicate social hierarchies in their struggles for social change. See especially Ava Baron, ed., *Work Engendered: Toward a New History of American Labor* (Ithaca: Cornell University Press, 1991); Roediger, *Wages of Whiteness*. My study of the 1909 shirtwaist strike builds on these recent trends in labor history and attempts to add to them a reconsideration of "agency."

4. Seidman, ed., *Jürgen Habermas on Society and Politics: A Reader*.

5. Middle- and upper-class suffragists were particularly successful in getting their views represented in the press. Some members of the WTUL and SP worked for suffrage, but the strike captured the attention of additional suffragists who had no prior experience with trade union issues. I use the word "suffragist" to refer to women who did not also belong to Socialist or union groups. Middle- and upper-class suffragists saw the shirtwaist strike partly as an opportunity to dramatize the need for votes for women. Their voice became significant in the public debate when they were quoted in articles and when they wrote special columns about the strike.

6. Nancy Fraser, "Struggle over Needs: Outline of a Socialist-Feminist Critical Theory of Late-Capitalist Political Culture" in Linda Gordon, ed., *Women, the State and Welfare* (Madison: University of Wisconsin, 1990), 206.

7. Historians do not comment overtly about their decisions not to use newspaper sources. My interpretation that they believed newspaper sources to be biased is rooted in widely known historical methods aimed at uncovering an accurate picture of past events. Newspapers, as all well-trained historians know, are not reliable sources of the "facts" if uncorroborated by other types of materials. However, a number of historians have recently called for a shift in historical inquiry from a positivist search for "accuracy" to a recognition of the socially situated nature of historical sources (and historians) and their role in the production of knowledge and meaning. See Scott, "Experience," in Butler

and Scott, eds., *Feminists Theorize the Political*, 22–40; Ann-Louise Shapiro, ed., *Feminists Revision History* (New Brunswick, N.J.: Rutgers University Press, 1994). I am indebted in this passage to Nancy Fraser's prose describing the interpretations of political needs made by competing groups in a society as being "[more than] representations. . . . Rather they are acts and interventions." Fraser, "Struggle over Needs," 204.

8. My understanding of strike chronology is drawn primarily from Louis Levine, *The Women's Garment Workers: A History of the International Ladies Garment Workers' Union* (New York: B. W. Huebsch, 1924); Helen Marot, "A Woman's Strike—An Appreciation of the Shirtwaist Makers of New York," *Proceedings of the Academy of Political Science* (Oct. 1910): 199–28.

9. *New York Evening Journal*, November 26, 1909, 1.

10. These attitudes led to a certain social acceptance of harassment of unescorted women in public. See "The Girl Who Comes to the City," *Harper's Magazine* (July 1908):693 for one worker's experience of harassment. Working women's presence in the streets as workers or consumers was thus hotly contested in 1909. Fiction for middle-class readers often narrated working women's public mobility as sexually dangerous. See Laura Hapke, *Tales of the Working Girl: Wage-Earning Women in American Literature, 1890–1925* (New York: Twayne Publishers, 1992). Hazel Carby shows that there was a similar moral panic about African American women in public, that focused regulation on women's bodies rather than on the economic markets that constricted their opportunities. Carby, "Policing the Black Woman's Body in an Urban Context," *Critical Inquiry* 18 (Summer 1992), 738–755.

11. Sumner, "The Spirit of the Strikers," 553, 551.

12. In other words, police and thugs "cited" a preexisting discourse of power in an attempt to define strikers as transgressive. They did not originate the language they used, but their particular use introduced new meanings into that language. See Judith Butler, "Implicit Censorship and Discursive Agency" in *Excitable Speech: A Politics of the Performative* (New York: Routledge, 1997), 127–63 for a discussion of the ritual nature of language that bridges Bourdieu's attention to enacted daily life and Derrida's attention to language.

13. The *New York Evening Journal* was owned by William Hearst, the great newspaper mogul who used his papers to advocate for causes he found admirable. At the same time, Hearst won huge readerships for his papers by making them highly sensational. This accounts for the contradictory content of newspapers like the *New York Evening Journal*, which portrayed the strikers in highly sensationalized terms and yet carried prostrike editorials. See Michael Emery and Edwin Emery, *The Press and America: An Interpretive History of the Mass Media*, 6th ed. (New York: Prentice Hall, 1988), 253–54. A letter to the editor of the *New York Evening Journal* commented on the support for the shirtwaist strike on the editorial page, saying, "Some people call the journal the 'Sensational Sheet.' Well, it would be better for our class if we had just such a fearless news-

paper in every . . . city . . . for it seems to me the most of the daily papers are controlled by the rich. . . . Every working man or woman is or should be a daily reader of the Journal." *New York Evening Journal*, January 21, 1910, 22.

14. *New York Evening Journal* December 1, 1909, 3.

15. *New York Sun*, November 30, 1909, 5.

16. *New York Evening Journal*, November 26, 1909, 1; *New York World*, December 21, 1909, 3; *New York Times*, December 24, 1909, 3. Magistrate Breen, in contrast, dismissed a striker arrested for calling a strike breaker a "scab," and declared it legal to use the word. See *New York World*, December 25, 1909, 9.

17. *New York World*, December 24, 1909, 4; *New York Tribune*, December 25, 1909, 2; *New York Sun*, December 25, 1909, 10.

18. *New York Evening Journal*, December 31, 1909, 9. See also Kathy Peiss's discussion of the phrase "painted woman" in *Hope in a Jar*, 30–31.

19. *New York Sun*, November 30, 1909, 5.

20. See for example Norwood, *Labor's Flaming Youth*; Hall, "Disorderly Women"; Michelle Perrot, *Workers on Strike: France 1871–1890* (New Haven: Yale University Press, 1987).

21. *New York Evening Journal*, November 24, 1909, 1; *New York Sun*, December 6, 1909, 1; *New York Tribune*, November 25, 1909, 4. See also *New York Tribune*, November 28, 1909, 5.

22. *New York Evening Journal*, December 6, 1909, 5; *New York Times*, November 28, 1909, 3.

23. *New York Sun*, November 30, 1909, 5; *New York Tribune*, November 26, 1909, 10.

24. *New York World*, November 23, 1909, 2; *New York World*, November 24, 1909, 1; *New York World*, January 13, 1910, 3.

25. Comstock, "The Uprising of the Girls," 15–16.

26. *New York World*, November 26, 1909, 1; *New York Tribune*, November 27, 1909, 4; *New York Times*, November 27, 1909, 3; *New York World*, January 19, 1910, 2.

27. *New York Sun*, December 6, 1909, 1.

28. *New York Tribune*, December 19, 1909, 1.

29. *New York Evening Journal*, December 6, 1909, 5; *New York Sun*, December 4, 1909, 6; *New York Sun*, December 3, 1909, 6.

30. Kessler-Harris, *A Woman's Wage*, 14–44.

31. Eric Foner, *Free Soil, Free Labor, Free Men: The Ideology of the Republican Party Before the Civil War* (New York: Oxford, 1970); Roediger, *Wages of Whiteness*; Lawrence Glickman, "Inventing the 'American Standard of Living': Gender, Race and Working-Class Identity, 1880–1925," *Labor History* 34 (2–3)

(Spring-Summer 1993): 221–35; Glickman, *A Living Wage: American Workers and the Making of Consumer Society* (Ithaca: Cornell University Press, 1997).

32. Kessler-Harris, *A Woman's Wage*, 31–32; Glickman, "Inventing the 'American Standard of Living'," 224. The idea of an exclusively male living wage was an overt part of the public debate in the shirtwaist strike. One letter to the *New York Times* stated, "It must be perfectly evident that, if a single woman is getting enough to support herself or even to help in the support of her family, the working man, with a wife and two or three children to support on the same wage must be falling far below the reasonable standard." *New York Times*, January 2, 1910, 12. It should be noted that some of the female labor organizers challenged this apparent point of agreement between male union officials and female reformers. Both Pauline Newman and Mary Anderson extended the rhetoric of a "living wage" to women workers in the years after the 1909 strike.

33. Beatrice Fairfax, "Bravo, Little Sisters, Keep to the Fight," *New York Evening Journal*, December 19, 1909, 18.

34. Dorothy Dix, "Shirtwaist Strike Shows Woman's Need of the Ballot," *New York Evening Journal*, January 6, 1910, 17.

35. *New York Evening Journal*, November 27, 1909, 3.

36. *New York Evening Journal*, January 6, 1910, 17; see also *New York Evening Journal*, January 12, 1910, 16.

37. *New York Times*, December 25, 1909, 2. Despite the preponderance of Jewish strikers, the press paid a great deal of attention to Christmas as a hardship for the strikers.

38. *New York Call*, January 3, 1909, 1; *New York Call*, December 29, 1909 (special issue), 1; *New York Evening Journal*, December 4, 1909, 3; *New York Times*, January 3, 1909, 1.

39. *New York Call*, December 29, 1909, 1. Christmas fell on a Saturday in 1909; the special issue was published the following Wednesday.

40. Scott, "What the Women Strikers Won," 480; Marot, "A Woman's Strike," 126; "When You Go Out Shopping Remember the Shirt-Waist Girl," *Ladies' Garment Worker* 1 (1) (Apr. 1910): 1; William Mailly, "How Girls Can Strike," *Progressive Woman* 3 (33) (Feb. 1910); Teresa Malkiel, "The Jobless Girls," *New York Call*, December 29, 1909 (special issue): 2; see also Clark and Wyatt, *Making Both Ends Meet*, 85.

41. *New York Call*, December 24, 1909, 6.

42. Malkiel, "The Jobless Girls," 2.

43. Ibid.; Tom Price, "Fighting to Live," *International Socialist Review* 10 (8) (Feb. 1910): 679.

44. *New York Call*, January 3, 1910, 6.

45. *New York Call*, December 29, 1909.

46. The leaders' strategic moves were part of what Linda Gordon and

Nancy Fraser term "the genealogy of dependency." "A Genealogy of *Dependency*: Tracing a Keyword of the U.S. Welfare State," *Signs* 19 (2) (Winter 1994): 309–36. Such notions of women's dependency became codified in the 1930s welfare system and underpin long-lasting understandings of welfare and citizenship. See Linda Gordon, *Pitied But Not Entitled: Single Mothers and the History of Welfare, 1890–1935* (New York: Free Press, 1994); Barbara Nelson, "The Origins of the Two-Channel Welfare State: Workmen's Compensation and Mother's Aid," in Linda Gordon, ed., *Women, the State, and Welfare* (Madison: University of Wisconsin Press, 1990), 123–51. I am greatly indebted in this analysis to lawyer Lucie White's discussion of her own legal representation of a woman on welfare who had been accused of fraud. White identified two potential "stories" about Mrs. G. to narrate to the judge: a story that pled innocence on the basis of the abrogation of Mrs. G's rights by welfare regulators and a story that asked for mercy due to Mrs. G's exceptional poverty—demonstrated by the material evidence of her children's shoes. White knew the first story would be empowering to Mrs. G. because it asserted her rights as a citizen and that the second story would be demeaning; but she also believed the second story would be more likely to be effective because it would place the state in a comfortable position of benefactor. White quoted lawyer Patricia Williams, who said about her advocacy of poor people: "I learned to undo images of power with images of powerlessness; to clothe the victims of excessive power in utter, bereft naiveté; to cast them as defenseless supplicants . . . *pleading*. . . . I learned that the best way to give voice to those whose voice had been suppressed was to argue that they had no voice." Lucie White, "Subordination, Rhetorical Survival Skills, and Sunday Shoes: Notes on the Hearing of Mrs. G.," *Buffalo Law Review* 38 (1) (Winter 1990): 1–58. Quote of Williams is on 28. Thanks to John Sayer for sharing this article with me.

47. *New York Times*, January 4, 1910, 20.

48. Althusser, "Ideology and Ideological State Apparatuses," 170–86; see also de Lauretis, *Technologies of Gender*, 6–12.

49. Butler, *Excitable Speech*, 24–38. See also Jacqueline Rose, *Sexuality in the Field of Vision* (London: Verso, 1986), introduction.

50. I am not arguing that working women had a "postmodern" subjectivity or that they did not see identity as essential. Rather, I am using Butler and Althusser as a model for understanding political subjectivity as a historically constructed convention. Working-class women were largely excluded from the realms in which an Enlightenment rational subject made cultural sense and was rewarded; that is, public life, which was dominated by white, middle-class men. We should thus expect their subjectivities to be different, and trace the terrain of those subjectivities in the working women's daily lives and social relations.

51. Butler, *Excitable Speech*, 33.

52. Teresa Malkiel notes the importance of the English-language newspapers to the strikers in her fictionalized account, *The Diary of a Shirtwaist Striker* (1910;

reprint, Cornell: ILR Press, 1990), 83; Helen Marot also notes that working women read the English-language newspapers, "A Woman's Strike," 121.

53. The *New York Call* also carried stories and articles written particularly for working women. In the weeks after the strike, Teresa Malkiel published *The Diary of a Shirtwaist Striker* in serial form in the *Call*, and Gertrude Barnum (who was not a Socialist) wrote a weekly column the year of the strike entitled "Talks With the Girl Who Works." Malkiel's story did not much address working women's popular culture, but it also did not attack fashion or dime novel fiction. Indeed, Malkiel mentions women's desire for clothing in fairly positive terms and borrows some dime novel conventions in relating one strike event. Most other print material either ignored women's mass-produced popular culture or portrayed it in negative terms. Barnum's columns in the *Call* were consistent with her work in the *Ladies Garment Worker*: they routinely chastised women for their popular culture activities. See Malkiel, *Diary of a Shirtwaist Striker*; a sampling of Barnum's columns, "Talks With the Girl Who Works," are *New York Call*, March 6, 1909, 8; March 13, 1909, 8; March 20, 1909, 8; April 17, 1909, 8; May 1, 1909, 8.

54. See for example "When You Go Out Shopping Remember the Shirt-Waist Girl," 1. As in the dime novel convention, however, the *Ladies Garment Worker*'s emphasis on "frailty" sometimes served to draw attention to the bravery of the strikers. Becky Fischer was described as a "frail young girl," but also was celebrated as being arrested 39 times in 11 weeks. See "Loyalty and Self-Sacrifice of the Cleveland Strikers," *Ladies Garment Worker* 2 (11) (Nov. 1911): 15.

55. Pamela L. Gaddy, "Appealing to Working Women: Constructing Identity in *Ladies Garment Worker* and *Life and Labor*, 1910–1913," unpublished paper in possession of the author, 26.

56. Charlotte C. Barnum, "The Girl Who Lives at Home: Two Suggestions to Trade Union Women," *Life and Labor* (Nov. 1911): 346.

57. This call for reform could sound familiar to working women. As historian Lawrence Levine argues, the middle class has pursued cultural hegemony since the nineteenth century both through exclusions and through demands that the working class conform to middle-class values of social order. Levine, *Highbrow/Lowbrow*, 177.

58. Gertrude Barnum, "This Style—Six Twenty Nine," *Ladies Garment Worker* 4 (5) (May 1913): 29.

59. Barnum, "At the Shirtwaist Factory," 3.

60. Pauline Newman, "Our Women Workers: Educational Work for the Winter," *Ladies Garment Worker* 4 (10) (Oct. 1913): 16–17; "Our Women Workers: When You Have Time to Read," *Ladies Garment Worker* 4 (7) (June 1913): 34; "Our Women Workers: When You Have Time to Read," *Ladies Garment Worker* 4 (8) (July 1913): 24.

61. Orleck, *Common Sense and a Little Fire*, 74.

62. These leaders were similar to German Socialists who tried to reform the

tavern-based working-class culture that later critics came to see as resistant. Geoff Eley compellingly reviews German labor histories that engage the everyday practices of workers in "Labor History, Social History, Altagsgeschichte: Experience, Culture, and the Politics of the Everyday—a New Direction for German Social History?" *Journal of Modern History* 61 (June 1989): 297–343. Socialists frowned on the German Beer Riots of 1873, and the "schnapps-casinos" in Ruhr mining colonies before World War I. Roy Rosenzweig similarly argues that everyday drinking cultures in Worchester, Massachusetts provided a locus for working-class identity formation and an ethic of mutuality, though he does not document a parallel opposition to that culture from a working-class leadership concerned with respectability. However, the eight-hour movement did include an number of working-class leaders, including Ira Steward, who promoted a notion of working-class respectability. Roy Rosenzweig, *Eight Hours for What We Will* (New York: Cambridge University Press, 1983); David Roediger and Philip Foner, *Our Own Time: A History of American Labor and the Working Day* (New York: Greenwood, 1989).

63. Mary Anderson, "Letter," *Life and Labor* (Dec. 1911): 384.

64. For an excellent discussion of Newman's organizing in the context of the small cadre of women organizers see Orleck, *Common Sense and a Little Fire*, 57–80. Ann Schofield, *To Do and To Be: Portraits of Four Women Activists, 1893–1986* (Boston: Northeastern University Press, 1997), 24–47, 88–94, discusses Barnum's and Newman's organizing activities.

65. I am indebted to Butler's phrasing in this passage. See *Excitable Speech*, 30.

66. See for example, "What is the Reason?" *Ladies Garment Worker* 5 (3) (Mar. 1914): 21.

67. Butler, *Gender Trouble*, 149.

68. Dye, *As Equals and as Sisters*, 7.

69. Butler, *Gender Trouble*, 142–49; Scott, "Experience" in Butler and Scott, eds., *Feminists Theorize the Political*, 22–40.

4. Ladies and Orphans

1. Clara Lemlich, "Leader Tells Why 40,000 Girls Struck," *New York Evening Journal*, November 26, 1909, 3. Though Lemlich was listed as the author of this article, a preamble to the article explained that Lemlich told her story to a reporter. Thus, while this is perhaps the best source available by a striking worker produced during the strike itself, it is a mediated source.

2. Quoted in Orleck, *Common Sense and a Little Fire*, 49.

3. Lisa Lowe, *Immigrant Acts: On Asian American Cultural Politics* (Durham: Duke University Press, 1996), 2.

4. Mary Dreier, the wealthy president of the Women's Trade Union League, was the only woman on the program to speak. Barbara Mayer Wertheimer, *We Were There: The Story of Working Women in America* (New York: Pantheon, 1977), 300.

5. Glenn's *Daughters of the Shtetl* is the only account that references this article. See page 165.

6. Orleck, *Common Sense and a Little Fire*, 25–27.

7. See Jennifer Maria Guglielmo, "Donne Sovversive: The History of Italian-American Women's Radicalism," *Italian America* (Sept. 1997):8–11; Donna Gabaccia, *Militants and Migrants: Rural Sicilians Become American Workers* (New Brunswick, N.J.: Rutgers University Press, 1988); Mary Jo Buhle, *Women and American Socialism, 1870–1920* (Urbana: University of Illinois Press, 1981), 298–99.

8. James C. Scott, *Domination and the Arts of Resistance: Hidden Transcripts* (New Haven: Yale University Press, 1990). The New Labor History quickly moved from a focus on workers' experiences at the shop as the foundations of "consciousness" to a broader examination of home, neighborhood, and leisure as well. E. Thompson's *The Making of the English Working Class* (New York: Vintage, 1966) was pathbreaking in this respect and since then the idea that "class-consciousness" is formed at least in part through culture, and cannot be measured simply by the presence or absence of strikes, has become dominant.

9. See Gayatri Chakravorty Spivak, "Subaltern Studies: Deconstructing Historiography" in *In Other Worlds* (New York: Routledge, 1988); Ranajit Guha and Gayatri Chakravorty Spivak, *Selected Subaltern Studies* (New York: Oxford University Press, 1988); Ranajit Guha, *Elementary Aspects of Peasant Insurgency in Colonial India* (Delhi: Oxford University Press, 1983). See also Walter Benjamin, "Theses on the Philosophy of History" in Hannah Arendt, ed., *Illuminations*, trans. Harry Zohn (New York: Schocken, 1969), 253–64.

10. Rose Strunsky, "The Strike of the Singers of the Shirt," *International Socialist Review* 10 (6) (Dec. 1909): 623–24. Rose Schneiderman, a principle organizer of the strike, also claimed that the strike surprised and amazed everyone, catching the union unprepared for such a sizable walkout. Schneiderman with Goldthwaite, *All for One*, 91.

11. *Ladies Garment Worker* 1 (2) (May 1910): 1. The article quoted the delegate's report to the union's Executive Board, from the ILGWU records that no longer exist. Local 25 had only about 100 members and a budget of four dollars, three months prior to the strike; and from one to two thousand members at the beginning of the strike. Louis Levine, *The Women's Garment Workers* (New York: B. W. Huebsch, 1924), 151, 153.

12. Quoted in Jeremy Brecher, *Strike!* (San Francisco: Straight Arrow Books, 1972), 236.

13. Ibid., 244.

14. Maxine Schwartz Seller, "The Uprising of the Twenty Thousand: Sex, Class, and Ethnicity in the Shirtwaist Makers' Strike of 1909" in Dirk Hoerder, ed., *Struggle and Hard Battle: Essays on Working Class Immigrations* (DeKalb: Northern Illinois University Press, 1986), 260–61; Tax, *The Rising of the Women*, 217–18.

15. Brecher discusses this tendency on pp. 245–46.

16. Ida Richter, quoted in Glenn, *Daughters of the Shtetl*, 200.

17. Glenn estimates that Jews comprised 66–77 percent of the strikers but only 55 percent of the labor force. Italian women, she estimates, comprised 34 percent of the labor force but only about 6 percent of the strikers. See ibid., 191–92. Glenn arrived at these estimates by looking at Marot's WTUL figures during the strike, and at the 1913 official industry census conducted by the Joint Board of Sanitary Control in the Dress and Waist Industry.

18. See Marot, "A Woman's Strike," 120. Secretary of the WTUL, Marot saw the "instinctive" resistance of Russian Jews as a positive thing in 1910. However, her willingness to resort to racial characteristics to explain radicalism proved double-edged. In 1911 she announced that the WTUL should dedicate its resources to organizing "American" (i.e., native-born Protestant) women because Jews were too ideological and strained the "generosity" of American women. See Orleck, *Common Sense and a Little Fire*, 67.

19. For a discussion of the effects of historical memory on the strikers see Glenn, *Daughters of the Shtetl*, 35–36, 176–78; Gerald Sorin, *The Prophetic Minority: American Jewish Immigrant Radicals, 1880–1920* (Bloomington: Indiana University Press, 1985), 124–40. See also Paula Hyman, "Immigrant Women and Consumer Protest: The New York City Kosher Meat Boycott of 1902," *American Jewish History* 70 (1) (Sept. 1980): 91–105.

20. This view first appeared in Charlotte Baum, Paula Hyman, and Sonya Michel's important early work on the history of Jewish women, *The Jewish Woman in America* (New York: Dial, 1976), 137–40.

21. Nixola Greely-Smith, "'Strike of the Shirtwaist Girls Reveals Big Growth of Trade Unions Among Women," *New York World*, January 8, 1910, 3, quotes Helen Marot of the WTUL saying that until recently, working women demonstrated an "unconquerable apathy to the advantages of organization."

22. Glenn, *Daughters of the Shtetl*, 199; see also discussion on 184–85, 192. For a discussion of factors influencing Italian women's participation see also Colomba M. Furio, "The Cultural Background of the Italian Immigrant Woman and its Impact on Her Unionization in the New York City Garment Industry, 1880–1919" in George E. Pozzetta, ed. *Pane e Lavoro: The Italian American Working Class* (Toronto: The Multicultural History Society of Ontario, 1980): 81–98.

23. Glenn, *Daughters of the Shtetl*, 199–200, 184.

24. Gerald Sorin, *A Time for Building: The Third Migration 1880–1920* (Baltimore: Johns Hopkins University Press, 1992), 126.

25. Orleck, *Common Sense and a Little Fire*, 57.

26. Rose Schneiderman, "The White Goods Workers of New York: Their Struggle for Human Conditions," *Life and Labor* 3 (5) (May 1913): 132.

27. Fania Cohn also worked full-time in a Brooklyn white goods shop, which she also struggled to organize. Orleck, *Common Sense and a Little Fire*, 38, 45–46.

28. This is not the only way historians narrate Jewish history and its relationship to consumerism. Andrew Heinze, Barbara Schreier, and Jenna Joselit all show convincingly how consumption became a means through which Jews created themselves as Americans. However, these studies do not address radicalism and strikes in the Jewish community, and tend to narrate the story not only of Americanization but of the making of a Jewish middle class. Thus, they greatly privilege consumption over radicalism as a foundation of Jewish identity. While for many labor historians the Jewish immigrant subject is a hardworking radical, for some historians of culture the same subject is a hardworking consumer. Both narratives illuminate crucial aspects of Jewish history. Both also are in danger of being assimilated to a liberal pluralist story of American inclusion and progress that obscures ongoing U.S. power relations and material inequalities. See Heinze, *Adapting to Abundance*; Schreier, *Becoming American Women*; Jenna Weissman Joselit, *The Wonders of America: Reinventing Jewish Culture, 1880–1950* (New York: Hill and Wang, 1994). See also Lowe, *Immigrant Acts*, 30–39, 64, for a superb critique of immigration, "aestheticization" and the "discourse of citizenship."

29. Lipsitz, *Time Passages*, vii, 133–62, 233–56.

30. "Americanizing Jewish Alien Girls," *The American Hebrew*, October 12, 1917, 652. Many German Jews had emigrated to the United States in the midnineteenth century and felt compelled to aid the Eastern European Jews in their Americanization process. For a discussion of Jewish attempts to Americanize new immigrant women see Riv Ellen Prell, *Fighting to Become Americans: Jews, Gender and the Anxiety of Assimilation* (Boston: Beacon, forthcoming [1999]). Thanks to Prell for sharing this source with me.

31. Glenn, *Daughters of the Shtetl*, 168; Seller, "The Uprising of the Twenty Thousand," 261.

32. Frowne, "The Story of a Sweatshop Girl," 56; Laughlin, *The Work-a-day Girl*, 143.

33. Marot, "A Woman's Strike," 121.

34. "40,000 Girls to Join Great Strike of New York Waistmakers," *New York Evening Journal*, November 10, 1909, 2.

35. "Girl Strikers Form Band to Fight Thugs," *New York Evening Journal*, November 18, 1909, 1. Hyperbole characterized much of the *Evening Journal*'s coverage. It announced the Cooper Union meeting on November 17 under the headline GOMPERS WILL START 75,000 GIRLS IN STRIKE. However, this article was on page eleven of the paper and was not large. Some women probably heard of the meeting this way, but undoubtedly many learned of it through the leafletting in the streets of the garment district conducted by union organizers in the days before the meeting.

36. Richardson, *The Long Day*, 197–98. See also Mary Kingsbury Simkhovitch, *The City Worker's World in America* (New York: Macmillan, 1917), 133. The phenomenon of "lady friends" is in need of greater study. Fragmentary

evidence suggests it may have been an ongoing aspect of female-dominated workplaces, and that employers found it threatening. George Lipsitz, in his study of 1940s labor, quotes Donald Laird's *The Psychology of Supervising the Working Woman* as follows: "those wonderful 'friendships' which spring up quickly are usually crushes between the girls. They walk around together during the lunches . . . buy birthday presents for each other, temporarily lose interest in boys. When a crush is just starting the alert executive will transfer one of the girls." George Lipsitz, *Rainbow at Midnight: Labor and Culture in the 1940s* (Urbana: University of Illinois Press, 1994), 54.

37. This statement sounds a bit like the kind of hubris for which characters are often punished. However, the villain does not drown, and Leonie does not pay for her deed in any way. Libbey, *Leonie Locke*, 134.

38. Malkiel, *The Diary of a Shirtwaist Striker*, 83.

39. The *Forverts* went from a circulation of 19,502 in 1900 to 122,532 in 1911. It continued to gain dominance over the other Yiddish papers of New York and reached 37 percent of the total readership of Yiddish papers in 1916. See Heinze, *Adapting to Abundance*, 150.

40. For example, see "Triangle Company Issues an Appeal to all Manufacturers," *Forverts*, November 1, 1909, 1; Advertisement, *Forverts*, November 1, 1909, 2; "Theater Benefit for the Striking Ladies Waist Makers' Union," *Forverts*, November 3, 1909, 2; "Who are the Special Detectives?" *Forverts*, November 11, 1909, 1; "50,000 Waistmakers Want to Strike," *Forverts*, November 17, 1909, 3; "Gompers at the General Assembly of the Ladies Waistmakers," *Forverts*, November 17–22, 1909, 2. The *Forverts* was so strongly prostrikers that the Triangle Company sued the paper for its coverage of the dispute before the general strike began. *New York Call*, November 19, 1909, 3.

41. "Some Measures Against the Ladies Waist Makers," *Forverts*, November 12, 1909, 1; "50,000 Waist Makers Want to Strike," *Forverts*, November 17, 1909, 3; "A Group of Striking Ladies Waistmakers From the Triangle Company," *Forverts*, November 16, 1909, 1.

42. "Triangle Company Issues an Appeal to All Manufacturers," *Forverts*, November 1, 1909, 1; "Our Dirty Money," *Forverts*, November 12, 1909, 3.

43. Indeed, one editorial compared the Triangle and Leiserson owners to "the pogromchiks in Russia—but these perpetrators are Jews! So much the worse!" See "Our Dirty Money," *Forverts*, November 12, 1909, 3.

44. George J. Sanchez, *Becoming Mexican American*, 229.

45. Announcements appeared in the *Bolletino della Sera* on November 8, 1909 and November 22, 1909. "Lo Sciopero delle Sartine," *Bolletino della Sera*, November 2, 1909. After the strike began, the paper ran an article about a "riot" between strikers and scabs on Greene Street in almost identical terms as the English-language dailies: "The battle lasted about one hour, and at random intervals many women's hats feel to the street. The little hands of some of the

girls held huge chunks of hair." "Lo Sciopero delle Sartine," *Bolletino della Sera*, November 27, 1909, 1. *Il Proletario* first covered the strike on December 3, 1909, and then again on December 24, 1909. *Il Progresso Italo-americano* only covered the strike on November 25, 1909.

46. Jennifer Guglielmo, "Donne Ribelli: Recovering the History of Italian Women's Radicalism in the United States," Philip Cannistraro, ed., *The Lost World of Italian American Radicalism* (Albany: SUNY Press, forthcoming); Guglielmo, "Italian Women Garment Workers and the Politics of Labor Organizing, 1900–1945," Donna Gabaccia and Franca Lacoretta, eds., *Foreign, Female and Fighting Back: Italian Women, Work and Activism in the Diaspora* (Toronto: University of Toronto Press, forthcoming).

47. For discussion of IWW attempts to provide speakers, see "Sciopero generale di lavoratori in Camicette 40,000 Scioperanti," *Il Proletario*, December 3, 1909. For 1913 coverage, see articles titled "Il Colossale Sciopero del Sarti," *Il Progresso Italo-americano* in January and February 1913. Another reason for increased participation in later garment strikes is that Italian organizers such as Angela Bambace visited the homes of Italian workers to provide information about the strike in Italian, and gained admittance where Jewish organizers had not been welcome. See Jean A. Scarpaci, "Angela Bambace and the ILGWU: The Search for an Elusive Activist," George Pozzetta, ed., *Pane e Lavaro*, 101–3; Colomba M. Furio, "Immigrant Women and Industry: A Case Study. The Italian Immigrant Woman and the Garment Industry, 1880–1950," Ph.D. diss., New York University, 1979.

48. *New York Call*, December 15, 1909, 1; *New York Tribune*, December 20, 1909, 2.

49. Quoted in Clark and Wyatt, *Making Both Ends Meet*, 66.

50. William Mailly, "The Working Girls' Strike," *Independent* 67 (December 23, 1909): 1416.

51. Quoted in Wertheimer, *We Were There*, 301; Newman's emphasis.

52. Employers began settling with the union immediately, so that some workers only struck for a few days. However, recalcitrant employers formed the Manufacturer's Association to oppose the union's efforts collectively. The union dealt with the employers who joined the Manufacturer's Association as a group. Nevertheless, all strikers met both in their own shop meetings and in large mass meetings, and at the beginning of the strike, when grievances were discussed, all believed that the union would confront their bosses personally.

53. Historians do not draw attention to this assumption. Rather, it lies embedded in the way they narrate the strike. Glenn writes that "striking workers demanded a 52-hour work week"; Meredith Tax similarly writes that "strikers also demanded the abolition of subcontracting." Seller's language is more precise, stating that "the union demanded a 52-hour week." The slick way that the difference between the workers' stories and the union story gets lost in Glenn's and Tax's accounts demonstrates how historians' narratives take up theoretical perspectives even when they

intend to be just relating the story. Glenn, *Daughters of the Shtetl*, 169; Tax, *The Rising of the Women*, 218; Seller, "The Uprising of the Twenty Thousand," 263. See also Scott, "Experience," in Butler and Scott, eds., *Feminists Theorize the Political*, 22–40.

54. Marot, "A Woman's Strike," 125.

55. Clark and Wyatt, *Making Both Ends Meet*, 67.

56. Marot, "A Woman's Strike," 124.

57. Fannie Shapiro (pseudonym) in Sydelle Kramer and Jenny Masur, eds., *Jewish Grandmothers* (Boston: Beacon Press, 1976), 12.

58. Jennie Matyas, oral history transcript 43, Tamiment Library.

59. Nancy Fraser, "Rethinking the Public Sphere: A Contribution to the Critique of Actually Existing Democracy," in Craig Calhoun, ed., *Habermas and the Public Sphere* (Cambridge: MIT Press, 1992), 109–42.

60. Clara Lemlich, "Leader Tells Why 40,000 Girls Struck," *New York Evening Journal*, November 26, 1909, 3.

61. Comstock, "The Uprising of the Girls," 21.

62. William Mailly, "Working Girls' Strike Result of Oppression," *New York Call*, December 29, 1909 (special issue), 1.

63. Lipsitz, *Rainbow at Midnight*, 53.

64. Mary Bularzik, "Sexual Harassment at the Workplace: Historical Notes" in James Green, ed., *Workers' Struggles, Past and Present: A "Radical America" Reader* (Philadelphia: Temple University Press, 1983), 121.

65. Nancy Fraser, *Unruly Practices: Power, Discourse and Gender in Contemporary Social Theory* (Minneapolis: University of Minnesota Press, 1989), 171–73.

66. Glenn, *Daughters of the Shtetl*, 146–48; 175.

67. Fraser, *Unruly Practices*, 164–65.

68. Libbey, *Leonie Locke*, 9–10; *Willful Gaynell*, 3.

69. For a discussion of Lemlich's education, see Orleck, *Common Sense and a Little Fire*, 21.

70. Schneiderman with Goldthwaite, *All for One*, 41.

71. Frowne, "The Story of a Sweatshop Girl," 56.

72. "Girls' Stories," *Life and Labor* 4 (8) (Aug. 1914): 243. There is another story of sexual harassment in this same set of stories, collected by a WTUL member.

73. See Roediger, *Wages of Whiteness*, 43–92. Striker Anna McGinty used a similar rhetorical device in opposing sexual harassment in the Cleveland strike: "No wonder a contractor who has been offering the girls in the shop the same insult the overseer offered the negro girl before the war, does not want a union." Anna McGinty, "Letter to the Editor: Forced to Strike," *Ladies Garment Worker* 2 (8) (Aug. 1911): 6.

74. Women's Trade Union League Papers, reel 3039.

75. Katherine Coman, "A Sweated Industry," *Life and Labor* 1 (1) (Jan. 1911): 14; the article "Chicago at the Front" in the same issue describes Coman's process of interviewing a set of strikers to arrive at her list of grievances. See 6–7.

76. For example, Anna Shapiro reported her experience of being required to do personal errands for the boss: "The foreman was ugly, too, and he made me do all his errands for him—running down stairs to buy his cigars or matches, or to get him a glass of water, or anything else—and he said many things to me which no nice girl wants to hear, and no nice girl wants to run and buy cigars and things for a man. "The Girls' Own Stories," *Life and Labor* 1 (2) (Feb. 1911): 51. See also the National Women's Trade Union papers, reel 3039, Tamiment library.

77. McGinty, "Letters to the Editor: Forced to Strike," 5–6; "Warning to Merchants issued by the Committee," *Ladies Garment Worker* 3 (1) (Jan. 1912): 8.

78. Leonora O'Reilly, "The Story of Kalamazoo," *Life and Labor* 2 (8) (Aug. 1912): 228–30; see also "Editorial," *Ladies Garment Worker* 3 (5) (May 1912): 12–13; "Contempt of Court or Contempt for a Vicious System," *Ladies Garment Worker* 3 (6) (June 1912): 1–4; Max Danish, "Kalamazoo Corset Co. Breaks on Union Wheel," *Ladies Garment Worker* 5 (10) (Oct. 1914): 24–26.

79. Quoted in Glenn, *Daughters of the Shtetl*, 175; see also "Public Education and the Employer," *Ladies Garment Worker* 4 (5) (May 1913): 19–20 for a discussion of sexual harassment as a grievance in this strike.

80. Schneiderman with Goldthwaite, *All for One*, 86; Harry Lang, *"62"— Biography of a Union* (New York: Astoria Press, 1940), 178–79.

81. The fact that striking women focused on their own identities as "ladies" or "orphans" but did not develop a term for sexual harassment probably limited their effectiveness because they did not label the act itself as criminal. Despite women's clear perspective on the effects of sexual harassment, in the public eye it remained too much an issue of polite treatment and thus, for some, a simple infraction of manners. Nevertheless, it was a great accomplishment to bring the issue into formal political debate and collective action at such an early period.

82. Quoted in Orleck, *Common Sense and a Little Fire*, 48.

83. Mailly, "Working Girls' Strike Result of Oppression," 1.

84. Marot, "A Woman's Strike," 126–27; Clark and Wyatt, *Making Both Ends Meet*, 76–77.

85. *New York Times*, January 4, 1910, 20.

86. Malkiel, "The Jobless Girls," 2.

87. Malkiel, *The Diary of a Shirtwaist Striker*, 108, 95, 110.

88. Clark and Wyatt, *Making Both Ends Meet*, 67. In late December, lawyer

Miles Dawson created a new list of picket rules that further infer the behavior women exhibited on the picket lines: "[Strikers do not have the right] to continue to walk beside a strike breaker for a long distance, such as a block or more, even though only arguing, persuading and entreating; To stop others as by halting them or turning them aside; To threaten or attempt to intimidate; To lay hands on them or otherwise to assault them; to apply vile and improper names to them so as to endanger a breach of the peace; To congregate in front of or about a shop in such numbers as to be a menace." Dawson, noting the unfair practices of the police and thugs, repeated twice the opaque warning that pickets "should, under no circumstances, do that which they have no right to do merely because they are interfered with." Miles Dawson, "Dawson Defines Pickets' Rights," *New York Call*, December 29, 1909 (special issue), 1.

89. See, for example, *New York Evening World*, November 26, 1909, 1; *New York Times*, November 27, 1909, 3; *New York Tribune*, November 27, 1909, 4; *New York Evening World*, November 27, 1909, 2; *New York Sun*, December 2, 1909, 1; *New York Evening World*, January 19, 1910, 2;

90. *New York Evening Journal*, January 26, 1910, 1.

91. Parker, *Working With the Working Woman*, 127–28.

92. *New York Evening Journal*, December 24, 1909, 4. This was written in the day's editorial. The editor of the *Evening Journal* supported the strike.

93. *New York Evening Journal*, December 9, 1909, 9; *New York Sun*, December 16, 1909, 1; *New York Evening Journal*, December 16, 1909, 8; *New York Sun*, December 11, 1909, 5. See also *New York Evening Journal*, December 17, 1909, 10; *New York World*, December 16, 1909, 11; *New York Sun*, December 21, 1909, 2.

94. Malkiel, *The Diary of a Shirtwaist Striker*, 90, 95, 135.

95. *New York Times*, December 25, 1909, 2; *New York Times*, December 2, 1909, 3; *New York Sun*, December 2, 1909, 1; *New York Tribune*, January 20, 1910, 4; *New York Evening World*, December 20, 1909, 1; *New York Evening World*, January 13, 1910, 3; *New York Times*, December 24, 1909, 3.

96. Hall, "Disorderly Women"; Norwood, *Labor's Flaming Youth*.

97. Violence played a similar role in later strikes. Shirtwaist worker Angela Bambace once told her sister Maria how to handle a strike breaker: "Don't talk to her, punch her in the nose." Bambace, who would become an important union leader, may have acted both out of the culture of young workers and as part of an Italian female tradition. Her mother, Guiseppina Bambace, not only encouraged her daughters in their strike efforts, but joined them on the picket line, armed with her rolling pin. Quoted in Scarpaci, "Angela Bambace and the ILGWU," 102; Ardis Cameron, *Radicals of the Worst Sort: Laboring Women in Lawrence, Massachusetts, 1860–1912* (Urbana: University of Illinois Press, 1993), 130–31.

98. The term is Nancy Fraser's. See "Rethinking the Public Sphere," 109–42. See also Leela Fernandes's application of the notion of subaltern counterpublics in "Beyond Public Spaces and Private Spheres: Gender, Family and

Working-Class Politics in India," *Feminist Studies* 23 (3) (Fall 1997): 525–47.

99. Quoted in Orleck, *Common Sense and a Little Fire*, 64.

100. *New York World*, December 3, 1909, 1. The photograph held in the ILGWU archives has no identification except that it is from the shirtwaist strike, and bears the caption, "Linked arm-in-arm on their way down the Bowery to City Hall." The origin in the *New York World* is not noted, nor are the individuals identified. Historians have thus reasonably assumed that all of the women pictured were strikers. The *New York World*, however, printed the names of the women pictured, though not in order to correspond with the women's placement in the picture: Ida Raub, Rena Bosky, Mary Effers, Yetta Raff, Mary Dreier, and Helen Marot. From comparison to other pictures of Dreier and Marot, I believe Dreier is third from the left and Marot is fifth from the left. Glenn reprinted this picture as evidence of the American styles worn by some Jewish immigrants; this differs from my interpretation of the strikers' dress in this photograph as particularly crafted to be tasteful (and indistinguishable from Marot and Dreier's "respectable" dress) in ways quite different from the popular styles of working women. See *Daughters of the Shtetl*, 165.

101. Malkiel, *The Diary of a Shirtwaist Striker*, 95; Wald, *The House on Henry Street*, 203.

102. *New York Tribune*, December 16, 1909, 3.

103. Steedman, *Landscape for a Good Woman*.

104. Butler, *Excitable Speech*, 26–29.

105. As with the other newspaper sources, it is necessary to reserve some skepticism about whether this really happened. The papers reported that the strike breaker made this statement to Rose Pastor Stokes, who herself was a working-class woman who married a millionaire. The papers focused considerable attention on Stokes's involvement in the strike, and her wealthy status and the well-known dime novel trope meant that this could have been fabricated by reporters to gain public interest. Indeed, one headline read ONE ON MRS. STOKES (*New York Tribune*, December 16, 1909, 3). Nevertheless, such a formulation was also very available to strike breakers, so even if this particular story is not true, we should consider the potential uses of this trope.

106. *New York Herald*, April 7, 1905, 6; *New York Evening Journal*, April 28, 1905.

107. Comstock, "The Uprising of the Girls," 21; see also *New York Evening Journal*, November 29, 1909, 3; *New York Times*, January 2, 1910, 6, 8.

108. Libbey, *Willful Gaynell*, 241.

109. Philip Davis, "The Shirtwaist Makers' Strike," *The Chautauquan* 59 (1) (June 1910): 103; Max Danish, "The Wrapper Makers— Before and After the Strike," *Ladies Garment Worker* 4 (4) (Apr. 1913): 1; "The Unrest in the Garment Trades," *Ladies Garment Worker* 2 (12) (Dec. 1911): 10.

5. Movie-Struck Girls

1. Ruth True, *The Neglected Girl* (New York: Russell Sage, 1914), 67.

2. "What Happened to Mary," *The Ladies World* (Aug. 1912): 3.

3. I am indebted to Miriam Hansen's brilliant work on cinema as a public sphere. See Hansen, *Babel and Babylon*, 1–19, 90–126. Roy Rosenzweig also talks about the importance of the early motion picture theaters as a public space in *Eight Hours for What We Will*. See also Peiss, *Cheap Amusements*.

4. Ibid., 148.

5. Michael M. Davis, *The Exploitation of Pleasure: A Study of Commercial Recreations in New York City* (New York: Sage, 1911), 21; Steven J. Ross, *Working-Class Hollywood: Silent Film and the Shaping of Class in America* (Princeton: Princeton University Press, 1997), 19; Peiss, *Cheap Amusements*, 146, 148.

6. Hansen, *Babel and Babylon*, 14.

7. Peiss, *Cheap Amusements*, 226n53; 154–58; Elizabeth Ewen, "City Lights: Immigrant Women and the Rise of the Movies," *Signs* 5 (3) Supplement (Spring 1980): S45–S66. Comedies were the most numerous of the motion pictures before 1908, but with the advent of new filming techniques and more complex narratives, they became less central. See Eileen Bowser's superb *History of the American Cinema, vol. 2: The Transformation of Cinema, 1907–1915* (New York: Charles Scribner's Sons, 1990), 56.

8. The scholar most associated with this view is Lewis Jacobs, *The Rise of the American Film* (New York: Teachers College Press, 1939). See also Garth Jowett, *Film: the Democratic Art* (Boston: Little, Brown, 1976). The most recent application of this perspective is Ross, *Working-Class Hollywood*. See Hansen's excellent critique of this view in *Babel and Babylon*, 68–70.

9. Ross, *Working-Class Hollywood*, 56–85.

10. My understanding of early film history relies principally on Bowser, *History of the American Cinema, vol. 2*. See especially 28–32 for a discussion of the early crisis in the industry. I also draw on Charles Musser, *The Emergence of Cinema: The American Screen to 1907* (New York: Scribner, 1990); David Bordwell, *On the History of Film Style* (Cambridge: Harvard University Press, 1997); Robert Sklar, *Movie-made America: A Cultural History of American Movies* (New York: Vintage, 1994).

11. Bowser, *History of the American Cinema, vol. 2*, 28–32, 217.

12. See ibid., 19, 53–54; Hansen, *Babel and Babylon*, 16, 23.

13. Cook, *The Fiction Factory*; "Writing the Movies: A New and Well-Paid Business," *New York Times*, August 3, 1913 (printed in Gene Brown, ed., *New York Times Encyclopedia of Film 1896–1979* [New York: Times Books, 1983]).

14. Cook, *The Fiction Factory*, 155–56, 167.

15. Bowser, *History of the American Cinema, vol. 2*, 54, 167–68.

16. Hansen, *Babel and Babylon*, 84.

17. Lary May, *Screening Out the Past: The Birth of Mass Culture and the Motion Picture Industry* (New York: Oxford University Press, 1980).

18. Snyder, *The Voice of the City*. For a discussion of regulation of the early cinema, see Janet Staiger, *Bad Women: Regulating Sexuality in Early American Cinema* (Minneapolis: University of Minnesota Press, 1995).

19. Bowser, *History of the American Cinema, vol. 2*, 44.

20. Ross, *Working-Class Hollywood*, 48, 57, 74. See also Kay Sloan, *The Loud Silents: Origins of the Social Problem Film* (Urbana: University of Illinois Press, 1988), 62–69. Sloan claims, "After the long shirtwaist strike in New York in 1909 and 1910, films starring courageous, beautiful women strike leaders inundated theaters" (64). I have been unable to substantiate this claim. There were a number of films, such as *The Struggle* (Kalem, 1913) in which the daughter of a striker played a significant role among a group of male strikers, but even in these movies the female character did not play a role as a recognized leader. Sloan claims that *The Long Strike* (Essanay, 1911) "featured a labor leader who courted the boss' son to win the demands of the women strikers." However, the *Moving Picture World* review that Sloan cites as her only evidence does not indicate a strike of women workers. Indeed, the heroine meets the boss's son when on her way to the factory at the noon hour, carrying her father's lunch pail. She is the daughter of a striker, not a striker herself. See "The Struggle," *Moving Picture World* 16 (June 7, 1913): 1009; "The Long Strike," *Moving Picture World* 10 (December 23, 1911): 989.

21. Ross, *Working-Class Hollywood*, 57.

22. "The Girl Strike Leader," *Moving Picture World* 7 (July 23, 1910): 193.

23. Ross, *Working-Class Hollywood*, 74; Sloan, *The Loud Silents*, 64–66.

24. Bowser, *History of the American Cinema, vol. 2*, 178, 185. The episodes of *What Happened to Mary* could be understood if viewed separately, as each traced a particular adventure that was resolved within the time of the short. This has caused some not to classify *What Happened to Mary* as a serial. See Bowser 206. However, themes of Mary's mysterious origin, her struggle in the work world, and romance all were pursued across different segments and tied the stories together. Indeed, *What Happened to Mary* had far more narrative continuity than *Hazards of Helen*, which is always classed as a serial. In *Hazards of Helen*, a romance between Helen and another worker provides a very loose continuity between rather interchangeable episodes of adventure. However, by the time *Hazards of Helen* began in 1914, serials were an established genre, and the film fit the bill in terms of its sensational content and its release schedule.

25. Some of these films drew quite directly on the "Laura Jean Libbey" dime novel formula, while others drew on other cheap fiction conventions, including the dime novel romances featuring wealthy heroines that were read by working women. As chapter 1 argued, even these characters usually figured class inequities in some way. Female characters could also be found in Westerns and other dime novels targeting a primarily male audience. The film industry

creatively mixed a number of dime novel conventions in creating the female adventure short.

26. "What Happened to Mary," *Bioscope* (July 31, 1913): 368–69; Rothvin Wallace, "The Activities of Mary," *The Ladies' World* (Mar. 1913): 11.

27. Frank Luther Mott, *A History of American Magazines* (Cambridge: Harvard University Press, 1957), 4:360–68. *The Ladies World* was bought by McClure Publications, Inc., in February of 1912. Charles Dwyer discussed the impact of *What Happened to Mary* on subscription rates in "The Editor and the Reader," *The Ladies World* 33 (12) (Dec. 1912): 1. 42.

28. Lewis E. Palmer, "The World in Motion," *The Survey* 22 (June 5, 1909): 356; Bowser, *History of the American Cinema, vol. 2*, 93, 106–19; Kathryn Fuller, *At the Picture Show: Small-Town Audiences and the Creation of Movie Fan Culture* (Washington, D.C.: Smithsonian Institution Press, 1996), 115–33; Richard de Cordova, *Picture Personalities: The Emergence of the Star System in America* (Urbana: University of Illinois Press, 1990).

29. Mary Fuller with Bailey Millard, "My Adventures as a Motion-Picture Heroine," *Collier's* 48 (15) (Dec. 30, 1911): 16–17; "What Happened to Mary," *Bioscope* (July 31, 1913): 369. (*Bioscope* was a British film magazine; *What Happened to Mary* opened in England in 1913.)

30. "Miss Mary Fuller Wearing the 'Mary' Hat," *The Ladies World* (June 1913): 4; Wallace, "The Activities of Mary," 11.

31. *The Ladies World* 33 (8) (Aug. 1912): 4; 33 (9) (Sept. 1912): 1. For winners that matched plot developments, see 33 (11) (Nov. 1912): 40; 34 (1) (Jan. 1913). Later serials overtly promised that winners would determine the upcoming plot. See "The Perils of Pauline: Today's Prize Offer," *Atlanta Georgian*, June 14, 1914. See also Kathryn Fuller's description of a Thanhousser contest for an ending to the serial *A Million Dollar Mystery* (1913) in *At the Picture Show*, 128.

32. Buck Rainey, *Those Fabulous Serial Heroines: Their Lives and Films* (Metuchen, N.J.: Scarecrow Press, 1990), 459; Ben Singer, "Female Power in the Serial-Queen Melodrama: The Etiology of an Anomaly," *Camera Obscura* 22 (Jan. 1990): 91–129; "Perils of Pauline," *Variety* (April 10, 1914); see also "The Trey O' Hearts," *Variety* (August 7, 1914).

33. Simkhovitch, *The City Worker's World in America*, 124; Sherman C. Kingsley, "The Penny Arcade and the Cheap Theatre," *Charities and the Commons* 18 (Jan. 1907): 295. For discussions of the role of theaters in ethnic working-class neighborhoods during the silent era see Peiss, *Cheap Amusements*, on New York, 139–53; and on Chicago in the 1920s see Cohen, *Making a New Deal*, 120–29.

34. True, *The Neglected Girl*, 116; Jane Addams, *The Spirit of Youth and the City Streets* (New York: Macmillan, 1909), 86; Robert A. Woods and Albert J. Kennedy, *Young Working Girls: A Summary of Evidence from Two Thousand Social Workers* (Boston: Houghton Mifflin, 1913), 114. See also Louise de Koven

Bowen, *Five and Ten Cent Theaters* (Juvenile Protection Association of Chicago, 1909, 1911). Addams and de Koven Bowen were both talking about Chicago. Patterns of motion picture projection and attendance were very specific to each city at this time. I have only used Chicago sources when I also have a source from New York City that corroborates its basic point.

35. Harriet McDoual Daniels, *The Girl and Her Chance* (New York: Fleming H. Revell, 1914), 73; Simkhovitch, *The City Worker's World in America*, 131. See also Peiss, *Cheap Amusements*, 53–55, 110–13.

36. Addams, *The Spirit of Youth and the City Streets*, 80–81; Hasanovitz, *One of Them*, 247; Laughlin, *The Work-a-day Girl*, 147.

37. Odencrantz, *Italian Women in Industry*, 204, 235. Filomena Ognibene quoted in Ewen, "City Lights," S58. Laughlin reported that working women typically attended motion picture theaters more than twice per week. Laughlin, *The Work-a-day Girl*, 143.

38. Esther Packard, *A Study of Living Conditions of Self-Supporting Women in New York City* (New York: Metropolitan Board of the YWCA, 1915), 51, 86.

39. Mary Heaton Vorse, "Some Picture Show Audiences," *Outlook* 98 (June 24, 1911): 443, 446.

40. Fuller, *At the Picture Show*, 115.

41. Buck-Morss, *The Dialectics of Seeing*, 253–55; see also McRobbie, "The *Passagenwerk* and the Place of Walter Benjamin in Cultural Studies," 96–120; and Leo Charney and Vanessa R. Schwartz, eds., *Cinema and the Invention of Modern Life* (Berkeley: University of California Press, 1995) for discussions about the connections among modernity, the city, and motion pictures. In particular, see Marcus Verhagen, "The Poster in *Fin-de-Siècle* Paris: "That Mobile and Degenerate Art'," 103–29.

42. William R. Leach, "Transformations in a Culture of Consumption: Women and Department Stores, 1890–1925," *Journal of American History* 71 (2) (Sept. 1984): 319–42.

43. Laughlin, *The Work-a-day Girl*, 142.

44. Addams, *The Spirit of Youth and the City Streets*, 91; Woods and Kennedy, *Young Working Girls*, 114.

45. Louise de Koven Bowen, *Safeguards for City Youth at Work and at Play* (New York: Macmillan, 1914), 19.

46. Daniels, *The Girl and Her Chance*, 73. Some white-collar workers did attend motion pictures on their lunch hours. In addition, the Strand theater on Broadway opened an inexpensive lunchroom for "working girls" within the massive theater structure. Many factory workers, however, would not have had time to walk there to have lunch. See "A Theater with Four Million Patrons a Year," *Photoplay Magazine* 7 (Apr. 1915): 84.

47. Davis, *The Exploitation of Pleasure*, 54.

48. See Lauren Rabinowitz, *For the Love of Pleasure: Women, Movies, and Culture in Turn-of-the-Century Chicago* (New Brunswick, N.J.: Rutgers University Press, 1998), 22–26, 82–97, for discussions of the meaning of the female gaze in public and in cinema.

49. Quoted in Mary Field, " 'On Strike' A Collection of True Stories," *American Magazine* (Oct. 1911): 736. In the Women's Trade Union League Papers, Tamiment Library.

50. Addams, *The Spirit of Youth and the City Streets*, 86.

51. Palmer, "The World in Motion," 356.

52. Quoted in Peiss, *Cheap Amusements*, 153.

53. Sarah Helen Starr, "The Photoplay: An Entertainment, An Occupation," *The Ladies' World* 33 (6) (June 1912): 9; Ernest A. Dench, "Our Brooklyn Jungle," *Illustrated World* 26 (Oct. 1916): 222–23; William A. Page, "The Movie-Struck Girl," *Woman's Home Companion* 45 (June 1918): 18. See also Fuller, *At the Picture Show*, 129.

54. Page, "The Movie-Struck Girl," 18; Bowser, *History of the American Cinema, vol. 2*, 24; Fuller, *At the Picture Show*, 130.

55. Richard de Cordova, "The Emergence of the Star System in America," in Christine Gledhill, ed., *Stardom: Industry of Desire* (London: Routledge, 1991), 17–29.

56. "Acting for the 'Movies' " *Literary Digest* 48 (Feb. 28, 1914). This first-person article about Mary Fuller was reprinted from the newspaper the *Indianapolis Star*.

57. Starr, "The Photoplay," 9.

58. "Mary Pickford Has a Word to Say" *Harper's Bazaar* (Apr. 1917): 55.

59. Charles Musser, "Ethnicity, Role-playing, and American Film Comedy: From *Chinese Laundry Scene* to *Whoopee* (1894–1930)" in Lester D. Friedman, ed., *Unspeakable Images: Ethnicity and the American Cinema* (Urbana: University of Illinois Press, 1991), 54.

60. I have chosen to look closely in this chapter at only two of the serials, but my analysis of these two is informed by a broader examination of the genre. I viewed a number of serial episodes at the Library of Congress, Motion Picture Division, including episodes from *Lucille Love, Girl of Mystery, The Ventures of Marguerite, Hazards of Helen, Girl and the Game, Pearl of the Army, The Lightening Raider, The Purple Mask*, and *A Woman in Grey*. I read print versions of *What Happened to Mary, Who Will Marry Mary, Plunder, The Adventures of Kathlyn*, and *The Perils of Pauline*.

61. Cowie, *Representing the Woman*, 4.

62. Advertisement for *What Happened to Mary*, Edison Archives; "What Happened to Mary," *Bioscope* (July 31, 1913): 368–69; " 'Mary' and the Movies," *The Ladies' World* 33 (10) (Sept. 1912): 1.

63. Ibid.

64. "What Happened to Mary: The Remarkable Story of a Remarkable Girl," *The Ladies' World* 33 (8) (Aug. 1912): 3.

65. Ibid.

66. Quoted in Cowie, *Representing the Woman*, 51.

67. For example, in episode 2 Mary buys some new clothes to replace her clothes from the island. (For immigrant women whose purchases of new clothes were among their first acts in the new country this scene could have particular appeal.) The female shopkeeper, however, treats her rudely because she is so plainly dressed. When Mary picks out the loveliest clothes in the shop, she repeats the common dime novel convention of the working girl instinctively dressing herself impeccably once she becomes an heiress. The presence of the storekeeper who degrades Mary because of her plain dress invokes class distinction, and invites indignation on Mary's behalf and enjoyment of Mary's purchases as a vindication of her ill treatment. "What Happened to Mary in the City," *The Ladies World* 33 (10) (Sept. 1912): 12.

68. Rachel M. Brownstein, *Becoming a Heroine* (New York: Viking Press, 1984), xxi. See also Cowie, *Representing the Woman*, 6–7.

69. "What Happened to Mary," *Bioscope* (July 31, 1913): 369. Note that for this reviewer, sensationalism was necessary to achieve a "realistic" effect.

70. Walter Licht, *Working for the Railroad: The Organization of Work in the Nineteenth Century* (Princeton: Princeton University Press, 1983), 163, 160.

71. The producer's decision to make Helen a telegraph operator for a railroad dovetailed men's heroic stories of labor with formulas based on female heroines. Women did work in the railroad industry at this time; however, their positions were redefined to exclude them from men's promotional track. In 1918, only 2.6 percent of all women railroad workers were telegraph operators. Helen served, like Mary, not as a representation of the "real" working opportunities or experiences of working-class women, but as a fantasy of women in the (masculine) workplace, privy to masculine adventures and amenities. See Maureen Weiner Greenwald, "Women Workers and World War One: The American Railroad Industry, A Case Study," *Journal of Social History* 9 (Winter 1975): 154–77.

72. Film critic Ben Singer argues that this combination of power and vulnerability undergirded a desire for sensationalist films and images by the turn of the century; sensationalist images particularly focused on new and dangerous forms of transportation such as the train, the streetcar, and the automobile. Singer, "Modernity, Hyperstimulus, and the Rise of Popular Sensationalism" in Charney and Schwartz, eds., *Cinema and the Invention of Modern Life*, 72–99. See also Singer's discussion of the *Hazards of Helen* serial in "Female Power in the Serial-Queen Melodrama," 102–3.

73. The stage melodrama version of "Bertha, the Sewing Machine Girl"

when revived in early 1900s, for example, featured a "realistic" train collision. "Labor's Grandest Demonstration," *Union Labor Advocate* (Sept. 1909): 15; advertisement, *Moving Picture World* 14 (3) (Oct. 1912): 262.

74. Episode 58, "The Wrong Order" is at the Motion Picture Division, Library of Congress.

75. A number of reviews and synopses of episode 31 can be found in the Helen Holmes clipping file, New York Public Library for Performing Arts.

76. Information on episodes gained from promotional material found in the *Hazards of Helen* clipping file, New York Public Library for Performing Arts. In *The Girl and the Game*, a railroad series starring Helen Holmes, the heroine refuses a proposal in the first episode. The camera cuts between two romantic close-ups: the man proposing, and Helen smiling slightly, shaking her head, "no." The romantic film techniques, all the more startling because true close-ups were rare at this time, served to highlight the narrative innovation of the refusal. For information on episode 13, see Bowser, *History of the American Cinema, vol. 2*, 187.

Conclusion: A Place to Dream

1. Bertha Levy, "Regina's Disappointment," *Ladies Garment Worker* 3 (10) (Sept. 1913): 19–20.

2. Warren Susman, " 'Personality' and the Making of Twentieth-Century Culture," 271–85.

3. Janice Radway, *A Feeling for Books: The Book-of-the-Month Club, Literary Taste, and Middle-Class Desire* (Chapel Hill: University of North Carolina Press, 1997), 371n. Jackson Lears offers a new interpretation of consumer society in *Fables of Abundance: A Cultural History af Advertising in America* (New York: Basic Books, 1994) which seeks to move beyond an opposition between "authenticity" and "consumerism" by tracing an "alternative language of objects" (395). Lears credits artists and intellectuals for these (authentic) alternatives. My argument here focuses not on such alternatives but on the daily, ordinary practices of the unprivileged with mass-produced consumer culture.

4. Glenn, *Daughters of the Shtetl*, 166; Ross, *Working-Class Hollywood*, 10, 24.

5. "Pauline Newman," in Joan Morrison and Charlotte Fox Zabusky, eds., *American Mosaic: The Immigrant Experience in the Words of Those Who Lived It* (New York: Dutton, 1980), 9–14.

6. For example, see Newman, "When You Have Time to Read," *Ladies Garment Worker* 4 (7) (June 1913): 34. Newman urged, "Don't read books that take you into a fairy land and introduce you to a Prince who falls in love with you. You are wasting your time reading such books."

7. Buck-Morss, *The Dialectics of Seeing*, 253–54, 125–26. My last statement paraphrases Benjamin's language and theoretical framework here, though my view differs from his in key respects. Benjamin thought that the dreamworld of

commodities was collective, but that people were immersed in individual imaginative experiences and were blind to their collective element. They needed to "wake up" from that state and recognize the "dream *as* a dream" in order to see the experience as collective and thus seize its political potential. Benjamin stated that at the moment of this recognition of collectivity, "the historian takes upon himself the task of dream interpretation." See Buck-Morss, 261. However, as Angela McRobbie notes, Benjamin's *Passagenwerk* studied popular culture *objects* rather than social relations, and so may have missed the shared meanings of actual consumers' experiences. Though I do not endorse Benjamin's opposition between sleeping and waking, I agree that historical "dream interpretation" is called for to discern the collective meanings of the "dream." See McRobbie, "The *Passagenwerk* and the Place of Walter Benjamin in Cultural Studies," 114.

INDEX

Americanization, 55–56; sales of, 34, 217n48; sensationalism in, 36, 43; serialized, 34; sexual vulnerability in, 74, 142–43; social recognition in, 192; strikers' reading of, 134; use of suspense, 71; wish images in, 69; working girl formula in, 37–43; working ladyhood in, 74, 143, 144; working women's consumption of, 13, 37, 49, 51–52, 55–60, 68, 202, 203, 206. *See also* fiction

dime novels, romance genre of, 14, 37, 38, 40–41; freedom in, 73; lending of, 54–55; middle-class values in, 43–44

Dix, Dorothy, 101, 105, 108

Douglas, Ann, 5, 209n8

dream worlds, 52, 220n14, 250n7

Dreier, Mary, 155, 233n4, 242n100; arrest of, 128, 129, 130

dressmakers, "slop," 17, 18, 23; ready-made clothes from, 28

Dwyer, Charles, 245n27

Eastman Kodak Company, 167

economy: family, 63–64, 73, 211n22; leisure, 62; moral, 66, 223n64; sexual, 62, 177

Edison Company, 162, 166–67, 192, 248n69; advertising by, 174; Progressive views of, 170; rationalization of production by, 172

Effers, Mary, 242n100

eight-hour movement, 233n62

Eley, Geoff, 232n62

Enlightenment: political subjectivity in, 3, 85, 96, 105, 159, 203, 226n2; view of rationality, 226n2, 231n50

eroticism, in fashion, 215n27

ethnicity: in American political culture, 226n2; and autonomy, 52; in consumer culture, 211n13, 212n30; role of commodities in, 204; role of fashion in, 18, 62; in shirtwaist strike, 98; in working-class culture, 6, 51; in working ladyhood, 13

evening gowns, ready-made, 28, 29

Ewen, Elizabeth, 163, 210n9

Ewen, Stuart, 210n9

Fairfax, Beatrice, 100

family, working women's role in, 63–64, 73

Family Story Paper, The 34, 35

fan culture, of motion pictures, 15, 173–74, 178–79, 181, 183–86, 200

fashion: African-American, 68; class distinction in, 18, 23–24, 27, 61–62; constricting, 27, 30, 215n27; consumption of, 8, 18, 49, 50, 52, 68; as creative process, 51; cultural meanings of, 85; eroticism in, 215n27; grades of, 18, 19, 28–29; immigrant women's use of, 61; inexpensive, 17; middle-class taste in, 24, 26–30, 81, 204, 215n27; moral value in, 26, 29–30, 31, 78; mystification of, 25; in production process, 215n19; reform in, 30–31; relationship to fiction, 51; role in Americanization, 2; self-improvement through, 24; sentimental style in, 25; "sincere" style in, 25, 26; social uses of, 18, 61, 68; working women's consumption of, 49, 50, 51, 66, 68, 202, 203. *See also* clothing; garment industry

fashion, working-class, 1–2, 21–22, 28, 63; color in, 81; conspicuous, 18, 29–30, 48–49, 67, 77–81, 82, 85, 113–15; in family economy, 211n22; as frivolous, 211n16; hats in, 9–12, 16, 77, 79–80, 133, 146–47; importance of, 60–63; as investment, 62; and ladyhood, 10; moral value in, 28, 29; restrictive, 30; in shirtwaist strike, 85, 88, 94, 98–100, 103–105, 113–14, 130, 131, 133, 148, 155; shoes in, 77, 80–81; Stokes on, 29, 80; underwear in, 81–82; WTUL on, 113

femininity: in consumer culture, 4–5, 210n9; and physical labor, 14–15, 198

feminism, subject position in, 3, 208n3

fiction: consumption of, 18; domestic, 41, 43, 218n69; effect of market on, 46; modes of production for, 18, 31; moral value in, 31–32, 41; relationship to fashion, 51; serial, 18, 46; standardization of, 35–36

fiction, formulaic, 17–18; effect of industrialization on, 31, 32; emergence of, 18–19; honest mechanic stories in,

audience identification with, 186–91, 195–98

Hitchcock, Alfred, 190

Hoffman, Ada, 154

Hollywood: market interests in, 165; melodramas of, 77, 225n100

Holmes, Helen, 194, 249n76

honest mechanic stories, 37, 38, 39–40, 42

Horkheimer, Max, 209n9

identity: effect of motion pictures on, 15, 187; historical representation of, 14; of immigrant women, 50; middle-class, 27, 44; in movie serials, 191; political, 13, 159; resistant, 121; role of consumption in, 204; of shirtwaist strikers, 145–46, 154, 203; social construction of, 205; and subjectivity, 13; working-class, 233n62; of working-class women, 6, 73, 83, 85, 119, 120, 145, 163, 179, 180, 200, 231n50; in working ladyhood, 145–46, 154, 202

immigrants: Americanization of, 9, 55–56, 59, 61, 127; in consumer culture, 210n11; culture of, 54; Jewish, 127, 136, 236n28; in Socialist movement, 125. See also women, immigrant

industrialization: as democratizing force, 214n14; effect on consumption, 21; effect on popular fiction, 31, 32

installment plans, 63

International Ladies' Garment Workers Union (ILGWU), 87, 90; local 25, 89, 123, 131, 160, 234n11; radicals in, 137; on sexual harassment, 145; in shirtwaist strike, 102, 103, 112, 118, 139, 150; view of working women, 3

International Workers of the World (IWW), 137, 238n47

interpellation theory, 109–10, 118

intertextuality, 51

Jacobs, Lewis, 243n7

Jameson, Fredric, 36

Joselit, Jenna, 235n28

journalists, middle-class, 100–101

journals: influence on commodities,

25–26; labor, 112–16; mail-order, 173

Kalamazoo corset strike (1912), 116, 145

Kalem Company, 169, 172, 184

Kelley, Robin D. G., 7, 51, 68

Kennedy, Albert, 180

Kessler-Harris, Alice, 98, 99

Keystone Cops, 172

Knights of Labor, 40

labor, slave versus free, 4

labor history, 3, 88–89, 210n11; consciousness in, 234n8; strikes in, 227n3; women's, 6

labor journals, 112–16

labor leaders: account of shirtwaist strike, 88–89, 92; addresses to strikers, 111–12, 116; control of women strikers, 149–50; depiction of women strikers, 85, 106, 108, 109, 111, 117, 118, 122–23; Forverts on, 136; motivations of, 123; on picketing, 149; strategies of, 230n46; views of working women, 3; women among, 115–16. See also unions

labor politics, working-class women in, 51

labor rationalization, 140; effect on creativity, 57; in print media, 32, 34–36, 43, 45

labor relations, in commodity production, 25

ladies: in dime novels, 69; dress of, 26–27; working women as, 49, 50–51, 68, 69–71, 77–78. See also ladyhood, working

Ladies Garment Worker (journal), 112, 113, 201; on fiction, 114, 206; on women's popular culture, 232n53

Ladies' Home Journal, 173

Ladies' World, The (journal): audience of, 173; movie production by, 162, 172–74, 192; Oppenheim in, 44, 45; serial fiction in, 19

ladyhood: cultural value of, 81; definition of, 24; for immigrant women, 2; social practices of, 69

ladyhood, working, 49, 50–51, 68, 69–71, 78–79; agency of, 109, 110, 118, 206; amusements in, 77; and class identity, 13; cultural practices of, 120, 123, 157, 158; as cultural resource, 86, 121; in dime novels, 74, 143, 144; entitlement in, 2, 104, 120, 155–56; and fashion, 10; in interpellation theory, 109–11, 118; language of, 121, 142, 143; politics of, 82; as public identity, 145–46, 154, 202; role of consumption in, 50, 203; role of movies in, 162, 183; in shirtwaist strike, 83, 85, 86, 116; subjectivity of, 13, 14, 225n103; violence in, 134. *See also* working-class women

language: of entitlement, 104; ritual nature of, 228n12; of working lady-hood, 121, 142, 143

Laughlin, Clara, 129, 178, 246n37

Lawrence Strike (1912), 20, 46, 154, 213n5

Leach, William, 180

Lears, Jackson, 249n3

Lee, Martyn, 19

Leiserson shirtwaist factory: owners of, 237n43; police brutality at, 124; strike in, 89, 91, 132, 136, 137

leisure: and consumption of commodities, 20; for working women, 7, 178

Lemlich, Clara, 16, 90, 233n1; arrest of, 132; on clothing, 146; at Cooper Union, 119; rhetoric of, 8–9, 11, 121, 143, 147–48; on sexual harassment, 144, 145; and shirtwaist strike, 119–20, 126, 127; in Socialist Party, 147–48, 159; on workers' grievances, 8, 140–41, 146

Levine, Lawrence, 219n73, 232n57

Levy, Bertha, 201–202

Lewis, Lisa, 7

Libby, Laura Jean, 37, 41, 57, 217n58; cost of novels, 34; *The Heiress of Cameron Hall,* 72; heroes of, 40; influence on movies, 244n25; *Leonie Locke,* 41, 134, 237n37; marriage in, 157; plots of, 56; political action in, 42

Licht, Walter, 193

Life and Labor (journal), 58, 112, 113, 115; on sexual harassment, 143–44, 145

lingerie waists, 131

Lippard, George, 36–37

Lipsitz, George, 7, 142, 236n36

literacy, 32; and dime novel reading, 54, 58

literature: canonical, 218n69, 219n76; political discussion in, 46; working women's access to, 206

Little Women (Alcott), 70, 77

Lonedal Operator, The (film), 172

Long Strike, The (film), 244n20

Lowe, Lisa, 120

magazines. *See* journals

Mailly, William, 141

makeup, 61, 95, 215n20, 229n18

Malkiel, Theresa, 105, 155; *Diary of a Shirtwaist Striker,* 135, 150–51, 153–54, 231n52, 232n53

Manufacturers' Association, in shirtwaist strike, 90, 108, 150, 238n52

market: effect on cultural commodities, 165; effect on fiction, 46; freedom from, 219n76; newspapers in, 93; for ready-made clothes, 28; working women's place in, 2, 18, 19, 21, 30–31

Marot, Helen, 129, 139, 155, 235n17, 242n100; on picketing, 149; on reading, 231n52; on resistance, 235n18

marriage: in dime novels, 13, 76, 157–58; in fiction, 192; working women's view on, 157

Marx, Karl, 215n18

mass production: of commodities, 17, 18; effect on middle-class, 23; of print media, 20–21, 31. *See also* clothing, ready-made

Matyas, Jennie, 140

McClure's (journal), 46

McGinty, Anna, 239n73

McRobbie, Angela, 12, 65, 68, 211n16

media: active reception of, 220n12. *See also* motion pictures; print media

melodrama: in dime novels, 41, 44, 58, 70; in formula fiction, 39; in movies, 77, 162, 199, 225n100; train wrecks in, 195; virtue in, 76; working-girl, 37

Merwin, Bannister, 168, 173, 188

Mexican Americans, 7

Meyerowitz, Joanne, 43–44, 72

middle class: as consumers, 19, 23–25, 44, 204, 214n11; consumption of motion pictures, 165, 170, 171, 185;

consumption of print media, 92, 96; cultural hegemony of, 232*n*57; effect of mass production on, 23; emergence of, 23, 213*n*11; fear of disorder, 99–100; idea of character, 23, 27, 203–204; reading habits of, 44; taste in fashion, 26–30, 81, 204; view of shirtwaist strike, 100, 108, 117, 132; view of working-class women, 27, 37, 74, 77

modes of production, for fiction, 18, 31

Modleski, Tania, 4, 209*n*8

Moresco, Filomena, 64

motion picture industry: crisis in, 243*n*10; economic relations of, 160–65; rationalization of production in, 166, 172, 199; regulation of, 170, 244*n*18, 248*n*69

Motion Picture Patents Company (MPPC), 166–67

motion pictures: "actuality," 167; audience identification with, 186–91, 195–98; comedies, 163, 243*n*7; depiction of strikes, 171–72; depiction of working women, 170, 176; dime novels' influence on, 164, 172, 244*n*25; distribution of, 168; educational, 170; effect on self-identity, 15, 187; extras in, 184; fan culture of, 173–74, 178–79, 181, 183–86, 200; female adventure in, 162, 172; and gender hierarchies, 200; influence on dating, 176–77; "labor-capital," 166, 170–71, 195; middle-class audience of, 165, 170, 171, 185; mode of narration in, 167–70; modernity in, 246*n*41; posters for, 15, 179–82, 184, 200; as public sphere, 243*n*3; railroad dramas, 172; relations of production in, 165; role in working ladyhood, 162; scenario writers of, 168–69, 173; self-censorship of, 170; sensation in, 195, 199, 248*n*68, 249*n*72; "social problem," 170; standardization of, 169–70, 173; star system of, 15, 173–74, 181, 183–85; Westerns, 245*n*25; white-collar workers at, 246*n*46; working women's consumption of, 161–64, 176–87, 199–200, 212, 246*n*37. *See also* serials, motion picture

Murolo, Priscilla, 219*n*3

"Mysteries of the city" (formula), 36–37, 39

narrative: film, 167–70; participation in, 174–75; mass-produced, 7, 10

Newman, Pauline, 51, 109, 110–11; as labor organizer, 115, 127, 233*n*64; in shirtwaist strike, 120, 138, 155; Socialist principles of, 159; on wages, 230*n*32; on women's reading, 205–206, 249*n*6

newspapers: coverage of working women, 38; Democrat-owned, 217*n*59; expansion of, 32–33; Italian, 137; middle-class culture in, 33; sensationalism in, 32–33, 92–93, 128, 134, 218*n*59, 225*n*92, 228*n*13; as sources, 227*n*7; working women's reading of, 128–29, 231*n*52; Yiddish, 125, 135–36, 237*n*39

newspapers, penny, 31, 32–33; middle-class readers of, 33; working-class interests in, 34

New York Call, 94, 102, 118, 231*n*53; cartoons in, 103–107; on sexual harassment, 141; on wages, 148

New York Evening Journal, 8; audience of, 93; Lemlich in, 120; ownership of, 228*n*12; readers of, 10; strikers in, 98, 131–33, 136; on strike violence, 94, 132, 133, 134; support of strike, 130, 241*n*92; use of hyperbole, 236*n*35

New York Evening World, 129

New York Hat, The (film), 10–11, 213*n*27

New York Herald, 32, 157

New York Sentinel, 34

New York Sun, 32, 98

New York Times: coverage of shirtwaist strike, 92, 97; on movies, 168

New York Tribune, 92

New York World, 93, 155, 242*n*100

nickelodeons, 162, 163–64, 170; expansion of, 166; as social centers, 179

Norwood, Stephen, 7, 8, 154

novelists, dime, 42

Odem, Mary 223*n*55

Odencrantz, Louise, 178

Ognibene, Filomena, 178
Oppenheim, James: "Bread and Roses,"
20, 46, 213n5; creative autonomy of,
45–46; movie scenarios of, 168, 173;
"Peg O'the Movies," 18, 19, 20, 21,
45, 46; radicalism of, 44, 46
Orleck, Annelise, 114, 126, 221n29
orphans, 146; in dime novels, 72, 73; in
film serials, 191; freedom of, 145, 191

Parker, Cornelia Stratton, 222n40
Pastor, Rose. See Stokes, Rose Pastor
Pathé-Frères, 166
patriarchy: effect of popular culture on,
212n26; women's freedom from, 11
peddlers, immigrant, 53
"Peg O'the Movies" (Oppenheim), 18,
19, 20, 21, 45, 46
Peiss, Kathy, 6, 52, 62, 77, 215n20; on
makeup, 229n18; on movies, 162,
164, 177
penny press, 18, 31, 32–33, 34
personality: culture of, 19–20, 203; role
of consumption in, 204
Peterson, Joyce Shaw, 43, 72
Philadelphia Public Ledger, 32
Phillips, John S., 45
picketing, by Appalachian strikers, 7
picketing, in shirtwaist strike, 90, 91–95,
122, 128; defense of, 102; labor
leaders on, 149; obstructions to, 118;
rules for, 240n88; strategies of, 123,
152; violence in, 94–95, 97–98, 105,
131–33, 148, 149, 151, 237n45;
women's behavior during, 149–54
Pickford, Mary, 10–11
piecework, 57; sexual harassment in, 142;
wages for, 67, 140
police: brutality of, 124, 155; discourse of
power, 228n12; Forverts on, 136; in
shirtwaist strike, 95, 96, 105, 106,
131–32, 148, 153, 241n88
politics: and consumption, 4, 14, 205; in
formula fiction, 42–43; identity in,
13, 159. See also subjectivity, political
posters, motion picture, 179–82, 184, 200
Postman, Neil, 210n9
power: fantasies of, 198; and gender, 182;
police discourse of, 228n12

print media: class divisions in, 44, 45;
coverage of shirtwaist strike, 84, 87,
88, 89, 92–107, 111, 128–37; format
of, 35; labor rationalization in, 32,
34–36, 43, 45; market divisions in, 44;
mass-produced, 20–21, 31; middle-
class audience of, 92, 96; narratives of,
10; in public sphere, 86–87; Socialist,
88, 94, 115
private sphere, 85, 226n2
production: of fashion, 215n19; labor
process in, 25, 57; modes of, 18, 31;
rationalization of, 166, 172, 199, 202;
relations of, 22, 165; socioeconomic
factors in, 12
Progresso Italo-americano, Il (newspaper),
137, 237n45, 238n47
Proletario, Il (newspaper), 137
prostitutes, 91–92, 95, 148
public debate: in movies, 166; on sexual
harassment, 144; on shirtwaist strike,
154, 159, 227n5
public space: access to, 226n2; gaze in,
247n48; movie theaters in, 162–63,
179, 245n33; in shirtwaist strike, 148;
women's occupation of, 91–93, 94,
102, 117, 161, 182, 203, 228n10
public sphere: economic decisions in, 87;
motion pictures as, 243n3; political
exchange in, 85, 226n2; print media
in, 86–87; shirtwaist strikers in, 86,
93, 102; virtue in, 91; women's exclusion from, 106, 118, 134
publishers, of dime novels, 34. See also
print media
pushcarts, 2, 52–54, 65, 80

R. J. Reynolds Corporation, 213n27
race, 212n30; in American political
culture, 226n2; and style, 215n27
radicalism: and fashion consumption, 8;
Italian, 120, 137; of Jewish immigrants, 236n28; of Jewish women,
125, 127, 235n18; Oppenheim's, 44,
46; of shirtwaist strikers, 122; subculture of, 120, 121, 124, 148; of
working women, 5–6
Radway, Janice, 49, 57, 204; on romance,
7, 224n85; on social grammar, 69

Raff, Yetta, 242n100

railroads: in motion pictures, 172, 193–95, 248n71, 249n76; nationalization of, 228n13; women employees of, 248n71

rationality: in consumer culture, 5; Enlightenment view of, 226n2, 231n50; gendered ideology of, 117; in political subjectivity, 206; of shirtwaist strikers, 98, 105, 106, 111, 112, 116; of working women, 113

Raub, Ida, 242n100

readers: cultural competency of, 93; as movie fans, 173

reading: as creative process, 51–52; Jewish women's, 221n29; role in Americanization, 55–56; of romances, 224n85; social context of, 49, 57–58; working women's experience of, 69–70, 205–6. See also dime novels

remnants, fabric, 65, 66–67

resistance, 121–22, 205; to consumer culture, 209n9; of immigrant Jews, 235n18; in shirtwaist strike, 150

Richardson, Bertha, 31; on fashion, 29, 48, 81–82

Richardson, Dorothy, 82, 222n40; on name changing, 60; on reading habits, 56, 57–58; on workers' dress, 67–68, 216n37

Richardson, Samuel, 36, 192

Roediger, David, 4

romances. See dime novels, romance genre of

Rose, Tricia, 7

Rosen, Anna, 153

Rosenzweig, Roy, 233n62

Ross, Steven, 162, 166, 170, 171, 205

Ruiz, Vicki, 7, 211n13

Sanchez, George, 136, 211n13

Saxton, Alexander, 34, 37, 217n59

scabs, 90, 241n97; in shirtwaist strike, 92, 95, 105, 151, 229n16, 237n45, 242n105

Schneiderman, Rose: on dime novels, 54, 55; on sexual harassment, 145; in shirtwaist strike, 126, 234n10; in WTUL, 127

Schreier, Barbara, 235n28

Scott, James, 121–22

Scott, Joan, 117

secret inheritances, in dime novels, 13, 76, 154

self: character model of, 19–20; formation of, 207; personality model of, 19–20, 204; and subjectivity, 13

Selig Company, 175

Seller, Maxine Schwartz, 128, 238n53

sensationalism: in dime novels, 36, 43; in motion pictures, 195, 199, 248n68; in newspapers, 32–33, 92–93, 128, 134, 218n59, 225n92, 228n13

serials: fiction, 18, 34, 46; suspense in, 190

serials, motion picture, 19, 164, 172–76, 186–99, 247n60; class in, 189; contradictions in, 198, 199; identity in, 191; railroads in, 172, 193–95, 248n71, 249n76; sensationalism in, 199, 248n68, 249n72

settlement houses, 48, 77, 82

Seven Arts (little magazine), 46

sewing machine, 28

sexual harassment: in Cleveland strike, 239n73; in dime novels, 72, 142–43; political import of, 142; public debate on, 144; of shirtwaist workers, 8, 141–45, 240nn76&79&81

Shapiro, Anna, 240n76

shirtwaist strike (New York, 1909), 83; causes of, 89–90; chronology of, 228n8; collective memory in, 127; cultural meaning in, 128; effect on films, 244n20; egg throwing in, 152–53; ethnicity in, 98; fashion discussion in, 85, 88, 94, 98–100, 103–105, 113–14, 133, 148, 155; Gompers on, 119; grievances in, 8, 122, 138–42, 146, 240n79; as holiday, 96, 149; influence of, 159; Italian women in, 125–26, 136–37, 235nn17&22, 238n47; Jewish women in, 125–26, 135, 136, 230n37, 234n17; labor's account of, 88–89, 92; Lemlich on, 119–20; limitations of, 160; management in, 136; Manufacturers' Association in, 90, 108, 150, 238n52; media coverage of,

84, 87, 88, 89, 92–107, 111, 128–37; middle-class view of, 100, 108, 117, 132; police in, 95, 96, 105, 106, 131–32, 148, 153; political discourse on, 120; political subjectivity in, 15, 120, 122, 138, 148, 158; prostrike editorials on, 228n13; public debate on, 154, 159, 227n5; publicity for, 128–34, 137, 236n25; scabs in, 92, 95, 105, 151, 229n16, 237n45; settlements in, 237n52; "stars" of, 134, 135; strike committee in, 90, 108; suffragists and, 87, 90, 100, 108–109, 227n5; union demands in, 139, 142; violence in, 94–95, 97–98, 105, 131–33, 148, 149, 151, 237n45; walkout in, 15, 119, 122, 123, 137–38; women organizers of, 126–27; working ladyhood in, 85, 86, 116. *See also* picketing

shirtwaist strikers: as Amazons, 97; Americanization of, 136; arrest of, 94, 102, 124, 128, 129, 130, 131, 132, 148, 229n16, 232n54; bravery of, 148, 150–54, 157, 232n54; cartoons of, 103–107; charges of immorality against, 91–92, 98, 148; as charitable subjects, 101–102, 171; at Christmas, 101–102, 230n37; as clients, 108; as consumers, 210n11; dress of, 80, 84–85, 130, 131, 242n100; effect of historical memory on, 235n19; ethnicity of, 98; exclusion from strike debate, 154, 159; gendered attacks on, 91; grievances against bosses, 8, 141–46, 240n79; labor leaders' depiction of, 85, 106, 108, 109, 111, 117, 118; labor's control over, 149–50; negative depictions of, 96–98; number of, 118, 123; political legitimacy of, 87–89, 91–93, 96–97, 122; political subjectivities of, 15, 120, 122, 138, 148, 158, 203; public identity of, 145–46, 154, 303; radicalism of, 122; rationality of, 98, 105, 106, 111, 112, 116; rejection of compromise, 150; shop meetings of, 138–40; as transgressive, 228n12; union recognition for, 101, 116

shoes: quality of, 30; of working women,

2, 77, 80–81, 216n37

Shomer (Yiddish writer), 56

Sider, Gerald M., 213n6

Simkhovitch, Mary, 177

Singer, Ben, 248n72

sizing, improvement in, 28

Sloan, Kay, 244n20

Smith, Francis S.: "Bertha, the Sewing Machine Girl," 38–39, 249n73

Socialist Party (SP), 87, 102, 103, 112, 118; German, 232n62; Jewish women in, 120, 125; Lemlich in, 147–48, 159; organizing by, 139; publications of, 88, 94, 115; on suffrage, 5

Sorin, Gerald, 126

Spelman, Elizabeth, 3–4

stage plays: strikes in, 42; train wrecks in, 195, 248n73; working-girl, 38, 39

Stallybrass, Peter, 33

Stansell, Christine, 23, 28

steam presses, 32

Steffens, Lincoln, 45–46

Stein, Leon, 154

Steward, Ira, 233n62

Stokes, Graham Phelps, 157, 242n105

Stokes, Rose Pastor: marriage of, 157, 242n105; reading experiences of, 222n36; on reading habits, 49, 55, 58–59, 72, 220n4; on sexual harassment, 141; in shirtwaist strike, 157–58, 242n105; on working-class dress, 29, 80, 81

story papers, 31, 32, 35, 217n49; working girl formula in, 34

Street and Smith (publishers), 34, 38, 217n48

strike breakers. *See* scabs

strikes: by Appalachian women, 6–7; in dime novels, 40; in dramas, 42; effect of social forces on, 227n3; in garment industry, 90, 115, 123, 145, 159, 160; in labor history, 227n3; mass, 123, 124; in movies, 171–72; in popular literature, 20–21; rent, 134; scabs in, 90; sexual harassment in, 145; steel, 124; violence in, 241n97; working-class women in, 5. *See also* shirtwaist strike (New York, 1909)

Struggle, The (film), 244n20

subaltern counterpublics, 154, 242n98

subjectivity: definition of, 12; formation of, 13, 51, 109, 110–11, 117, 121–22, 203, 206; hidden transcripts of, 121; and identity, 13; of ladyhood, 13, 14, 225n103; limits to, 14; in movie consumption, 162; postmodern theories of, 225n103, 231n50; resistant, 205; role of consumption in, 13, 182

subjectivity, political, 3; and consumer culture, 4; and dime novels, 114; Enlightenment-based, 3, 85, 96, 105, 159, 203, 226n2; historical construction of, 231n50; rationality in, 206; of shirtwaist strikers, 15, 120, 122, 138, 148, 158; of working women, 85, 86, 95–96, 100, 106, 108, 109, 116–18, 119, 120, 121, 145, 159

Sue, Eugene, 36

suffragists: access to press, 227n5; advocacy of working women, 101; and shirtwaist strike, 87, 90, 100, 108–109, 227n5

Sumner, Mary Brown, 8, 91–92

Susman, Warren, 19–20, 203–204

suspense, in serials, 190

sweatshops, 60

tailors, "slop," 22

taste: class distinction in, 31; in consumption, 23; in fashion, 25, 26–27; middle-class, 77

Tax, Meredith, 238n53

Taylor, Rebecca, 105

technology, in movie serials, 193–95

telegraph lines, nationalization of, 228n13

Tentler, Leslie, 210n9

textile production, mechanization of, 23

Tompkins, Jane, 41

Triangle Shirtwaist Company, 124; fire of 1911, 8, 160; owners of, 237n43; police brutality at, 124; strike at, 89, 90, 91, 132, 136, 137

True, Ruth, 161, 177

"Two Phases of Yuletide" (cartoon), 103–104

underwear, silk, 81–82

Union Labor Advocate, 195

unions: depiction in movies, 166; recognition of shirtwaist strikers, 101; role in Americanization, 136; in shirtwaist strike, 87; women organizers in, 233n64; women's participation in, 112; on working women, 73; working women's views of, 60, 235n21. *See also* labor leaders

Uprising of the 20,000, 123, 213n27

Urosova, Natralya, 138, 149

Valesh, Eva McDonald, 101–102, 108; on picketers, 150

Variety (magazine), 175–76

vaudeville, 219nn73&76

violence: in dime novels, 133; in rent strikes, 134; in shirtwaist strike, 94–95, 97–98, 105, 131–33, 148, 149, 151, 237n45; of strikers, 241n97

virtue: in melodrama, 76; in public sphere, 91; of shirtwaist strikers, 91–92, 98, 148

Vitagraph Company, 168–69

voluntary associations, 214n11

Wage Earners, The (motion picture), 195

wages, 25; "American Standard" of, 99, 230n32; in piecework, 67, 140; in shirtwaist strike, 147–48; "woman's," 98–99

Wald, Lillian, 82; on dress, 29, 48, 81; on makeup, 61; on strikers, 155

Walkowitz, Judith, 12

weddings, 77

welfare system, women's dependency under, 231n46

"What Happened to Mary," 187–93; antecedents of, 172; class distinction in, 189, 248n67; consumer input into, 174–75; as melodrama, 191; romance in, 192–93; sensationalism in, 248n68; social recognition in, 192, 195; suspense in, 190

What Happened to Mary (movie version), 45, 162; audience identification with, 186, 187; versus print version, 187–88; production of, 172–73; scenario writers for, 168; as serial, 244n24

CPSIA information can be obtained
at www.ICGtesting.com
Printed in the USA
JSHW041920040822
28903JS00005B/127

9 780231 111034